AF773614

Contributions to Political Science

More information about this series at http://www.springer.com/series/11829

Anna Fill

The Political Economy of De-liberalization

A Comparative Study on Austria, Germany and Switzerland

Springer

Anna Fill
University of Bern
Bern, Switzerland

ISSN 2198-7289 ISSN 2198-7297 (electronic)
Contributions to Political Science
ISBN 978-3-030-01065-2 ISBN 978-3-030-01066-9 (eBook)
https://doi.org/10.1007/978-3-030-01066-9

Library of Congress Control Number: 2018956321

© Springer Nature Switzerland AG 2019
This work is subject to copyright. All rights are reserved by the Publisher, whether the whole or part of the material is concerned, specifically the rights of translation, reprinting, reuse of illustrations, recitation, broadcasting, reproduction on microfilms or in any other physical way, and transmission or information storage and retrieval, electronic adaptation, computer software, or by similar or dissimilar methodology now known or hereafter developed.
The use of general descriptive names, registered names, trademarks, service marks, etc. in this publication does not imply, even in the absence of a specific statement, that such names are exempt from the relevant protective laws and regulations and therefore free for general use.
The publisher, the authors and the editors are safe to assume that the advice and information in this book are believed to be true and accurate at the date of publication. Neither the publisher nor the authors or the editors give a warranty, express or implied, with respect to the material contained herein or for any errors or omissions that may have been made. The publisher remains neutral with regard to jurisdictional claims in published maps and institutional affiliations.

This Springer imprint is published by the registered company Springer Nature Switzerland AG
The registered company address is: Gewerbestrasse 11, 6330 Cham, Switzerland

For my family and the dogs

Acknowledgements

Writing a doctoral thesis is like climbing a mountain: at times it can be exciting and inspiring; at other times it can be truly exhausting. Sometimes it seems as if your progress has stalled. Yet finishing a dissertation certainly feels as rewarding as reaching the summit. I would not have been able to complete this climb without several special people who were there for me the whole way.

First and foremost, I would like to thank my dissertation supervisor, Prof. Klaus Armingeon, who continuously supported and motivated me throughout this dissertation project and was always on hand with help and advice. I would also like to give a special thank you to my second dissertation supervisor, Prof. Lucio Baccaro, who often provided me with thought-provoking suggestions and helped me recognize the strengths and limitations of my argument. Moreover, I would like to thank Prof. Peter Hall who helped me advance my argument during my time researching at the Department of Government at Harvard University.

My work would not have been possible without the Swiss National Science Foundation, which sponsored the liberalization research project on which my dissertation is built and granted me a generous doc.mobility scholarship to fund my research visit abroad.

I would also like to thank my colleagues and friends at the Institute of Political Science at the University of Bern who have supported me both emotionally and professionally. Thank you Sarah E., David, Kai, Sara K., Maya, Rafael, Alex, Flo, and Laura. Last but not least, I would like to thank my family and friends who were really always there for me.

Contents

List of Abbreviations

ALMP	Active labor market policy
BAK	Bundesarbeitskammer Österreich
BDA	Bundesvereinigung der Deutschen Arbeitgeberverbände
BDI	Bundesverband Deutscher Arbeitgeber
CDU	Christlich Demokratische Union Deutschlands
COMP	Competition policy
CSU	Christlich-Soziale Union (in Bavaria)
CVP	Christlichdemokratische Volkspartei der Schweiz
DGB	Deutscher Gewerkschaftsbund
DHKT	Deutscher Handelskammertag
EDU	Education policy
EEA	European Economic Area
EEC	European Economic Community
EPL	Employment protection legislation
EU	European Union
EVP	Evangelische Volkspartei
FIN	Financial policy
FPD	Freie Demokratische Partei
FPÖ	Freiheitliche Partei Österreichs
GOV	Corporate governance
HC	Healthcare policy
IR	Industrial relations
IV	Industriellenvereinigung
LK	Landwirtschaftskammer
LPS	Liberale Partei der Schweiz
NEB	Non-employment benefits
OECD	Organisation for Economic Co-operation and Development
ÖGB	Österreichischer Gewerkschaftsbund
ÖVP	Österreichische Volkspartei
PEN	Pension policy
PRI	Privatization policy

SAV	Schweizer Arbeitgeberverband
SGB	Schweizer Gewerkschaftsbund
SGV	Schweizer Gewerbeverband
SPD	Sozialdemokratische Partei Deutschlands
SPS	Sozialdemokratische Partei der Schweiz
SPÖ	Sozialdemokratische Partei Österreichs
SVP	Schweizer Volkspartei
TAX	Taxation policy
VOCTR	Vocational training
WKÖ	Wirtschaftskammer Österreich

List of Figures

List of Tables

Chapter 1
Introduction

Over the past 40 years, the relationship between states and markets has changed: since the late 1970s, markets have increasingly taken over the traditional policy domains of governments, while states have opened up their national economies to global market forces. As a consequence, many Western democracies have become more liberalized across all major political economic fields (Streeck and Thelen 2005; Simmons and Elkins 2004). This transformation has resulted in the corporatization and subsequent privatization of many state-owned companies, particularly in the field of transportation, energy, water, and telecommunications, in all OECD countries (Clifton et al. 2006). Financial practices have been de-regulated, taxes and import quotas have been universally reduced, and exchange rates have been unified to encourage free global movement of capital and goods (Simmons and Elkins 2004). Policymakers have adjusted their monetary strategies and switched from Keynesian macroeconomic policies to neoclassical policies (Scharpf 1991, 1987). Global capitalism has undergone a neoliberal transformation (Baccaro and Howell 2011). On the distributional side, welfare states, labor markets, and collective labor relations were liberalized (Baccaro and Howell 2011, 2017; Streeck 2009). Mature welfare states have been modernized, including cuts to benefit levels, reforms of financing mechanisms, and more restrictive eligibility requirements for welfare claimants (Häusermann 2010). The Great Recession further increased the pressure for liberalization and austerity in certain industrialized countries (Armingeon and Baccaro 2012).

The comparative literature on the welfare state and capitalism is mostly in agreement that the majority of industrialized economies have been liberalized to varying degrees (Baccaro and Howell 2017; Streeck and Thelen 2005; Höpner et al. 2011). Hence, liberalization is perceived as the common denominator unifying many of the reform changes that have been implemented in Western political economies since the early 1980s. Even though the extent and the shape of liberalization varies in different countries, the primary direction of reform is considered to be towards greater liberalization (Streeck and Thelen 2005).

© Springer Nature Switzerland AG 2019

A. Fill, *The Political Economy of De-liberalization*, Contributions to Political Science, https://doi.org/10.1007/978-3-030-01066-9_1

Without denying common trends towards liberalization, I argue that liberalization is not, as widely perceived, the only direction that reform has taken in the past decades. Contrary to the majority of recent academic research, this book states that industrialized economies have also engaged in de-liberalizing reform processes throughout their political-economic development. I am not claiming that de-liberalizing policies were as present as liberalizing policies; instead, my research shows that de-liberalization processes in the form of policy reforms are responsible for a fair share of reform developments. New data from the Liberalization Database, which covers policy reforms in the welfare state, the labor market, and the privatization, finance, competition and tax nexus, as well as in healthcare and education over the last 30 years in 38 countries, indicates that out of 12,539 reform changes *4906* reform changes are de-liberalizing—representing *an absolute share of 39.1% of all reforms* in the database (Armingeon et al. 2019).

In this contribution, *liberalization* processes are defined as the politically enacted and legitimated delegation of allocation and distribution decisions affecting markets. Liberalizing reforms aim to promote market principles and remove market barriers. De-liberalization follows the reverse principle; however, this does not mean that de-liberalization can only happen in the form of reversing liberalization policies. This means that de-liberalizing reforms hamper market principles (Höpner et al. 2014). In other words, de-liberalization comprises all policies that constrain the role of markets and promote a stronger role of the state.

1.1 De-liberalization Processes in the Age of Liberalization

Even though popular science has taken up the topic of de-liberalization—for example, the Economist recently reported on the new period of protectionism and retreat (The Economist 2017; McKinsey 2016), while other outlets have mainly discussed a new era of de-globalization (Forbes 2016; Barbieri 2016)—current scientific literature mostly disregards the topic of de-liberalization (Streeck and Thelen 2005; Höpner et al. 2011). Yet, based on recent findings from the Liberalization Database (Armingeon et al. 2019), a newly compiled data set, I am able to demonstrate that, despite many opposing academic accounts, policy reforms in industrialized countries are not exclusively aimed at liberalization, but can also be reformed towards de-liberalization.

This distinctive dataset covers data on liberalizing and de-liberalizing policy reform changes in the following fields: labor market policies, industrial relations, financial policies, welfare state policies, competition and privatization policies in 38 countries from 1973 up to 2013. This database has the advantage of directly measuring liberalizing and de-liberalizing changes and is therefore optimally suited for this study.

The data set includes a policy reform if the change was the result of a political decision maker, the outcome of a collective bargaining process, or court-mandated events, and if it had a socio-economic effect. The database does not cover informal institutional change, such as new practices in the field of industrial relations[1] or neglecting to update old institutions in order to face new challenges (e.g., tailoring policies for new at-risk groups such as atypical workers) (Armingeon et al. 2019).

The database illustrates the incisiveness of these reforms through Peter Hall's concept of policy changes (1993) and Baumgartner's status quo change (2013).[2] Hall's concept depicts the extent of a reform by analyzing the spectrum of change: a first-order change occurs when the means (instrument settings) for a given policy are altered, for example if the amount of social security benefits is modified. A second-order change happens when the instruments of the given policies are changed. An example would be the introduction of a new active labor market policy where the state temporarily finances 50% of the social security costs in order to combat unemployment. A third-order change occurs when the goal of a given policy is changed, such as the permission to run private, profit-oriented job agencies focusing on temporary work. Baumgartner's status quo change depicts a major change that challenges an existing status quo of a given policy; an example would be a drastic cut in the unemployment benefit replacement rate resulting in a shift from a 79% replacement rate to a 55% replacement rate, or the abolishment of a mandatory retirement age in the public sector.

Based on the weighted incisiveness as well as on the amount of reforms in a distinct policy field in a given year, a weighted liberalization index has been established. This index provides insights on reform dynamics in terms of the extent, gravity, and timing of liberalization and de-liberalization policies. The index captures the *reform development* from the 1970s up to the current period and also depicts the rate of reform changes over time. It does not, however, provide any insight in terms of the overall level or base level of liberalization or de-liberalization.

Typical cases of liberalizing reforms in welfare states and on labor markets include reductions in unemployment benefits, the implementation of performance-dependent financing mechanisms in hospitals, higher co-payments for patients, introductions/expansions of atypical contracts, and cutbacks in pension expenditures through the adoption of a higher retirement age or cuts in benefits. In the realm of the privatization-finance nexus, typical examples include the privatization of state-owned companies, the reduction of credit controls for banks, and the expansion of private public utility services. Classic de-liberalizing reform examples include increasing social security benefits, expanding collective wage agreements, the launch of a statutory minimum wage, the abolition of university fees, state subsidized employment, the restriction of foreigners to national labor markets, and the transformation of private companies to state-owned-enterprises.

[1]With regards to policy changes in industrial relations—the Liberalization Database incorporated the Database on Institutional Characteristics of Trade Unions, Wage Setting, State Intervention and Social Pacts, 1960–2010 (ICTWSS) (Visser 2013).

[2]Both Hall's policy change (1993) and Baumgartner's status quo change (2013) will be explained in greater detail in Chap. 3 of this book.

The following graphs, which are based on the index, deliver the first evidence that de-liberalization processes make up a reasonable amount of enacted reforms. The first figure depicts reform trajectories across all policy fields, while the second figure focuses on salient policies[3] that are important for the public such as welfare, labor market, healthcare, education, industrial relations, and tax policies. The indices of all graphs are based on data of the Liberalization Database[4] and depict a 3-year moving average in order to fully capture a policy trend cycle. The index is standardized by the number of countries and policy fields.

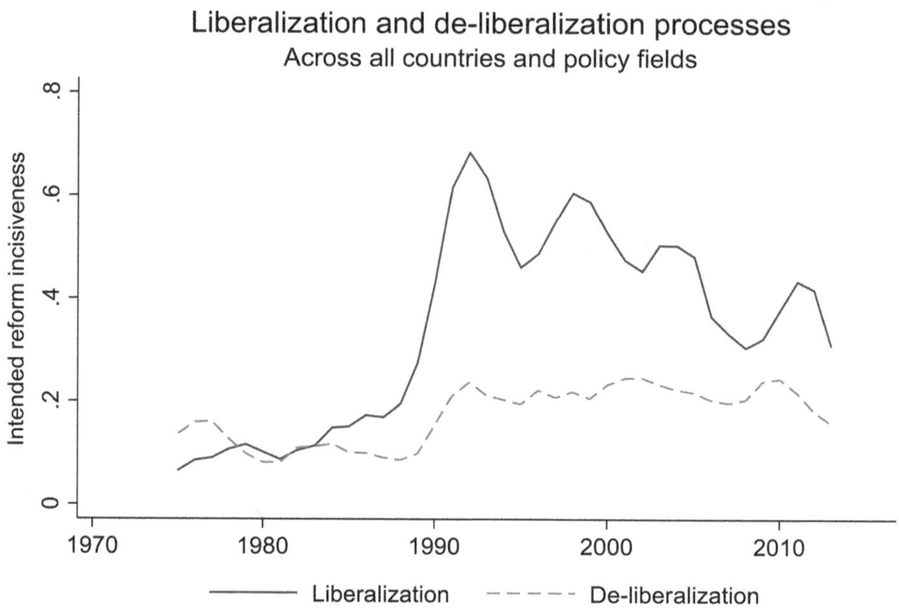

Fig. 1.1 Liberalization and de-liberalization processes across all countries and policy fields. Source: Liberalization Database (Armingeon et al. 2019)

[3]Politically salient policy fields will be explained in greater detail in Chap. 2. Politically salient policy fields include active labor market policies, education policies, employment-protection legislation, healthcare policies, industrial relation policies, unemployment benefit policies, pension policies, tax policies and vocational education training policies. Source: Liberalization Database (Armingeon et al. 2019).

[4]Country abbreviations correspond to the international ISO 3166-1 numeric format.

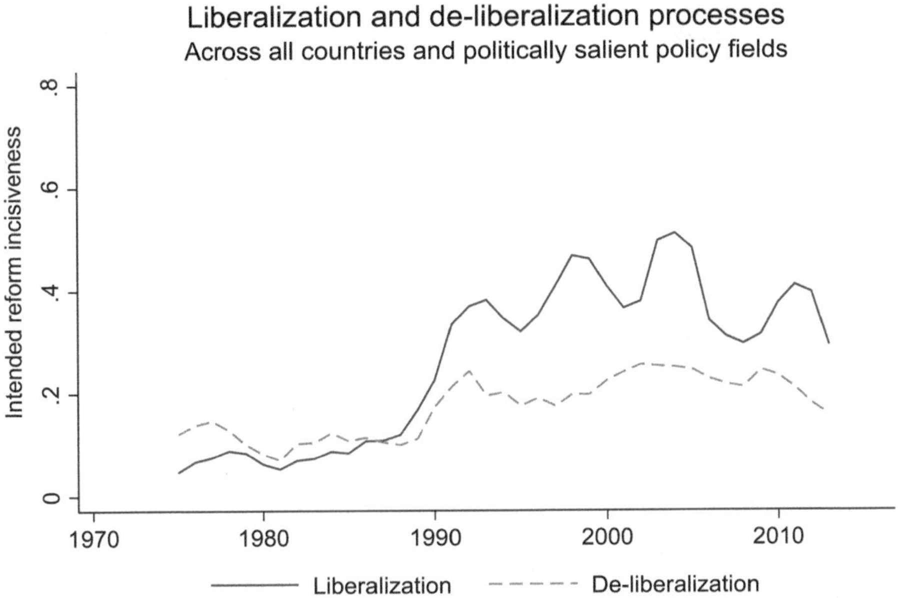

Fig. 1.2 Liberalization and de-liberalization across all countries and politically salient policy fields. Source: Liberalization Database (Armingeon et al. 2019)

While these graphs confirm that liberalization reforms took place, they also demonstrate that a significant amount of de-liberalization also occurred in all countries, and even dominated the policy changes in certain countries in certain years. In particular, de-liberalization dominates in almost 20% of all years across all countries, meaning that in almost 20% of all years across all countries, the calculated value (weighted index) was higher for de-liberalization than for liberalization.[5]

Moreover, the overall distribution[6] between liberalization and de-liberalization *based on the weighted index* shows that around 40% of all reforms across all fields in the Liberalization Database have been de-liberalizing. While the liberalizing changes have generally been graver than de-liberalizing reforms, de-liberalization processes constitute a decent portion of reform activities in Western economies.

[5]Calculations: Three-year moving averages standardized according to countries and policy fields.

[6]Ibid.

Table 1.1 Distribution of de-liberalizing and liberalizing reform changes across all policy fields, all countries, and all years

Policy changes	Share of liberalizing reforms as a percentage (%)	Share of de-liberalizing reforms as a percentage (%)
First-order changes across all countries and policy fields	60.9	39.1
Second order changes across all countries and policy fields	67.8	32.2
Third order changes across all countries and policy fields	73.7	26.3
Status quo changes across all countries and policy fields	75.2	24.8

Source: Liberalization Database (Armingeon et al. 2019)

Hence, contrary to the prevalent wisdom in political science, the graphs and the policy redistribution in the data set emphasizes the puzzling fact that de-liberalization is a common reform option in Western nations. Yet, when we take a closer look at the data, we also see that the amount of de-liberalization varies between countries as well as between country groups.

Traditional comparative welfare state accounts have presumed a relationship between various groups of welfare states and policy reform patterns (Thelen 2014; Häusermann 2010; Esping-Andersen 1990, 1996). Different reform and liberalization processes are assigned to distinct welfare state typologies (Esping-Andersen 1990) based on these states' specific political and economic legacies, such as the strength of labor, the power of employers, and the influence of interest groups, as well as distinctive institutional configurations of social security systems and the economic openness of a country (Thelen 2014; Esping-Andersen 1990; Pierson 1996). Following this approach, we can also see that various types of welfare states[7] engage differently not only in liberalizing but also in de-liberalizing policy reforms.[8]

[7]Anglo-Saxon countries: AUS, CAN, GBR, IRL, NZL, USA; Continental European countries: AUT, BEL, DEU, FRA, LUX, NLD, CHE; Eastern European countries: HRV, BGR, CZE, EST, HUN, LVA, LTU, POL, ROU, SVK, SVN; Nordic countries: DNK, FIN, ISL, NOR, SWE; Southern European countries: CYP, ESP, GRC, ITA, MLT, PRT.

[8]Calculations are based on the Liberalization Database (Armingeon et al. 2019).

Table 1.2 Distribution of de-liberalizing and liberalizing reform changes according to country groups across all policy fields and all years

	First order reform changes as a percentage		Second order reform changes as a percentage		Third order reform changes as a percentage		Status quo changes as a percentage	
Country groups	LIB	DE-LIB	LIB	DE-LIB	LIB	DE-LIB	LIB	DE-LIB
Anglo-Saxon	55.5	44.5	59.2	40.8	64.4	35.6	67.3	32.7
Continental European	55.1	44.9	60.3	38.7	77.2	22.8	69.2	28.8
Eastern European	68.4	31.6	72.8	27.2	81.5	18.5	78.9	21.1
Nordic	62.3	37.7	75	25	72	28	77.6	22.4
Southern European	61.4	38.6	63.7	36.3	64.1	35.9	71.5	28.5

Source: Liberalization Database (Armingeon et al. 2019)

Continental European countries in particular show a high proportion of de-liberalizing reforms (44.9%) relative to the number of liberalizing reforms (55.1%) based on the absolute number of reforms.

In terms of the Continental European welfare states, three countries—namely Austria, Germany, and Switzerland—stand out in particular due to several aspects: firstly, all three countries demonstrate prominent recent de-liberalizing reforms. Secondly, all three countries are Bismarckian-type welfare states and share many institutional similarities with regards to politics and industries, a successful economy, and similar cultural aspects. Thirdly, all three countries exhibit a high ratio of de-liberalizing reforms overall *even though, to various extents*, Austria displays a proportion of 43.0% de-liberalizing reforms to 57.0% liberalizing reforms, Germany shows 37.4% de-liberalizing reforms to 62.4% liberalizing reforms, and Switzerland implemented 43.5% de-liberalizing reforms to 56.5% liberalizing reforms.

Austria has been quite active when it comes to introducing de-liberalization policies in the welfare state and labor market, for example the introduction of an anti-wage-dumping law, the implementation of a means-tested basic income scheme, the repeal of university fees, and the enactment of legislation to anchor social partners into the constitution (Obinger et al. 2010; Armingeon et al. 2019). Germany has also enacted a number of new de-liberalizing policies. A new pension package for employees who can retire at the age of 63 if they have worked for 45 years,[9] an extended mothers' pension, a statutory minimum wage, and a law to strengthen collective bargaining—the *Law to Reinforce Collective Bargaining Autonomy* (*Tarifeinheitsgesetz*), as well as a law to protect German companies from foreign takeovers have all been enacted in recent years (Walwei 2015; Armingeon et al. 2019; DieZeit 2017). Even Switzerland has attracted attention due to the introduction of various de-liberalizing laws such as the introduction of obligatory healthcare, the expansion of pension policies, and, recently, the mass immigration initiative, which aims to reduce the amount of foreign workers in Switzerland (Armingeon et al. 2019).

[9]This privilege is only accorded to those born before 1 January 1953 and receiving their pension for the first time on or after 1 July 2014 (Eurofund 2015).

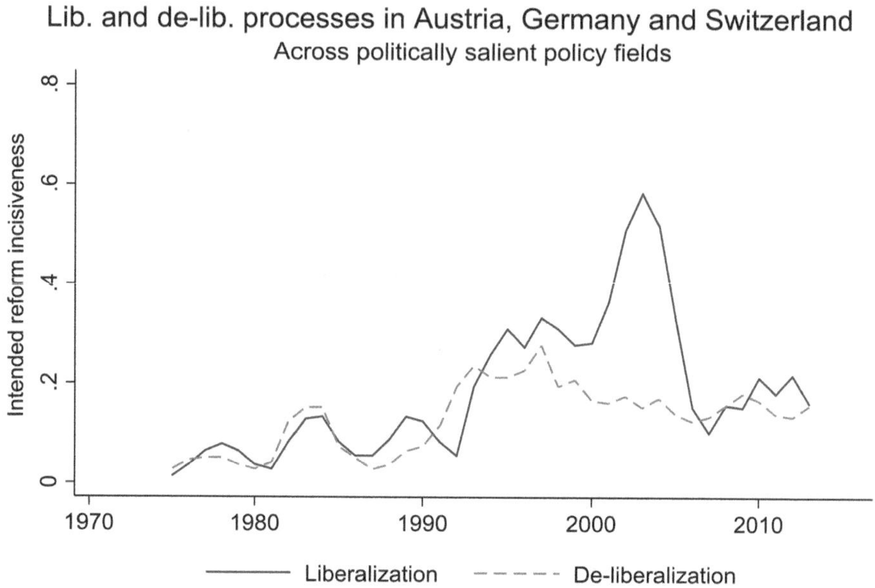

Fig. 1.3 Liberalization and de-liberalization processes in Austria, Germany, and Switzerland across politically salient policy fields. Source: Liberalization Database (Armingeon et al. 2019)

Since liberalization is assumed to be the 'privileged direction' of reform change within the comparative capitalism and welfare state literature, the fact that there has been a double movement in reform—both liberalizing and de-liberalizing policy changes—seems to be at odds with the current research (Baccaro and Howell 2017; Höpner et al. 2014; Streeck and Thelen 2005). The majority of academic studies in these fields would clearly predict liberalization in the case of reform. From a theoretical standpoint, this diagnosis is sensible as stated by Streeck and Thelen (2005: 33): *a liberal regime is one in which exit is favored as a dominant logic of action over voice, individual actors may find it easier to start a movement toward liberalization than one toward constraining market relations by institutional obligations.* Apart from collective action costs, de-liberalization might be hard to reconcile with political goals in times of austerity (Heyes 2013).

The observation of de-liberalizing reform policies in the age of liberalization reform suggests not only a more complicated picture of policy reform change, but also poses a puzzle for the corresponding literature. Why do countries engage repeatedly in *de-liberalizing* policy reforms? What role does de-liberalization play in the overall reform trajectories? Who are the main political actors pushing for de-liberalizing reforms and what are the interests and motives behind this reform strategy? Are de-liberalization processes mainly introduced out of functional necessity or political calculus? Why do continental European welfare states show such a high percentage of de-liberalizing policies? What influences the timing and the extent of liberalization?

The aforementioned facts and questions make it clear that de-liberalization policies have not only been an essential part of policy reform in Western countries, in particular in conservative Continental European welfare states such as Austria, Germany, and Switzerland, but also that the occurrence of de-liberalizing reform has not been adequately explained. In order to address the missing gap in the literature and combine these diverse research questions in an empirical case study, this book seeks to answer the following research question: *How can we explain the various de-liberalization processes in Austria, Germany, and Switzerland?*

1.2 De-liberalization Policy Reforms: The Argument in Brief

Analysis of the case studies shows that *political actors* and their *strategic use of policymaking* are particularly important in order to explain de-liberalization. Based on the premise that political parties are primarily vote- and office-seeking individuals, I argue that political parties have engaged in de-liberalization policies to compensate for liberalization in order to achieve liberalization processes or respond to existing liberalization processes. Throughout the late 1980s, when governing parties decided to pursue liberalization after market and budgetary pressures intensified, they chose strategies that were compatible with their political survival. Thus, policymakers used de-liberalization policies to appease liberalization reform opponents, build political coalitions, and strike policy deals. This allowed them to carry out liberalization processes. Moreover, political parties used de-liberalization to transform liberalizing reforms into electorally attractive propositions. By combining liberalizing and de-liberalizing welfare reform policies, political parties were able to target their voters via greater distributional benefits in some areas while pursuing cuts in other areas of the welfare state (Drazen and Eslava 2005; Pierson 1996). De-liberalization was therefore used to mitigate liberalizing reforms either by compensating for these reforms or by allowing the responsible political parties to avoid blame. De-liberalization therefore functions as an enabling mechanism for liberalization (Pierson 1996, 2004; Häusermann 2010).

As Pierson stated, however, time matters, and this is also true for policy reforms (2004). Once political parties gave in to far-reaching liberalization reforms in the realm of welfare state and industrial relations around the 2000s, the negative effects of these reforms became evident to both voters and the political parties themselves. These reforms resulted in negative feedback such as loss of votes for liberal reformers and a change in public opinion leading to resentment of liberalization and new policy demands shifting towards de-liberalization (Marx and Starke 2017). Political parties responded to these new positions from voters and engaged in de-liberalizing reforms as a response to earlier liberalization reforms in order to increase their political capital and win votes (Beramendi et al. 2015; Mabbett 2016; Bosch 2015; Obinger et al. 2010). Thus, political parties use de-liberalization policies to mitigate the effects of liberalizing reforms that were implemented earlier, as well as to claim credit for the new de-liberalizing reforms.

In order to achieve these de-liberalization policies, political parties forge coalitions with the organized left, which continues to support de-liberalizing welfare policies (Gordon 2015). The argument proceeds therefore in two steps. The first step focuses on the liberalization period, while the second step deals with the post-liberalization period (the period after far-reaching liberalization reform has been implemented in the continental welfare states) (Thelen 2014; Häusermann 2010). Consequently, de-liberalization occurs in relation to liberalization. Firstly, political parties use de-liberalizing reforms to compensate for and enable liberalization processes. Secondly, political parties use de-liberalizing reforms to mitigate the effects of earlier liberalization reforms and claim credit for the new de-liberalizing reforms after far-reaching liberalization has gone into effect. The extent of de-liberalizing policies is dependent on the political support of the actors involved in the governing process.

On the whole, this book attempts to show that de-liberalization reform processes have, despite conventional and academic wisdom, been more dominant throughout the last 30 years than generally presumed. Though I do not refute the extent of liberalization processes, I believe it is important to include de-liberalization as a possible direction of institutional change in order to gain a clearer understanding of political actors and their motives, as well as of reform processes in general. The main claim of this contribution—that de-liberalization patterns occur either as compensation or as a strategy to gain popularity and win votes—may very well be applied to other conservative Continental European welfare states. However, my argument has been tested and demonstrated on Austria, Germany, and Switzerland because these three countries are strong representatives of economically open and successful de-liberalizing Continental European welfare states. Moreover, the similarity of these three countries makes it possible to control for various institutional and cultural factors.

1.3 Contributions of This Book

This book is an evaluation of the dynamics of de-liberalization policy reform. As such, it makes several theoretical and empirical contributions to the academic and political communities. Firstly, it demonstrates that reform dynamics might be more focused on political strategies than usually assumed by many institutional accounts, which explain varieties of policy reform mainly based on micro- (institutional policy arrangements) and macro-institutions (consensus regimes) (Streeck and Thelen 2005; Hall and Soskice 2001). Secondly, this study deals with the relationship between liberalization and de-liberalization. Common political economic strands argue that de-liberalization either accompanies liberalization to compensate for difficult reform proceedings or in order to provide state rules and regulations (Vogel 1996; Pierson 1996), or that de-liberalization comes as response to capitalism, often induced by powerful social democratic interest groups and citizens (Polanyi 1944; Korpi 1983). However, this book argues that de-liberalization happens not only as part of liberalization processes or in response to them, but rather that it can occur as an enabling mechanism or correcting mechanism depending on the status quo of liberalization processes and options for political coalition-building. Thirdly, this work touches on the concept of institutional change by showing that this kind of change happens not only in a liberalizing direction, but also in a de-liberalizing direction.

Empirically, this study operates with a novel and large-scale data set—the Liberalization Database—which allows for a new operationalization and direct collection of liberalizing and de-liberalizing reform activities in 12 policy fields in 38 countries over more than 30 years from 1973 up to 2013[10] (Armingeon et al. 2019). Analysis based on this database was able to establish the existence of de-liberalization reform processes in various Western countries, despite many scientific accounts indicating otherwise. Additionally, this study also delivers specific insights on de-liberalization reform trajectories in Austria, Germany, and Switzerland. This research analyzed 21 comprehensive de-liberalizing reforms in Austria, Germany, and Switzerland with a focus on reform sequences, political actors, party coalitions, and policies. The result shows that de-liberalizing policies are often deployed in strategic policymaking. Furthermore, this book demonstrates that politically salient policies are more prone to de-liberalization, while politically non-salient policies are rarely de-liberalized or reversed.

1.4 Structure of This Book

This book follows the classical structure of an empirical social science work. It starts out by discussing the most prominent theories with regards to the research subject and their explanatory power. Subsequently, the argument of this book, which explains the different de-liberalization paths in Austria, Germany, and Switzerland, will be developed. Chapter 3 will lay out the research design and the research methods. This chapter will engage in the *small-N* comparative method and deliver criteria for the case selection. Additionally, the main sources and data will be discussed. Afterwards, the three case studies on Austria, Germany, and Switzerland will follow independently in Chaps. 4, 5 and 6. While also providing general information on the country cases, the main emphasis of these chapters is the analysis of de-liberalizing reforms in the specific countries. Chapter 7 summarizes the main findings of this book and discusses alternative explanations to the research question. The book will conclude with a brief outlook.

[10]The case study countries are analyzed up to the year 2015.

References

Armingeon K, Baccaro L (2012) Political economy of the sovereign debt crisis: the limits of internal devaluation. Ind Law J 41(3):254–275
Armingeon K, Baccaro L, Fill A, Galindo J, Heeb S, Labanino R (2019) Liberalization database 1973–2013 (20170619). Available online July 2019
Baccaro L, Howell C (2011) A common neoliberal trajectory: the transformation of industrial relations in advanced capitalism. Polit Soc 39(4):521–563
Baccaro L, Howell C (2017) Trajectories of neoliberal transformation. Cambridge University Press, Cambridge
Barbieri P (2016) The losers of deglobalization. Why states should fear the closing of an open world. Foreign Affairs. https://www.foreignaffairs.com/articles/2016-11-13/losers-deglobalization. Retrieved 4 July 2017
Baumgartner F (2013) Ideas and policy change. Governance: Int J Policy Admin Inst 26 (2):239–258
Beramendi P, Häusermann S, Kitschelt H, Kriesi H (eds) (2015) The politics of advanced capitalism. Cambridge University Press, New York
Bosch G (2015) Der holprige Weg zum gesetzlichen Mindestlohn in Deutschland. Sozialer Fortschritt Unabhängige Zeitschrift für Sozialpolitik, vol 64. Duncker & Humblot, Berlin, pp 173–181. ISSN:0038-609X, ZDB-ID 20886
Clifton J, Comín F, Fuentes D (2006) Privatizing public enterprises in the European Union 1960–2002: ideological, pragmatic, inevitable? J Eur Publ Policy 13(5):736–756
DieZeit (2017) Regierung erhöht Übernahmeschutz für Firmen. DieZeit 12. http://www.zeit.de/wirtschaft/unternehmen/2017-07/auslaendische-investoren-vetorecht-bundesregierung-uebernahme. Retrieved 1 July 2017
Drazen A, Eslava M (2005) Electoral manipulation via expenditure composition: theory and evidence. NBER Working Paper No. 11085. http://www.nber.org/papers/w11085. Accessed 1 Mar 2017
Esping-Andersen G (1990) The three worlds of welfare capitalism. Polity Press, Cambridge
Esping-Andersen G (ed) (1996) Welfare states in transition: national adaptations in global economies. Sage, London
Eurofund (2015) Germany: new retirement package. https://www.eurofound.europa.eu/publications/article/2015/germany-new-retirement-package. Accessed 1 Feb 2017
Forbes (2016) Trump, China, and the 'de-globalization' trade. Forbes, Foreign Affairs, 23 Nov 2016. https://www.forbes.com/sites/kenrapoza/2016/11/23/trump-china-and-the-deglobalization-trade/#7e7054ac4cd0. Accessed 1 July 2017
Gordon J (2015) Protecting the unemployed: varieties of unionism and the evolution of unemployment benefits and active labour market policy in the rich democracies. Soc Econ Rev 13 (1):79–99
Hall P (1993) Policy paradigms, social learning and the state. Comp Polit 25:275–296
Hall P, Soskice D (eds) (2001) Varieties of capitalism: the institutional foundations of comparative advantage. Oxford University Press, Oxford
Häusermann S (2010) The politics of welfare state reform in continental Europe. Modernization in hard times. Cambridge University Press, Cambridge
Heyes J (2013) Flexicurity in crisis: European labour market policies in a time of austerity. Eur J Ind Relat 19(1):15
Höpner M, Petring A, Seikel D, Werner B (2011) Liberalisierungspolitik. KZfSS Kölner Zeitschrift für Soziologie und Sozialpsychologie 63(1):1–32
Höpner M, Petring A, Seikel D, Werner B (2014) Liberalization policy—an empirical analysis of economic and social interventions in western democracies. Wirtschafts- und Sozialwissenschaftliches Institut Diskussionspapier 11/2014. https://ideas.repec.org/p/zbw/wsidps/192b.html. Accessed 1 Mar 2017
Korpi W (1983) The democratic class struggle. Routledge & Kegan Paul, Boston
Mabbett D (2016) The minimum wage in Germany: what brought the state in? J Eur Publ Policy 23 (8):1240–1258. https://doi.org/10.1080/13501763.2016.1186210

Marx P, Starke P (2017) Dualization as destiny? The political economy of the German minimum wage reform. Polit Soc 0(0):1–26. https://doi.org/10.1177/0032329217726793

McKinsey (2016) Digital globalization: the new era of global flows. McKinsey Company Global Institute. http://www.mckinsey.com/business-functions/digital-mckinsey/our-insights/digital-globalization-the-new-era-of-global-flows. Accessed 1 Mar 2017

Obinger H, Starke P, Moser J, Bogedan C, Gindulis E, Leibfried S (2010) Transformations of the welfare state. In: Small states, big lessons. Oxford University Press, Oxford

Pierson P (1996) The new politics of the welfare state. World Polit 48(2):143–179. https://doi.org/10.1353/wp.1996.0004

Pierson P (2004) Politics in time: history, institutions, and social analysis. Princeton University Press, Princeton

Polanyi K (1957, 1944) The great transformation. Beacon Press, Boston

Scharpf F (1987) Sozialdemokratische Krisenpolitik in Europa. Campus, Frankfurt a. M

Scharpf F (1991) Die Handlungsfähigkeit des Staates am Ende des Zwanzigsten Jahrhunderts. Politische Vierteljahresschrift 32(4):621–634

Simmons B, Elkins Z (2004) The globalization of liberalization: policy diffusion in the international political economy. Am Polit Sci Rev 98(1):171–189

Streeck W (2009) Re-forming capitalism: institutional change in the German political economy. Oxford University Press, Oxford, UK and New York

Streeck W, Thelen K (2005) Beyond continuity: institutional change in advanced political economies. Oxford University Press, New York

The Economist (2017) In retreat—global companies are heading home. And it's not only because of the threat of protectionism. The Economist (print version), 28 Jan 2017, p 11

Thelen K (2014) Varieties of liberalization: the new politics of social solidarity. Cambridge University Press, New York

Visser J (2013) ICTWSS Data base. Amsterdam Institute for Advanced Labour Studies (AIAS), University of Amsterdam, Amsterdam

Vogel SK (1996) Freer markets, more rules. Regulatory reform in advanced industrial countries. Cornell University Press, Ithaca

Walwei U (2015) From deregulation to re-regulation: trend reversal in German labour market institutions and its possible implications. IAB Discussion Paper, No.10/2015. https://www.econstor.eu/handle/10419/108844. Accessed 1 Mar 2017

Chapter 2
The Politics of De-liberalization

2.1 Is De-liberalization a New Phenomenon in Political Economy?

Why do Continental European welfare states engage in de-liberalization reform? How can we explain these de-liberalization processes in political economies and their various governments? The current political economy literature has produced various debates and compelling accounts which are highly relevant to the topic of de-liberalizing reform trajectories. The first strand of literature looks at the *party goals and the interests of political actors* and candidates. The second theoretical account focuses on *functional theories*. Lastly, the third strand focuses on *power resources* and *partisanship theory* before transitioning to institutional accounts.

2.1.1 Public Choice Approaches: Party Goals and Interests

Early public choice accounts, for instance Downs (1957), established the idea of utility-maximizing political candidates. This means the main motivation of a political actor is to gain and retain office. Consequently, political actors have no partisan preference or interest in which policy is implemented; they only care about office (Persson and Tabellini 2000: 47). In line with this assumption, political actors focus mainly on the median voter, since his or her preferences are assumed to have a significant effect on the election result (Meltzer and Richard 1981). Thus, political actors who want to win votes will choose policy reforms that are supported by the majority of voters (Persson and Tabellini 2000: 62).

Further approaches in the public choice literature assume that political actors can also be motivated by the direct *policy outcomes* (Persson and Tabellini 2000: 108). Policy-seeking political actors are not blind to the chosen policies; as a result, it is expected that political coalitions are built on conjuncture based on policies. It is

© Springer Nature Switzerland AG 2019

A. Fill, *The Political Economy of De-liberalization*, Contributions to Political Science, https://doi.org/10.1007/978-3-030-01066-9_2

assumed that political actors can differentiate between policies and deals that mirror the preferences or dislikes of their supporters (De Swaan 1973: 88; Strom and Müller 1999: 7). Moreover, political actors might also be motivated by vote seeking (Strom and Müller 1999: 7; Downs 1957). This suggests that political actors *formulate policies to win elections rather than win elections to formulate policies* (Downs 1957: 28). The underlying motivations of the political candidate are the desire for power, prestige, and wealth, while the primary objective is to be elected to public office.

All three motivations of political actors are compatible with the enactment of de-liberalizing reforms and provide a strong explanation for their implementation. If political actors are foremost vote- and office-seeking entities and their voters' support or even demand de-liberalizing policies, then political actors will enact de-liberalizing policies. If political actors are motivated by the policy outcome and their partisan policy preferences align with de-liberalizing policies, political actors will try to legislate de-liberalizing reform policies. Hence, de-liberalization arguments are in line with public choice approaches.

2.1.2 Functionalist Accounts

The next group of theories on liberalization and de-liberalization could be labeled as *functionalist*. The common denominator among these theories is the assumption that common pressures lead to common policy reactions (Armingeon and Fill 2016). In economics, it is assumed that pressures from international markets lead to a race to the bottom wherein countries compete over more flexible labor markets in order to attract business as well as foreign investment (Olney 2013: 193). The *race to the bottom* or *efficiency hypothesis* has been debated in comparative welfare state literature as well. After the 1990s, various welfare state accounts predicted that increased globalization would lead to a 'battle of taxes' (Genschel 2002). Representatives of these theories claim that trade liberalization and capital mobility create a competition between national states by attempting to attract firms, investors, and highly skilled labor. In order to win this competition, national governments have to reduce taxes, which in turn creates a downward pressure on states' budgets resulting in retrenchments and lean welfare state institutions (Simmons and Elkins 2004; Wunder 1999; Scharpf 1997). The effects of European economic integration on welfare states have been debated in a similar vein. The classic interpretation follows as well on the *race to the bottom* hypothesis: the different labor and wage standards as well as the direct competition between the various member countries promote a decrease in the regulation of taxes on companies and capital, resulting in increased tax burdens on consumers and workers coupled with a downsizing of social protections (Scharpf 1997; Kvist 2004; Menz 2009: 157–163).

Recent functional accounts center on the underlying 'logic of capitalism' wherein governments have no choice but to adhere to the growing demands of market pressures otherwise business will extricate itself through internationalization

(Streeck and Thelen 2005: 4; Armingeon and Fill 2016). Even though countries might still exhibit important differences, they all converge towards liberalization (Streeck and Thelen 2005; Baccaro and Howell 2017). Convergence is seen as a common (neoliberal) occurrence in which existing political-economic institutions are re-adapted towards new liberal functions (Baccaro and Howell 2017: 13–15). Accordingly, it is presumed that various pathways in various speeds—gradual or abrupt changes—lead to liberalization; national differences can be traced back to national political-economic inheritances. The substantial contribution of these accounts is the emphasis on gradual and informal institutional change (Streeck and Thelen 2005; Baccaro and Howell 2017). The state, as well as politicians, act merely as middlemen to readjust policies towards liberalization, while dynamic capitalism and markets set the tone (Baccaro and Howell 2017; Streeck 2009; Streeck and Thelen 2005). Thus, it is supposed that there will be no reversals of liberalization as long as the dynamics of capitalist regimes and markets remain the same (Armingeon and Fill 2016). If these *functional hypotheses* assuming the common occurrence of liberalization are correct, we should expect to find no occurrence of de-liberalization processes, since states have no choice but to cut their budgets.

In stark contrast to these *functional accounts*, the *compensation hypothesis* (Meinhard and Potrafke 2012; Rodrik 1998) predicts an increase in de-liberalization based on the internationalization and expansion of capitalism and markets. Polanyi (1944) posits that the state must play an adjusting role in order for the market economy to function. This implies not only the regulation of money and credit by the state, but also the protection of workers in terms of both unemployment and education. Polanyi (1944) claimed that society itself would continuously produce counter-movements to liberalization reforms in order to prevent a complete 'dis-embedding' of the economy. Katzenstein (1985) argues that small European economies, such as Austria, tend to complement their growing liberalizing tendencies in the international economy by introducing state-controlled, stabilizing policies. Rodrik (1998) argues moreover that economies that are greatly exposed to economic risks tend to spend more on public policies in order to mitigate the negative effects for those affected by increasing internationalization. Global integration might produce negative effects such as inequality and heightened insecurity. Therefore, governments employ de-liberalization strategies to secure support for further globalizing measures from affected workers and voters. Garrett (1998) formulates a similar argument by stating that governments are cushioning market dislocations by redistributing wealth in order to curb the negative effects resulting from a combination of globalization and economic insecurity. Furthermore, Iversen (2001) as well as Iversen and Cusack (2000) predict an expansionary welfare state with increasing levels of globalization. The majority of the aforementioned literature refers to a logic in which the pressure to liberalize manifests political demand for de-liberalization to compensate the public for rising economic risks.

If we assume that the compensation hypothesis is correct, we should see more de-liberalizing policies with a steady increase of global integration, since these occurrences imply a dependency between liberalization and de-liberalization.

2.1.3 Power Resource, Interest Group, and Partisanship Theory

The traditional producer group theory links successful non-liberal policy reform (de-liberalization) to the relative power of alliances between social-democratic parties and trade union movements (Korpi 1983). In particular, the mobilization of socio-structural classes forms the basis for party politics and the power of class actors, as observed through trade unions being decisive in determining the outcome of liberalizing or de-liberalizing welfare state policies. Thus, the extent of de-liberalizing social policies is ultimately dependent on the result of the democratic class struggle (Korpi 1983; Stephens 1979). Additionally, *power resource theory* assumes that welfare state arrangements, once effectively present, provide continuous support for labor because they have a de-commodifying effect on it (Esping-Andersen 1990). Therefore, it is presumed that the party in power, the strength of the trade union movements, and the existing arrangement of the welfare state are decisive for the outcome of de-liberalizing policies according to *power resource theory* (Stephens 1979; Korpi 1983; Esping-Andersen 1990).

Similar to the *power resource theory*, 'traditional accounts' of the *partisanship theory* link the occurrence of de-liberalizing policies directly to the strength of left parties and governments. Authors such as Hibbs (1977) or Hewitt (1977) were able to show that distinct ideological parties were linked to distinctive policies and re-distributional outcomes. Boix (1998) also supported the *parties matter hypothesis* and assumed that leftist governments design macroeconomic policies that coincide with their partisan values. He identified leftist political strategies that aim to generate growth and higher investment through high taxes and public investment, demonstrating de-liberalizing reform efforts (Boix 1998: 203). Esping-Andersen (1990) based his conceptualization of the three worlds of the welfare state on the power of political actors. He claimed that strong middle-class loyalties in Scandinavia and in conservative Continental European welfare states used to provide continuous support for generous welfare states and therefore it was difficult to reform or restrict these regimes. Amable et al. (2006) argue in a similar vein that party politics do play an important role in determining the outcome of welfare state reforms with regards to liberalization and de-liberalization. While left-wing governments tend to increase expenditures during an economic downturn, right-wing governments pursue a liberalizing agenda by applying even stronger cuts in economically difficult times.

The *party matters approach* has been challenged by new accounts of the partisanship theory referring especially to the change in constituency and voters' demands (Häusermann et al. 2013). These novel lines of theory address in particular the complexity of socio-economic cultural change on the relationship between politicians and the electorate (Beramendi et al. 2015; Häusermann 2010). Even if parties are still programmatic organizations with ties to specific social groups, their electorate has changed and demands new kinds of policies (Häusermann et al. 2013: 227; Beramendi et al. 2015). Novel constituencies are made up of a growing number of educated, managerial, service, technical, and client-interactive professions, while factory workers and office clerks have become less important and more threatened by low-skilled immigrant workers. At the same time, more women have entered the workforce, and labor markets have often become dualized, resulting in new policy requests and electorate compositions as well as altered objectives on the part of interest groups (Emmenegger et al. 2012). Due to growing conflict lines resulting from this increase in complex, varying voter profiles, de-liberalization reform is dependent on political coalitions overcoming these conflicts, as well as on the functional need of covering the new social risks faced by these new electorate groups (Beramendi et al. 2015: 6–8).

Häusermann (2010) assumes that the various demands of these new social risk groups force a state of 'politics of exchange' in which coalitions (built along diverse conflict lines) facilitate this political process. The literature on new social risks emphasizes explicitly that recent welfare state developments not only involved retrenchments, but that there were also various benefit extensions in some policy fields involving de-liberalization policies (Häusermann 2010). All of these strands clearly allow for the option of de-liberalizing reform strategies. However, while earlier accounts refer to de-liberalizing policies particularly with regards to leftist parties and interest group organizations, more recent accounts link de-liberalizing policies to new voter demands and political strategies of exchange. If we assume that the *power resource* and *old partisanship theories* are correct, we would see an increase in de-liberalizing policies as soon as leftist governments come into power. If *newer partisanship accounts* were true, we would see distinct patterns of liberalizing and de-liberalizing reform strategies over time based on the supply and demand of political actors and voters.

2.1.4 Institutionalist Accounts

The following section discusses a variety of institutionalist accounts, including theoretical frameworks on path dependency, varieties of capitalism, varieties of liberalization, corporatism, consociational or direct democracies, as well as federalism.

Since the 1990s, an important body of literature on welfare states has emerged. These (neo-) institutionalist accounts predict stability over change in the welfare state. This stability has been attributed to path dependency, inertia, and mechanisms of institutional equilibrium (Häusermann 2010). In his seminal work, Pierson (1996) refers to de-liberalization policies in the context of the difficulty of reforming institutions. The legacy of a specific institutional set-up can aggravate reform options: Pierson's prime example of a path-dependent contingent reduction of reform options is a pay-as-you-go pension system. The switch from a pay-as-you-go system to a funded pension system would require the working population to double their pension contributions, since they would have to finance their pensions as well as those of the people already in retirement (Pierson 1994). Hence, the cost of adopting an alternative is so high that *it inhibits the exit of the current path* (Pierson 1994: 42). Similarly,

Pierson reasons that path dependency could also impede welfare state retrenchment. Welfare states' programs have created their own constituencies of beneficiaries, making it too costly for politicians to cut generous welfare policy programs; rather governments are more likely to try to negotiate reform packages than impose unilateral reform. Through the reform path of policy packages, including both liberalizing and de-liberalizing policies, political actors are able to avoid blame and reduce the cost of reform (Pierson 1996, 2001). Thus, path dependency, once established and fueled by a dynamic of self-reinforcing or positive feedback process, makes reversal difficult (Pierson 2004: 10). The specific timing of a process might therefore not only determine its possible outcome, but also provide some indication about the *mechanisms that generate striking temporal relationships* (Pierson 2004: 176), be it path dependency or critical junctures (Pierson 2004: 176). Pierson's account clearly addresses possible difficulties of securing support for purely liberalizing reforms and points to the strategic employment of de-liberalizing reforms. His focus on timing and sequences also helps us examine changing patterns and critical junctures in time. Thus, this account supports not only de-liberalization, but also provides strong explanations for focusing on institutions and political actors over time.

Representatives of the *Varieties of Capitalism (VOC)* school also advocate for the idea of persistent institutions over time (Thelen 2009). Early VOC scholars (Hall and Soskice 2001) claim that businesses are responsible for stabilizing existing institutional welfare and labor market arrangements to foster skill development, and also need to provide diversified quality production to create a comparative institutional advantage. Accordingly, the complementarity of welfare state policies and existing institutions in production regimes creates an institutional equilibrium that ensures success in coordinated market economies (CMEs). The setup of this strategic coordination provides room for intensive cross-class cooperation (Hall and Soskice 2001; Mares 2003; Swenson 2002). Thus, de-liberalizing policies in CMEs are not only dependent on companies' national production strategies but are also preferred by these companies because they provide for an institutional comparative advantage. However, early VOC approaches resulted in a growing number of critical responses emphasizing the lack of a notion of power, the exclusion of the state and party politics, a static and functionalist focus, the misjudgment of employers' preferences, and the disregard of ongoing liberalization processes, particularly in the realm of industrial relations (Hall and Thelen 2008; Streeck and Thelen 2005; Hancké et al. 2007; Hassel 2011; Baccaro and Howell 2017).

More recent approaches such as Thelen's Varieties of Liberalization (Thelen 2012, 2014) try to bridge the gap between VOC and its critics by introducing a differentiation between coordinated capitalism and egalitarian capitalism as well as a new definition of liberalization: *(a) liberalization as deregulation, often associated with LMEs; (b) liberalization as dualization, associated especially with continental European political economies like Germany; and, (c) liberalization through what we might think of as socially embedded flexibilization* (Thelen 2012: 146). Thelen hinges the different liberalization outcomes, or de-liberalizing accounts, on the organizational strength of labor and its ability to build political coalitions as well as on the specific competitive interest of employer organizations, and thus couples her institutional analysis with a certain amount of *power resource* (Thelen 2012, 2014). While both theoretical strands, the original VOC as well as Thelen's recent approach, are compatible with the occurrence of de-liberalization, the theories focus on different advocates of de-liberalizing change. If the VOC account were true, we would expect employers to be the main drivers of de-liberalizing change. If Thelen's varieties of liberalization were correct, we would assume that countries with powerful, highly-organized, and dense labor unions, which are deeply integrated in the policy process, would display a great deal of de-liberalization; this would especially be true for Nordic countries.

Another early strand of institutional accounts features the multiple concepts of corporatism.[1]

Katzenstein coined the notion of democratic corporatism in small (Western) European states that is characterized by the involvement of social partnership, business, and unions in national politics, the centralization and concentration of interest groups, and the voluntary and informal coordination of conflicting objects (Katzenstein 1985: 80–90). Additionally, Katzenstein further distinguishes between *liberal* and *social corporatism*, whereby the first is marked by strong, internationally oriented business communities and weak labor, which is especially prevalent in Switzerland, while the latter is denoted by strong, centralized labor unions and business communities that are politically weak, e.g. those prevalent in Austria (Katzenstein 1985: 104, 105). Closely linked with the concept of corporatism is the political tradition of consociational rather than majoritarian politics (Siaroff 1999; Schmidt 2006: 333). *Consociational democracies refer to a political style according to which political parties and governments regulate conflict by compromise and mutual concessions* (Armingeon 2002: 143), whereby majoritarian (or competitive) democracies solve conflicts through the principle of majoritarian rule (Schmidt 2006: 328).

Both *corporatism* and *consociational democracy* indicate specific styles of policymaking pursued by several political actors in a political system (Armingeon 2002: 143). *Consociational democracies* and *corporatism* are inherently associated with more compromise in policymaking rather than a zero-sum game (Armingeon 2002: 162, 163; Schmidt 2006: 334). With regards to de-liberalizing policies, we can assume that more compromise would also entail more de-liberalizing policies. Lijphart also states that a consensus democracy provides for more

[1]Earlier concepts focused on the organizational characteristics: *Corporatism can be defined as a system of interest representation in which the constituents' units are organized into a limited number of singular, compulsory, non-competitive, hierarchically ordered and functionally differentiated categories, recognized or licensed* [...] *by the state and granted a deliberate representational monopoly within their respective categories in exchange for observing*" (Schmitter 1979 [1974]: 13), while later concepts centered around the corporatist policymaking: "*Corporatism* [...] *is an institutionalized pattern of policy formation in which large interest organizations cooperate with each other and with public authorities not only in the articulation* [...] *of interests, but* [...] *in the 'authoritative allocation of values' and in the implementation of such policies* (Baccaro 2003 cited after Lehmbruch 1979: 150).

de-commodifying measures set by Esping-Andersen welfare standards (Esping-Andersen 1990), since a consensus democracy promotes *a kinder, gentler democracy* (Lijphart 1999: 294). Moreover, Armingeon (2002: 162, 163) demonstrates that consociational democracies show a tendency of higher social security expenditure in comparison to competitive democracies, once again indicating a propensity towards de-liberalization. Additionally, corporatist economies display a high amount of industrial peace and are able to adjust to external challenges through corporatist policymaking (Armingeon 2002: 153). Liberal corporatist countries are said to accept market-driven change more easily, only making political gestures for disadvantaged firms, whereas social corporatist countries are better able to cushion market-driven change than their liberal counterparts (Katzenstein 1985: 128–135). While corporatism and consociational democracies are both theoretical concepts, showing variety and deviations when applied to countries, both concepts indicate, theoretically, the tendency for de-liberalizing reform processes due to the inclusion of various interest groups, including capital and labor, and the focus on compromise-based solutions, particularly in social corporatist countries with strong labor unions and social democratic parties.

While *direct democracies* share many features with non-majoritarian democracies, Lijphart states that direct democracies cannot be regarded as either typically majoritarian or typically consensual (Lijphart 1999: 31). Direct democracies are defined as *the right of citizens to directly decide on substantive political issues by mean of popular votes, i.e., independently of the wishes of government or parliament* (Initiative and Referendum Institute Europe 2005: 228). The policymaking style of direct democracies is said to have a complicating and decelerating effect on policy reforms. Since all political participants have to be informed, have to vote, and can also challenge a vote, it can take a long time before consensus is reached on a reform. It is suggested that direct democracy has a weakening effect on welfare state expansion since the voter is actively informed about the cost of welfare expansions. Thus, it is posited that direct democracies shy away from expensive social policy arrangements, including high taxes and high welfare state expenditure (Schmidt 2006: 363–367). In this case, we would expect fewer de-liberalizing reforms in states with strong direct democracies.

Although the concept of federalism has been defined in a variety of ways (Duchacek 1987: 189; Inman and Rubinfeld 1997), several concepts points towards the following indicators: *[a] set of institutional arrangements and decision rules at central government level for incorporating territorially based interests—these arrangements vary in degree* (Obinger et al. 2005: 9). Accordingly, this specific form of government also affects policymaking. We anticipated that highly federalist and decentralized countries will have smaller governments and lower social expenditure growth because the states' budgets and scopes become smaller as taxes and expenditure are decentralized; competitive federalism may even hamper social policy expansion. Moreover, it is claimed that federalism promotes political fragmentation that impedes political coalition building and *power resource* approaches, which in turn would have fostered welfare state development (Swank 2002: 48). Moreover, the amount of actors and interest in politically fragmented system tends to delay or hinder policy decisions and reactions, and may therefore impede welfare state expansion[2] (Obinger et al. 2005: 35–37). Hence, we would expect highly federal countries to show fewer de-liberalizing policy reforms during the welfare state expansion period than less federal ones, yet there are also no strong indicators for retrenchment, since federal units, once in place, are not likely to give up their de-liberalizing policies (Leibfried et al. 2005: 318–323; 332–337). However, the variety and level of decentralization also plays a role in the introduction of de-liberalizing policies (Obinger et al. 2005: 11).

2.2 Political De-liberalization Strategies

2.2.1 Different Paths to De-liberalization

As we have seen, the literature provides a variety of theoretical accounts concerning liberalization and de-liberalization processes. Some narratives disregard the occurrence of de-liberalizing policies, while others offer explanations based on political actors, increased market pressures, *partisan* and *power resource strategies*, as well as several institutional accounts. Many contributions also place an emphasis on the relationship between liberalization and de-liberalization. While all these accounts provide interesting and fruitful insights, the majority of them lack the explanatory power to provide an argument for the distinct patterns of de-liberalizing changes in Austria, Germany, and Switzerland over time. Thus, I develop my argument from the three theoretical accounts which offer strong explanations for the occurrence of de-liberalizing policies: the rational choice approach, the newer partisanship theory, and the path dependency argument.

Against this backdrop, I make an argument that allows for a 'dynamic change' focusing on governments and their strategic employment of policies over time. This argument starts, therefore, from the premise that political parties want to gain and retain office for as long as possible (Persson and Tabellini 2000: 62). While I do not deny that functional and institutional constraints as well as past legacies matter, this book builds on the approach that political actors are, first and foremost, vote and office seeking individuals who will pursue their survival to the extent possible within their means (Beramendi et al. 2015: 2–3; Persson and Tabellini 2000: 62; Armingeon and Fill 2016). Proceeding from this theoretical account, I argue, firstly, that governments use de-liberalizing reforms to compensate for, and thereby enable liberalization processes. Secondly, governments and political parties use de-liberalizing reforms to mitigate the effects of earlier liberalization reforms and

[2]Obinger et al. (2005: 35–37) demonstrated that distinct welfare state expansion in the nineteenth century was also dependent on the rule of democracy. Countries under more authoritarian rule often experienced faster, more intensive welfare state development despite being federalist.

claim credit for new de-liberalizing reforms after far-reaching liberalization has been implemented and resulted in negative feedback from the public.

2.2.2 *De-liberalization as Compensation for Liberalization*

In the late 1980s, institutional welfare state arrangements started to be contested (Häusermann 2010: 20–23). Markets and national budgets began to apply pressure and legitimate welfare state policy reform (Streeck and Thelen 2005: 5–8; Häusermann 2010: 20–24). Thus, governments made their first attempts at welfare state retrenchment through a policy mix of liberalizing and de-liberalizing reforms. By using a combination of liberalization and de-liberalization, political parties were able to achieve liberalization despite opposing voters and interest groups. Firstly, the parties that were in office and relevant interest groups used de-liberalization policies to appease the political opposition by arranging policy deals and packages as compensation. The combination of de-liberalizing and liberalizing policies allowed governments to pursue liberalization while partly maintaining social policy and corporatist arrangements (Häusermann 2010; Pierson 1996). In particular, they were able to accommodate the demands of organized labor, which were, at this point in time, still powerful and dominant in shaping policy outcomes (Baccaro 2011).

Secondly, political parties used de-liberalizing policies to mitigate the negative effects for voters while also avoiding blame for liberalizing reforms (Pierson 1996, 2001). The mixture of liberalizing and de-liberalizing policies made it possible for governing parties to turn liberalizing reforms into electorally attractive propositions. In Austria, for example, the government reduced unemployment benefits in times of crisis, while at the same time introducing early retirement schemes for elderly citizens who have been particularly affected by layoffs due to an economic downturn (Armingeon et al. 2019). Thus, political parties could target their voters through the provision of more benefits in some areas while simultaneously pursuing welfare retrenchments in other areas.

This reasoning allows us to derive the following argument: political parties use de-liberalization to minimize conflict when introducing reforms and avoid blame from voters and interest groups (Drazen and Eslava 2005; Pierson 1996). Strategies often center on policy reform packages or *quid-pro-quo strategies* that combine both liberalizing and de-liberalizing policies (Häusermann 2010; Axelrod 1984; Obinger et al. 2010). The use of de-liberalizing policies therefore acts as an enabling mechanism for liberalization.

2.2.3 *Radical Liberalization Period*

As Pierson stated (Pierson 2004), however, timing matters because successful reform outcomes also depend on historical and institutional legacy as well as the context from which an issue emerges on the agenda (Häusermann 2010: 25). Some processes, such as liberalization, might only result in meaningful change over time (Pierson 2004: 90). By the end of the century, governments had fully committed to liberalizing strategies, while corporatist arrangements and industrial relations often deteriorated due to derogation and new practices that were introduced without formally adjusting these institutions (Baccaro and Howell 2017; Streeck and Hassel 2003; Häusermann 2010). Once governments were no longer dependent on unions to help them trade internal wage restraints for economic policy purposes, the 'meaningful corporatist exchange' between unions and politicians became a thing of the past (Goldthorpe 1984; Rathgeb 2016). Budget consolidation requirements from the European Union, mainly the Maastricht criteria, intensified the reform pressure on European member states (Scharpf 2002). Demographic stresses, rising unemployment, and declining productivity growth once again highlighted the public debt problem, while labor's power to resist was obliterated (Ebbinghaus 2006; Streeck 2009; Blyth 2013). The newly adopted status quo among governing parties was liberalization and austerity without the earlier compensation elements of reforms (Blyth 2013). This resulted in far-reaching transformations in continental European welfare states leading to welfare state reforms, rising inequality, and more precarious work (Kenworthy and Pontusson 2005; Häusermann 2010; Beramendi et al. 2015: 6–7). Hence, by the mid-2000s Austria, Germany, and Switzerland had undergone far-reaching liberalizing welfare state and labor market reforms (Obinger et al. 2010; Seeleib-Kaiser and Fleckenstein 2007; Streeck and Hassel 2003; Armingeon et al. 2019).

2.2.4 Post-liberalization: Mitigating Blame and Taking Credit

While governments accepted liberalization as the new status quo, voters were not unaffected by these negative changes (Blyth 2013). This shift resulted in a loss of votes for liberal reformers as well as new demands from voters and unions towards more de-liberalizing policies in the welfare state and on labor markets. (Obinger et al. 2010; Mabbett 2016; Beramendi et al. 2015; Dancygier and Walter 2015: 137–139).

These strong negative reactions to the politically salient topic of liberalization turned into negative feedback mechanisms on the part of voters and interest groups, which led to a dismissal of the political status quo (Jacob and Weaver 2015; Marx and Starke 2017). *When negative consequences of current policies are salient, in the sense that losses are cross-sectionally or temporally concentrated, the status quo becomes self-undermining* (Marx and Starke 2017: 6).

On the premise that politicians are vote- and office-seeking individuals, I argue further that political parties react to the altered circumstances resulting from the negative feedback to liberalization. Once far-reaching liberalizing reforms have produced negative circumstances which in turn have led to salient public debates, public and trade union support for liberalization and liberal reforms may wither, in particular where these changes in public opinion result in a loss of voters (Marx and Starke 2017). After liberalizing reforms have become unpopular among voters and interest groups, governments and political parties use de-liberalizing reforms to mitigate the effects of this earlier liberalization, which allows them to take credit for the introduction of new de-liberalizing reforms. Therefore, I argue that governments and political parties use de-liberalization to mitigate blame for earlier reforms. By introducing de-liberalizing policies, political parties can respond to negative critiques of earlier liberalizing reforms and demarcate themselves from liberal reformers or from the liberal reforms that they themselves had introduced previously. For example, the German Social Democrats changed course politically after being punished by their voters for their liberalizing *Hartz* reforms (Dostal 2016; Mabbett 2016). Moreover, political parties use de-liberalizing policies to take credit for new social protection measures against the backdrop of politically salient, negative liberalizing reforms. Once liberalizing reforms have become unpopular with voters and interest groups and political parties receive negative feedback, they can actively revisit these topics and introduce de-liberalizing policies to target the discontent voters and interest groups. In order to explain de-liberalization, I concentrate on endogenous political factors such as politicians' attempts to compensate for liberalizing reforms with corresponding de-liberalizing measures, and to mitigate negative feedback from voters through the introduction of de-liberalizing policies. However, I am not arguing that all countries de-liberalize to the same extent. De-liberalization policies, which are dependent on endogenous factors, need to have a majority appeal between political parties and interest groups, as well as the support (demand) of the public in order to be successfully enacted. Aiming to reach a powerful coalition, political parties often forge strategic alliances with organized labor to push for de-liberalization policies. Organized labor has continued to provide political support for de-liberalizing welfare policies despite trends towards neoliberalism (Gordon 2015; Thelen 2014; Naczyk and Seeleib-Kaiser 2015). The extent to which de-liberalizing reforms can be introduced depends on the relevant political parties' ability to form a coalition in support of de-liberalization.

Since political parties use de-liberalization mainly as a political strategy to compensate for liberalization policies, they primarily de-liberalize 'politically salient policies' (Culpepper 2011) which are highly salient such as social, labor, industrial relations, pension, tax and healthcare policies. As demonstrated by Culpepper, political parties take a stand on issues that are central to voters because these topics have a direct distributional outcome for these voters, and thus they might hold political parties accountable on these issues in future elections. Topics which are of importance to voters and about which voters are at least minimally informed are regarded as topics of *high political salience* (Culpepper 2011: 5–6).

In contrast, topics such as privatization, financial liberalization, and corporate governance are considered to be of low salience, and may be referred to as 'quiet policies'. These issues are not only of less interest to the electorate and trade unions given that there is no direct distributional outcome, but they are often deeply complex topics, and hence difficult to present to the public in a simple, straightforward manner. Thus, policymakers, interest groups, and the media mainly promote salient political topics to the public, while quiet policies such as financial regulation and corporate governance are often influenced by institutional and major shareholders as well as managers (Culpepper 2011: 5–6). Consequentially, quiet policies are not as prone to de-liberalizing reform (Armingeon and Fill 2016).

However, while political parties use de-liberalization to compensate for impending liberalization reform and mitigate blame for earlier liberalization reform, there still might be cases where national courts or international organizations such as the European Union arrange de-liberalization processes. These are examples of constraints that require political parties to adhere to the prescribed policies. In these cases, de-liberalization policies are not necessarily used to compensate for or prevent liberalization.

In summation, de-liberalizing policies can be introduced in the form of a reversal of earlier liberalizing processes, as a newly enacted institution or as an institutional change in either direction, denoting a policy reform package that includes both liberalizing and de-liberalizing changes. My argument in this book was developed in two steps. Based on the premise that governments and political parties are primarily vote- and office-seeking entities, I argued that most de-liberalization reforms are enacted to compensate for liberalization, to mitigate blame for earlier liberalization reforms, and to take credit for new de-liberalization policies after negative public feedback arises. On the whole, de-liberalizing reforms mainly concentrate on politically salient policy fields. The extent of the reforms, which varies from country to country, depends on the respective political parties' ability to form coalitions in support of de-liberalization.

During the first period of welfare state retrenchment, the overarching goal of the reforms introduced was to combine attempts at liberalization with compensatory policy elements that would be more attractive to voters. After far-reaching liberalization was implemented, de-liberalizing reforms were enacted not only to enable liberalization, but to respond to it or even reverse the previous liberalization trajectory.

References

Amable B, Gatti D, Schuhmacher J (2006) Welfare state retrenchment: the partisan effect revisited. Oxf Rev Econ Policy 22(3):426–444. https://doi.org/10.1093/oxrep/grj025

Armingeon K (2002) Interest intermediation: the cases of consociational democracy and corporatism. In: Keman H (ed) Comparative democratic politics: a guide to contemporary theory and research. Sage, London, pp 143–166

Armingeon K, Fill A (2016) Trajectories of liberalization and de-liberalization: actors matter. The cases of Austria, Germany, and Switzerland. Working paper presented at the annual conference of the Swiss Political Science Association on January 22, 2016

Armingeon K, Baccaro L, Fill A, Galindo J, Heeb S, Labanino R (2019) Liberalization database 1973–2013 (20170619). Available online July 2019

Axelrod R (1984) The evolution of cooperation. Basic Books, New York

Baccaro L (2003) What is alive and what is dead in theory of corporatism. Br J Ind Relat 41(4):683–706

Baccaro L (2011) Labor, globalization and inequality: are trade unions still redistributive? Comparing European workers. Part B: Policies and institutions. Res Soc Work 22:213–285

Baccaro L, Howell C (2017) Trajectories of neoliberal transformation. Cambridge University Press, Cambridge

Beramendi P, Häusermann S, Kitschelt H, Kriesi H (eds) (2015) The politics of advanced capitalism. Cambridge University Press, New York

Blyth M (2013) Paradigms and paradox: the politics of economic ideas in two moments of crisis. Governance 26(2):197–215

Boix C (1998) Political parties, growth & equality, conservative and social democratic economic strategies in the world economy. Cambridge University Press, Cambridge

Culpepper P (2011) Quiet politics and business power—corporate control in Europe and Japan. Cambridge University Press, Cambridge

Dancygier R, Walter S (2015) Globalization, labor market risks and class cleavages. In: Beramendi P, Häusermann S, Kitschelt H, Kriesi H (eds) The politics of advanced capitalism. Cambridge University Press, New York, pp 133–157

De Swaan A (1973) Coalition theories and cabinet formation. Elsevier, Amsterdam

Dostal J (2016) The crisis of German social democracy revisited. Polit Quart:1–11

Downs A (1957) An economic theory of democracy. Harper & Row, New York

Drazen A, Eslava M (2005) Electoral manipulation via expenditure composition: theory and evidence. NBER working paper No. 11085. http://www.nber.org/papers/w11085. Accessed 1 Mar 2017

Duchacek I (1987) Comparative federalism. The territorial dimension of politics. University Press of America, Lanham, MD

Ebbinghaus B (2006) Reforming early retirement in Europe, Japan and the USA. Oxford University Press, Oxford

Emmenegger P, Häusermann S, Palier B, Seeleib-Kaiser M (eds) (2012) The age of dualization: the changing face of inequality in deindustrializing societies. Oxford University Press, New York

Esping-Andersen G (1990) The three worlds of welfare capitalism. Polity Press, Cambridge

Garrett G (1998) Partisan politics in the global economy. Cambridge University Press, New York

Genschel P (2002) Globalization, tax competition, and the welfare state. Polit Soc 30(2):245–275

Goldthorpe J (1984) Order and conflict in contemporary capitalism. Oxford University Press, Oxford

Gordon J (2015) Protecting the unemployed: varieties of unionism and the evolution of unemployment benefits and active labour market policy in the rich democracies. Soc Econ Rev 13 (1):79–99

Hall P, Soskice D (eds) (2001) Varieties of capitalism: the institutional foundations of comparative advantage. Oxford University Press, Oxford

Hall P, Thelen K (2008) Institutional change in varieties of capitalism. Soc Econ Rev 7(1):7–34. https://doi.org/10.1093/ser/mwn020

Hancké B, Rhodes M, Thatcher M (eds) (2007) Beyond varieties of capitalism: conflict, contradictions, and complementarities in the European economy. Oxford University Press, Oxford

Hassel A (2011) The paradox of liberalization—understanding dualism and the recovery of the German political economy. LSE 'Europe in question' discussion paper series No. 42/2011. http://eprints.lse.ac.uk/53212/. Accessed 1 Feb 2017

Häusermann S (2010) The politics of welfare state reform in continental Europe. Modernization in hard times. Cambridge University Press, Cambridge

Häusermann S, Picot G, Geering D (2013) Partisan politics and the welfare state. Recent advances in the literature. Br J Polit Sci 43(1):221–240

Hewitt C (1977) The effect of political democracy and social democracy on equality in industrial societies: a cross-national comparison. Am Sociol Rev 42(3):450–464

Hibbs D (1977) Political parties and macroeconomic policy. Am Polit Sci Rev 71(4):1467–1487

Initiative and Referendum Institute Europe (2005) Guidebook to direct democracy, Amsterdam
Inman R, Rubinfeld P (1997) Rethinking federalism. J Econ Perspect 11(4):43–64
Iversen T (2001) The dynamics of welfare state expansion: trade openness, deindustrialization and partisan politics. In: Pierson P (ed) The new politics of the welfare state. Oxford University Press, Oxford
Iversen T, Cusack T (2000) The causes of welfare state expansion: deindustrialization or globalization? World Polit 52(3):313–349
Jacob A, Weaver K (2015) When policies undo themselves: self-undermining feedback as a source of policy change. Governance Int J Policy Admin Inst 28(4):441–457
Katzenstein P (1985) Small states in world markets industrial policy in Europe. Cornell University Press, Ithaca
Kenworthy L, Pontusson J (2005) Rising inequality and the politics of redistribution in affluent countries. Perspect Polit 3(3):449–471. https://doi.org/10.1017/S1537592705050292
Korpi W (1983) The democratic class struggle. Routledge & Kegan Paul, Boston
Kvist J (2004) Does EU enlargement start a race to the bottom? Strategic interaction among EU member states in social policy. J Eur Soc Policy 14(3):301–318
Lehmbruch G (1979) Liberal corporatism and party government. In: Schmitter P, Lehmbruch G (eds) Trends towards corporatist intermediation. Sage, London, pp 147–183
Leibfried S, Castles F, Obinger H (2005) Conclusion—'old' and 'new politics'. In: Obinger H, Leibfried S, Castles FG (eds) Federalism and the welfare state. New world and European experiences. Cambridge University Press, Cambridge, pp 307–353
Lijphart A (1999) Patterns of democracy: government forms and performance in thirty-six countries. Yale University Press, New Haven, CT
Mabbett D (2016) The minimum wage in Germany: what brought the state in? J Eur Publ Policy 23 (8):1240–1258. https://doi.org/10.1080/13501763.2016.1186210
Mares I (2003) The politics of social risk: business and welfare state development. Cambridge University Press, Cambridge
Marx P, Starke P (2017) Dualization as destiny? The political economy of the German minimum wage reform. Polit Soc:1–26. https://doi.org/10.1177/0032329217726793
Meinhard S, Potrafke N (2012) The globalization–welfare state nexus reconsidered. Rev Int Econ 20:271–287. https://doi.org/10.1111/j.1467-9396.2012.01021.x
Meltzer A, Richard S (1981) A rational theory of the size of government. J Polit Econ 89:914–927
Menz G (2009) European deregulation and national re-regulation: national response strategies revisited. In: Gamble A, Lane D (eds) The European Union and world politics: consensus and division. Palgrave Macmillan, Basingstoke, pp 157–176
Naczyk M, Seeleib-Kaiser M (2015) Solidarity against all odds: trade unions and the privatization of pensions in the age of dualization. Polit Soc 43(3):361–384
Obinger H, Castles F, Leibfried S (2005) Introduction: federalism and the welfare state. In: Obinger H, Leibfried S, Castles FG (eds) Federalism and the welfare state. New world and European experiences. Cambridge University Press, Cambridge, pp 1–46
Obinger H, Starke P, Moser J, Bogedan C, Gindulis E, Leibfried S (2010) Transformations of the welfare state. In: Small states, big lessons. Oxford University Press, Oxford
Olney W (2013) A race to the bottom? Employment protection and foreign direct investment. J Int Econ 91:191–203
Persson T, Tabellini G (2000) Political economics. Explaining economic policy. The MIT Press, Cambridge, MA
Pierson P (1994) Dismantling the welfare state? Reagan, Thatcher and the politics of retrenchment. Cambridge University Press, Cambridge
Pierson P (1996) The new politics of the welfare state. World Politics 48(2):143–179. https://doi.org/10.1353/wp.1996.0004
Pierson P (2001) The new politics of the welfare state. Oxford University Press, Oxford
Pierson P (2004) Politics in time: history, institutions, and social analysis. Princeton University Press, Princeton

Polanyi K (1957, 1944) The great transformation. Beacon Press, Boston
Rathgeb P (2016) Strong governments, precarious workers: labour market policy-making in the era of liberalization. EUI PhD theses. Department of Political and Social Sciences. http://hdl.handle.net/1814/43276. Accessed 1 Sep 2017
Rodrik D (1998) Why do more open economies have bigger government? J Polit Econ 106:997–1032
Scharpf F (1997) Economic integration, democracy and the welfare state. J Eur Publ Policy 4 (1):18–36
Scharpf F (2002) The European social model: coping with the challenges of diversity. J Common Mark Stud 40(4):645–670
Schmidt M (2006) Demokratietheorien—Eine Einführung. Verlag für Sozialwissenschaften, Wiesbaden
Schmitter C (1974) Still the century of corporatism? The Revof Politics 36(1):85–131
Schmitter P (1979) Still the century of corporatism? In: Schmitter P, Lehmbruch G (eds) Trends towards corporatism intermediation. Sage, London, pp 7–49
Seeleib-Kaiser M, Fleckenstein T (2007) Discourse, learning and welfare state change: the case of German labour market reforms. Soc Policy Adm 41(5):427–448
Siaroff A (1999) Corporatism in 24 industrial democracies: meaning and measurement. Eur J Polit Res 36(2):175–205
Simmons B, Elkins Z (2004) The globalization of liberalization: policy diffusion in the international political economy. Am Polit Sci Rev 98(1):171–189
Stephens JD (1979) The transition from capitalism to socialism. New studies in sociology. Palgrave, London
Streeck W (2009) Re-forming capitalism: institutional change in the German political economy. Oxford University Press, Oxford
Streeck W, Hassel A (2003) The crumbling pillars of social partnership. In Germany. Beyond the stable state. West Eur Polit 26(4):101–124
Streeck W, Thelen K (2005) Beyond continuity: institutional change in advanced political economies. Oxford University Press, New York
Strom K, Müller W (1999) Political parties and hard choices. In: Müller W, Strom K (eds) Policy, office, or votes? How political parties in Western Europe make hard decisions. Cambridge University Press, Cambridge, pp 1–36
Swank D (2002) Global capital, political institutions, and policy change in developed welfare states. Cambridge University Press, Cambridge
Swenson P (2002) Capitalists against markets. The making of labor and welfare state in the United States and Sweden. Oxford University Press, Oxford
Thelen K (2009) Institutional change in advanced political economies. Br J Ind Relat 47 (3):471–498. https://doi.org/10.1111/j.1467-8543.2009.00746.x
Thelen K (2012) Varieties of capitalism: trajectories of liberalization and the new politics of social solidarity. Annu Rev Polit Sci 15:137–159
Thelen K (2014) Varieties of liberalization: the new politics of social solidarity. Cambridge University Press, New York
Wunder HF (1999) International tax reform: its effect on repatriation decisions of multinational corporations. J Int Acct Audit Tax 8(2):337–353

Chapter 3
Methods and Research Strategies

The following chapter presents the methods used to test this book's argument. The chapter will start out by depicting the research strategy of a qualitative small-N study before discussing the criteria for the case selection. Subsequently, the chapter will introduce the data on which the main analysis is based.

3.1 Small-N Comparison

In order to investigate the policies and political processes of de-liberalization in Austria, Germany, and Switzerland, this work will engage in a comparative small-N case study by tracing de-liberalization reforms in all countries over a period of more than 30 years. Since the phenomenon of de-liberalization reform policies has not been widely acknowledged in the conventional scientific literature, a method which allows for not only generating theoretical content but also looking explicitly at the independent variables seems highly appropriate (Blatter and Haverland 2012: 27–29; Bennett and Elman 2008: 503).

However, since de-liberalization changes over time, this contribution adopts a combined approach, namely the co-variational approach (COV) complemented with causal process tracing (CTP); however, the co-variational approach generally dominates (Blatter and Haverland 2012: 205–207; Bennett and Elman 2008: 507). The first method investigates the differences between the cases and provides controls for explanatory factors influencing the outcome similar to a quantitative study. Causal process tracing also allows us to establish a connection between cause and effect within each case and over time (Blatter and Haverland 2012: 212–218; Bennett and Elman 2008: 507).

© Springer Nature Switzerland AG 2019

A. Fill, *The Political Economy of De-liberalization*, Contributions to Political Science, https://doi.org/10.1007/978-3-030-01066-9_3

3.1.1 Co-variational Comparison

This study will compare reform changes in the three countries over time, in particular de-liberalizing second order changes and/or third order changes or status quo changes in politically salient policy fields, namely active labor market policies, education, employment-protection legislation, healthcare, industrial relations, non-employment benefits, pension, tax and vocational education training, will be analyzed. The time period of the reform analysis runs from 1980 to 2015. The study starts in the 1980s—the onset of increased liberalization in many countries. The different periods of analysis in the case studies correspond largely to different governmental periods[1] to control for partisan accounts.

The framed de-liberalizing reforms will be analyzed according to the independent variables based on the literature review and the argument of this work. In order to control for the argument, the analysis will examine the reforms by looking at the timing, the actors and coalitions deciding on the reform, the political reasoning behind the reform, the decision-making process between the political actors, policy packages, and preceding or subsequent liberalizing reforms. The co-variational approach will be complemented with elements of causal process tracing based on the database and inferences from expert interviews that have been conducted for all three countries (Blatter and Haverland 2012: 205–207).

3.2 Case Selection

In order to provide for a good comparison, this study will select countries that are similar enough to be compared to one another, while at the same time different enough in their outcomes (*de-liberalization*) to probe the causes of different dimensions and shapes of de-liberalizing policy reform (Blatter and Haverland 2012: 42–45).

To investigate the phenomenon of de-liberalization, this book compares the reform trajectories of Austria, Germany, and Switzerland. Firstly, all three countries are Continental European welfare states that are particularly prone to de-liberalization reform. Even though Austria and Germany have been mature Continental European welfare states since the 1970s, while Switzerland only reached this status in the early 1990s,[2] they have all experienced similar welfare state pressures with respect to liberalization and new social risks (Häusermann 2010; Schulze and Schludi 2009; Obinger et al. 2010: 25–39, 193–198; Schmidt 2012;

[1]In the case of Switzerland, the period of analysis does not follow the governmental period at large since the party composition in the government did not change except between 2003 and 2007 (Obinger et al. 2010: 220).

[2]The case studies will provide a detailed picture of the economic, political, and welfare state related development of all three countries.

Manow 2005: 243–247). Secondly, all three countries share many similar institutional features in terms of politics and the economy. Austria, Germany, and Switzerland rely on the strategic interaction between the economy and the welfare state as observed in various social policies, corporatist arrangements, and extensive training systems (Hall and Soskice 2001). However, they each exhibit a slight variation in the coordination of these strategic interactions. While Austria has been characterized by a very strong neo-corporatism, including a powerful centralized union movement[3] that has also been referred to as *social corporatism,* Switzerland falls under the umbrella of a *liberal corporatism* characterizing a strong business community and more decentralized industrial relations (Heinisch 2001; Katzenstein 1985). Post-war Germany accommodated a robust model of industrial relations that ensured industrial peace and social cohesion at least until the 1990s when the system became more decentralized (Hassel 1999; Schmidt 2012; Streeck and Hassel 2003). Hence, all three countries display systems of corporatism, even though the manifestation in the political systems differs. Other important differences in the economy concern memberships in international organizations: Austria and Germany are members of the European Union and the eurozone, while Switzerland is only part of the Schengen Area (Vahl and Grolimund 2006; Lavenex and Schimmelfennig 2009; EU 2017). The political systems of these countries are similar in some ways and different in others. Switzerland has been regarded as a consociational democracy, Germany is considered as a hybrid between a consociational and a majoritarian democracy, and Austria is seen[4] as a hybrid with strong consociational tendencies (Schmidt 2006: 330; Schmidt 2010). All three countries are more or less federalist states to varying degrees (Obinger et al. 2005, 2010). The system of policymaking and the regulation of liberalizing and de-liberalizing reforms differs also. In Austria and Germany, policies are mainly legislated by governments occupying office which in return can also be held responsible for the enacted policies (Ucakar and Gschiegl 2009; Schulze and Jochem 2009; Onken 2013), while Switzerland is a direct democracy—a political system that is less dependent on specific legislation periods (Vatter 2013: 343).

Thirdly, all three countries exhibit a very similar ratio overall between liberalizing and de-liberalizing reforms[5]; however, all three countries have gone through phases of de-liberalization at different times and to varying degrees, which provides for an interesting comparison.

Austria, Germany, and Switzerland therefore make for an ideal comparison to investigate de-liberalization processes since all three countries embarked on de-liberalization and share many similar features, yet they exhibit an *important*

---

[3]Excluding a short interruption from 2000 to 2005 under the coalition of the Austrian People's Party and the right-wing Freedom Party (Hinterseer 2011).

[4]Austria was regarded as a consociational democracy until the 1990s, but subsequent political developments have raised questions about Austria's classification as consociational democracy (Schmidt 2010; Naßmacher 2010).

[5]Austria (57.0% lib to 43.0% de-lib), Germany (62.4% lib to 37.6% de-lib), and Switzerland (56.5% lib to 43.5% de-lib).

variance when it comes to possible influences and factors promoting de-liberalization, such as the partisan makeup of the government, the union density, and the interest mediation.

3.3 Data

The empirical analysis is based mainly on the Liberalization Database 1973–2013 of the University of Bern. The Liberalization Database systematically compiles liberalizing or de-liberalizing reform changes. The data set defines liberalization as the removal of market barriers or loosening of restrictions on free markets. De-liberalization implies a shift in the opposite direction—the tightening of restrictions on free market movements. Reform changes are tracked in the following policy areas: active labor market policies (almp), competition policy (comp), corporate governance (gov), education policy (edu), employment protection (epl), finance (fin), industrial relations (ir), healthcare (hc), nonemployment benefits (neb), pension systems (pen), privatization (pri), income and corporate taxes (tax), and vocational training (voctr).

In the Liberalization Database, each entry (row) refers to a specific reform activity. A reform is a change in the aforementioned policy fields. This change can take place in a liberalizing or a de-liberalizing direction. Based on Peter Hall's (1993) seminal work, this database differentiates between three different kinds of policy changes. A first-order change is a "process whereby instrument settings are changed. [. . .], while the overall goals and instruments of policy remain the same. [. . .]" (Hall 1993: 278). A second-order change occurs when the instruments of the given policies are altered, and a third-order change takes place when the goal of a given policy was changed via legislation. Since these changes are nested, a third-order change will most likely always involve a first- and a second-order change. In addition, the database captures the intended gravity of reforms with Baumgartner's (2013) concept of status quo change; this means if a policy change strongly challenges an existing status quo and greatly alters it, it qualifies as a status quo change.

The database covers 38 advanced, capitalist democracies, which are mostly members of the OECD states. The time period for of this database is set between 1973 and 2013[6]; however, countries that were not democratic in the year 1973 are included from the year when they became democratic.

A weighted liberalization index has been established based on the database. The index measures the intended incisiveness[7] or impact of all liberalizing and

[6]In the case of Austria, Germany, and Switzerland, the database includes data up to the year 2015 depending on the country.

[7]It is called intended incisiveness because the database as well as the index provide information only for the decision or the implementation of the law. However, the measurement of the actual political, economic, and societal outcome of the reform activity is not present in the Liberalization Database (Armingeon et al. 2019).

de-liberalizing reforms. The index adds the weighted policy changes together: each reform change is qualified according to the specific change and provided with a corresponding value: status quo changes and third-order changes are multiplied by 1, second-order changes are multiplied by 0.66, and first-order changes are multiplied by 0.33. All of the values for each single reform in every year are summed up. Calculations and analysis based on the weighted liberalization index will be an integral part of this research. Graphs created on the basis of this index will be based on a 3-year mean to fully account for policy reform legislation and an implementation circle (Armingeon et al. 2019).

In addition to the Liberalization Database, in this work I will draw on other information, such as primary national legal sources and scientific sources. Furthermore, I incorporate inferences from interviews with experts, party members, ministerial employees, and representatives of interest groups, foremost from the trade unions and employer associations of each country. Between January and April 2016, Klaus Armingeon and I conducted ten interviews in Austria, five in Germany, and three in Switzerland. The interviews lasted about an hour each. The questions were centered on liberalization and de-liberalization reform trajectories and the political actors behind these decisions.

References

Armingeon K, Baccaro L, Fill A, Galindo J, Heeb S, Labanino R (2019) Liberalization database 1973–2013 (20170619). Available online July 2019

Baumgartner F (2013) Ideas and policy change. Governance 26(2):239–258

Bennett A, Elman C (2008) Chapter 29: Case study methods. In: Reus-Smit C, Snidal D (eds) The Oxford handbook of international relations. Oxford University Press, Oxford

Blatter J, Haverland M (2012) Designing case studies—explanatory approaches in small-N research. Palgrave McMillan, Basingstoke

European Union (2017) Countries. https://europa.eu/european-union/about-eu/countries_en. Accessed 1 July 2017

Hall P (1993) Policy paradigms, social learning and the state. Comp Polit 25:275–296

Hall P, Soskice D (eds) (2001) Varieties of capitalism: the institutional foundations of comparative advantage. Oxford University Press, Oxford

Hassel A (1999) The erosion of the German system of industrial relations. Br J Ind Relat 37(3):483–505

Häusermann S (2010) The politics of welfare state reform in continental Europe. Modernization in hard times. Cambridge University Press, Cambridge

Heinisch R (2001) Defying neoliberal convergence: Austria's successful supply-side corporatism in the 1990s. Environ Plann Gov Policy 19(1):29–44

Hinterseer T (2011) Flexicurity in Österreich—Sozialpartner just renamed. Zentrum für Zukunftsstudien, Fachhochschule Salzburg. https://zfzsalzburg.files.wordpress.com/2011/08/03_hinterseer_flexicurity_neu.pdf. Accessed 1 Mar 2017

Katzenstein P (1985) Small states in world markets industrial policy in Europe. Cornell University Press, Ithaca

Lavenex S, Schimmelfennig F (2009) EU rules beyond EU borders: theorizing external governance in European politics. J Eur Publ Policy 16(6):791–812

Manow P (2005) Germany: cooperative federalism and the overgrazing of the fiscal commons. In: Obinger H, Leibfried S, Castles FG (eds) Federalism and the welfare state. New world and European experiences. Cambridge University Press, Cambridge, pp 222–263
Naßmacher H (2010) Politikwissenschaft. Oldenbourg Wissenschaftsverlag, München
Obinger H, Castles F, Leibfried S (2005) Introduction: federalism and the welfare state. In: Obinger H, Leibfried S, Castles FG (eds) Federalism and the welfare state. New world and European experiences. Cambridge University Press, Cambridge, pp 1–46
Obinger H, Starke P, Moser J, Bogedan C, Gindulis E, Leibfried S (2010) Transformations of the welfare state. In: Small states, big lessons. Oxford University Press, Oxford
Onken H (2013) Parteiensystem im Wandel—Deutschland, Grossbritannien, die Niederlande und Österreich im Vergleich. Springer Fachmedien, Wiesbaden
Schmidt M (2006) Demokratietheorien—Eine Einführung. Verlag für Sozialwissenschaften, Wiesbaden
Schmidt M (2012) Der mittlere Weg der Liberalisierungspolitik? Deutschland im internationalen Vergleich. In: Eckard J, Sturm R (eds) "Superwahljahr" 2011 und die Folgen. Nomos, Baden-Baden, pp 285–305
Schmidt T (2010) Hausbetreuung in Österreich—zwischen Legalisierung und Lösung? In: Scheiwe K, Krawietz J (eds) Transnationale Sorgearbeit, ihre Regulierung und die Praxis der Akteure—eine Einleitung. Springer Verlag für Sozialwissenschaften, Heidelberg, pp 171–198
Schulze I, Jochem S (2009) Germany: beyond policy gridlock. In: Immergut EM, Anderson K, Schulze I (eds) The handbook of west European pension politics. Oxford University Press, Oxford, pp 660–711
Schulze I, Schludi M (2009) Austria: from electoral cartels to competitive coalition-building. In: Immergut EM, Anderson K, Schulze I (eds) The handbook of west European pension politics. Oxford University Press, Oxford, pp 555–593
Streeck W, Hassel A (2003) The crumbling pillars of social partnership. In Germany. Beyond the stable state. West Eur Polit 26(4):101–124
Ucakar K, Gschiegl S (2009) Das politische system Österreichs und die EU. Facultas Verlags- und Buchhandels AG, Wien
Vahl M, Grolimund N (2006) Integration without membership: Switzerland's bilateral agreements with the EU. CEPS paperbacks. March 2006. Series: Centre for European Policy Studies (Brussels). CEPS paperbacks. Centre for European Policy Studies. ISBN 9290796162
Vatter A (2013) Das politische System der Schweiz. Nomos, Baden-Baden

Chapter 4
Austria: De-liberalization for the Voter

Austria has long been seen as a paragon of generous Christian Democratic welfare state in which the grand coalition government refused to bow to the pressures of liberalization (Obinger et al. 2010). Austro-Keynesianism and an extraordinary system of neo-corporatism made "*Austria the 'Island of the Blessed' in the Ocean of Globalization*" (Obinger et al. 2010: 24). However, in reality, Austria is no stranger to liberalization: In the early 2000s, a new governing coalition was formed by the conservative Austrian People's Party (Österreichische Volkspartei—ÖVP) and the Austrian Freedom Party (Freiheitliche Partei Österreichs—FPÖ). This coalition enacted far-reaching liberalization reforms; however, the liberalization processes in the welfare state came to a halt in 2006 and were superseded by a period of de-liberalizing reforms (Obinger et al. 2010: 24–78). As a result, Austria's reform path ended neither in a convergence towards Anglo-Saxon welfare and industrial relations institutions, nor in a frozen landscape. Rather, it is comprised of a mixture of both liberalizing reforms and de-liberalizing reforms (Hall and Soskice 2001; Esping-Andersen 1996; Armingeon et al. 2019).

© Springer Nature Switzerland AG 2019
A. Fill, *The Political Economy of De-liberalization*, Contributions to Political Science, https://doi.org/10.1007/978-3-030-01066-9_4

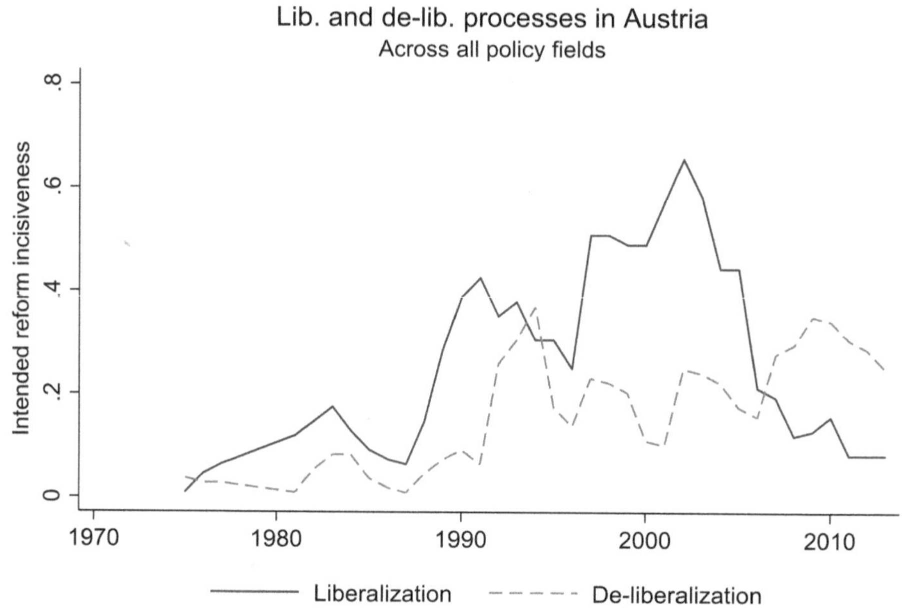

Fig. 4.1 Liberalization and de-liberalization processes in Austria across all policy fields. Source: Liberalization Database (Armingeon et al. 2019)

So how, then, can we explain the occurrence of de-liberalization processes in Austria?

One potential explanation, the *compensation hypothesis,* would link the occurrence of de-liberalization to the rise of globalization. However, looking closer at Austria's de-liberalization process, we can see that it was not a linear process despite an on-going liberalization process. Austria demonstrates two periods of comprehensive de-liberalization, yet these periods did not occur at the same time as liberalization; instead they followed afterwards. Additionally, there was a far-reaching liberalization period between 2000 and 2005 without any clear compensation measures (Armingeon et al. 2019). Hence, this approach does not allow us to fully explain the de-liberalizing reform developments that took place.

The *traditional partisanship explanation* links the rise of de-liberalizing policies to the Austrian Social Democratic Party (Sozialdemokratische Partei Österreichs—SPÖ) (Häusermann 2010; Pontusson 2011). Even though the Austrian Social Democrats have been very present in Austrian politics during periods of de-liberalization, they also have been in office during liberalization proceedings up to the 2000s (Obinger et al. 2010). During the first welfare state retrenchment period between 1980 and the early 1990s, as well as during the enactment of the two austerity packages in 1995 and 1996, the Social Democrats were not only in office, but also gained power in the executive branch by appointing a Chancellor. In that sense, the Social Democrats enacted market-sided policies and did not avoid a liberal path (Obinger et al. 2005: 211; Tálos and Wörister 1998). Another possible explanation—the *power resource approach* (Korpi 1983)—does not hold up either when confronted with Austria's distinct reform path. In 1995, the government passed the first austerity measure; however, it was doomed to fail when the social partners did not give their consent. In 1996, the social partners prepared another austerity package which included far-reaching liberalizing policy amendments and was successfully implemented thanks to the social partners' consent (Unger and Heitzmann 2003). Ultimately, the unions also opted for market-conforming policies.

An explanation based on *Varieties of Capitalism* cannot shed light on the inquiry how de-liberalizing policies came about in Austria. While VOC scholars would attribute de-liberalizing welfare state processes to the employers' preference for cross-class coordination and social policy investments to secure workers and skills (Hall and Soskice 2001; Mares 2003; Pastor 2014; Afonso 2012), the reality showed that it was mainly the grand coalition government and the unions who sought to initiate de-liberalizing reforms. Moreover, the Austrian association of employers, the Austrian Economic Chamber (Wirtschaftskammer Österreich—WKÖ) continually demanded welfare cuts (Rathgeb 2017; Interview BAK 2016a). Another producer group approach, Thelen's Varieties of Liberalization (Thelen 2014), is likewise not able to explain Austria's de-liberalizing outcome. Thelen would predict a dualistic de-liberalizing outcome for Austria, which may be true for Germany, but does not resemble Austria's de-liberalizing path (Rathgeb 2016). Furthermore, a corporatist approach *à la* Katzenstein (1985) is not able to illustrate the distinct reform pattern in Austria because his reasoning hinges market-cushioning policies on the emergence of liberalization processes, and yet there were no strong de-liberalizing policies during times of far-reaching liberalization.

Because of this, I contest the validity of the approaches specified above in order to explain the occurrence of de-liberalization policies in Austria. De-liberalization processes in Austria were strategically enacted by the Austrian government in order to compensate for and mitigate blame after liberalization processes while also taking credit for new de-liberalization policies.

The case study section proceeds as follows: Firstly, I provide a brief overview of Austria's welfare state and post-war economy from the point of view of liberalization and de-liberalization processes. Subsequently, different reform periods will be analyzed. Each period will provide for an overall development process of liberalizing and de-liberalizing reforms and the politics behind these actions before transitioning to the analysis of Austria's de-liberalizing second-order, third-order, and status quo policy changes in depth; these changes will be titled *comprehensive de-liberalization processes*. The selection for the comprehensive de-liberalization process is based on the availability of data and the importance of the case. Process tracing and interviews will be integrated into the analysis. In the conclusion, I will debate the main findings of this case relative to the central argument.

4.1 Austria's De-liberalization Processes: The Beginnings

Austria's de-liberalization process began in the 1980s at the same time that the first attempts to restrict the welfare state started. At the outset of these liberalization and de-liberalization processes, Austria was a fully matured welfare state with copious social democratic elements and a protected economy. Throughout the post-war period, Austria enjoyed an extensively nationalized industrial sector and a high level of public sector employment. Economic policy was based on Austro-Keynesianism, which combined Keynesian demand management with hard monetary policy towards the Deutsche Mark, moderate wage policies, and a high employment rate in nationalized industries (Obinger et al. 2010: 28–31; Nowotny 1996; Unger and Heitzmann 2003). The country was home to a large amount of state-owned companies because Austria nationalized most of its industries after the Second World War in order to safeguard the country's economic independence after German occupation. For that reason, it is estimated that by the end of the 1970s, 25% of the gross national product was produced by publicly owned firms (Armingeon and Fill 2016). Many of these sectors, such as telecommunications, energy supply, and the food industry, were sheltered from international competition (Belke and Schneider 2005).

Austria's post-war policy management was characterized by a strong cooperation between capital, labor, and the government. The most important interest groups have been the Austrian Economic Chamber (Wirtschaftskammer Österreich—WKÖ), the Chamber of Labor (Bundesarbeiterkammer—BAK), the Chamber of Agriculture (Landwirtschaftskammer—LK), the Austrian Trade Union Federation (Österreichischer Gewerkschaftsbund—ÖGB), and the Federation of Austrian Industries (Industriellen Vereinigung—IV). Political conflicts, cooperation, and interests have mainly been mediated between a few organizationally privileged peak associations of labor, capital, and the federal government. Additionally, these interest groups used to be closely linked to both major parties: the Austrian Social Democrats and the Austrian People's Party. The entanglement between the parties and the groups of capital and labor were not only based on the various groups' shared interests with regards to political issues, but the parties and the interest groups incorporated the same personnel. Therefore, the Austrian corporatism represented not only a horizontal linkage but also vertical linkage between parties and interest groups (Tálos 2008a; Ennser-Jedenastik 2016). The vertical linkages occurred both between the Social Democrats and BAK-ÖGB and between the Austrian People's Party and WKÖ-IV. The corporatist framework allowed for a close cooperation between capital and labor, which predominantly resulted in industrial peace and political stability (Eurofund 2017a; Tálos 2008a: 32–33, 43–44).

Consequently, Austria's de-liberalization and liberalization path started from a generous welfare state with a broad number of constituencies and a protected economy organized and strongly bolstered by the state. Policy-making processes were influenced by a pronounced corporatism.

4.2 Liberalization and De-liberalization Between 1980 and 1989

Whereas Austria demonstrated comparatively favorable outlooks with a low unemployment rate throughout the 1970s, things started to change throughout the 1980s. The Austrian economy was pressured by various endogenous and exogenous strains. The first challenge came from the nationalized industrial enterprises, which incurred major losses. The public industry crisis was the consequence of severe individual mismanagement, primarily in terms of investments and unqualified managerial board postings. Additionally, the industry was affected by an international steel crisis (Nowotny 1996). The breakdown of the national industry resulted in growing unemployment, with rates rising above 5% in 1987 (Trading economics 2017). Secondly, the national budget was also stressed due to increasing social security claims as a result of job losses and labor hoarding, all of which led to a budget deficit of nearly 5% the GDP in 1985 (Unger and Heitzmann 2003; Obinger et al. 2010: 41). Thirdly, the liberalization of capital made it more difficult to control interest rate policies and increased the importance of financial markets (Unger and Heitzmann 2003). Consequentially, the Austro-Keynesian policy management lost importance (Scharpf 1987).

4.2.1 Liberalization Policies Between 1980 and 1989

In an attempt to counter the aftershocks of the crisis in public structures, the government restructured the Austrian Industry Holding (Österreichische Bundes- und Industriebeteiligungen—ÖIAG) (Nowotny 1996). In 1987, the ÖIAG was privatized and allowed for up to 49% private ownership. The government also began introducing liberalization processes in other fields such as the financial market, which had been one of the most repressed financial markets in Europe prior to the late 1970s. The government reformed the financial sector by liberalizing interest rates and abolishing credit controls in 1980 and 1981, only to re-establish interest controls through the interest rate cartel in 1985. At the end of the 1980s, Austria liberalized its capital accounts, the interest rate cartel expired, and Austria opened up its capital market in 1987. The financial liberalization happened very gradually and did not entail a financial crisis (as in many other states). Austria later applied to join the European Economic Community (EEC) in 1989 (Braumann 2004).

The government also introduced small-scale reforms in terms of welfare state policies, for example in the area of pensions, which became unsustainable due to extensive labor hoarding; amendments included some cutbacks through changes in the linear accrual rates[1] and extensions of the reference period[2] that mostly affected women. In 1987, further modifications followed after hefty negotiations took place between the government and the unions. However, the adjustment was, compared to the discussion surrounding it, rather minor and included some changes in the treatment of the educational period, the accumulation of widowers' pensions, and liberalizing changes in the reference periods (Schulze and Schludi 2009; Obinger et al. 2010). The government reformed the labor market with both liberalizing and de-liberalizing measures, for instance, a rise in contributions for unemployment insurance and the suspension of unemployment benefits in cases of severance payments. Liberalizing reforms were implemented in both salient and non-salient policy fields; the changes in salient policy fields were rather minor while the changes in non-salient policy fields had a much greater impact.

4.2.2 De-liberalization Policies Between 1980 and 1989

Throughout the 1980s, the Austrian government also introduced de-liberalizing policies which deviated from earlier welfare state expansion. These de-liberalization policies happened in response to political strategies and the aim to liberalize. The reforms occurred in salient policy fields such as social and labor market policies (Pierson 1996; Häusermann 2010). These de-liberalizing policies resulted mostly in small adjustments and can therefore be categorized as first-order changes according to Hall (1993). In terms of pensions and unemployment benefits, the government expanded several benefit schemes. Additionally, the government introduced various training programs for the unemployed, in particular for the youth and in regions with high unemployment levels, as well as new forms of early retirement pensions. In the field of family benefits, the government began introducing some tax reforms to lower the burden on families with children while also extending the parental leave allowance from 12 to 24 months. Furthermore, it lengthened parental leave in 1990 (Obinger et al. 2010: 43, 44; Armingeon et al. 2019).

[1]An accrual rate is an important part of the pension formula: it is the rate at which a pension benefit is built up while the prospective retiree is an active member of a defined benefit scheme (Investopia 2017).

[2]Under automatic enrolment rules, the reference period is the period of time over which earnings are to be measured.

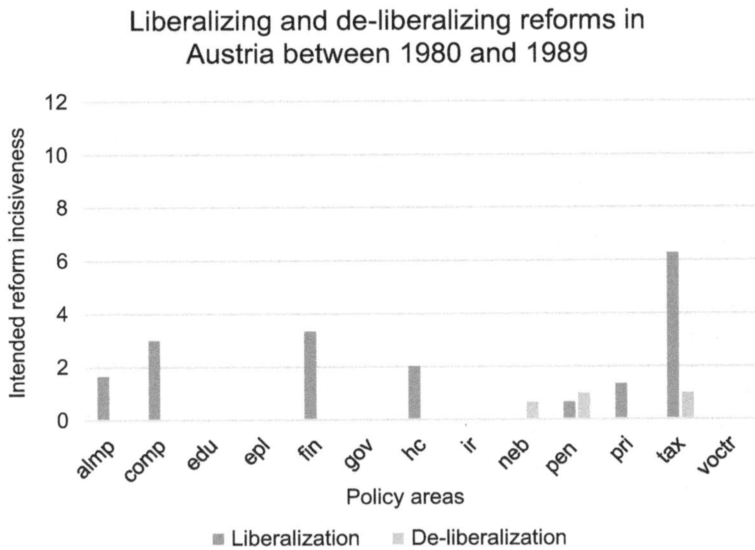

Fig. 4.2 Liberalizing and de-liberalizing reforms in Austria between 1980 and 1989 across all policy fields. Reforms are weighted according to the liberalization index (values: first-order changes: 0.33; second-order changes: 0.66; third-order and status quo changes: 1). Source: Liberalization Database (Armingeon et al. 2019)

4.2.3 Politics Between 1980 and 1989: Consolidation Attempts Result in De-liberalization

Despite growing economic obstacles and mounting expenditures in the welfare state, the political actors across all the different government formations opted for a mixture of modest de-liberalizing and liberalizing reforms in the welfare state (Obinger et al. 2010: 37–41; Unger and Heitzmann 2003). The majority of liberalizing reforms happened in the financial sector, yet some also occurred in politically salient areas, for example the restructuring of national industries. Damage to the state-owned industries resulted in heavy job losses which troubled typically stable SPÖ voters (Unger and Heitzmann 2003). However, the SPÖ-ÖVP coalition government under the Social Democratic Chancellor Franz Vranitzky refrained from heavy benefit cuts, despite the increased fiscal and economic pressures. On the contrary, the government expanded benefits that managed to outweigh retrenchment on the labor market until 1993. Even though the rise in expenditures led to criticism from employers, it also targeted the groups particularly affected by the privatization program. By reforming gradually while also expanding some social policies, the government was able to mitigate blame for reforms. The favored strategy was dichotomous—including both liberalizing and de-liberalizing changes. The focus on expenditure and fiscal stabilization also demonstrated that the government was not yet able to fully let go of its

Keynesian goals, which maintained low unemployment (Obinger et al. 2010: 40–42, 44–45). Overall, the government changed neither the basic goals nor the structures of the welfare state provision, but rather preserved the status quo (Obinger et al. 2010: 40–42, 44–45).

The cooperation between the government and the social partners showed slight fissures after the grand coalition adopted the above-mentioned liberalizing reforms, particularly the restructuring of the national industries. However, the overall trend of the relationship between the social partners and government demonstrated continuity more so than stark interruptions (Tálos and Kittel 2001: 83; Unger and Heitzmann 2003; Tálos 2008a: 90).

Between 1980 and 1989, the introduction of de-liberalization policies and political strategies of compensation were marketable. At the beginning of the 1980s, the Social Democrats governed alone. Later they governed with the inexperienced Freedom Party, which allowed the Social Democrats to determine the reform path. Throughout both government periods, the Social Democrats were able to follow a social democratic strategy focusing on expenditure rather than liberalization (Obinger et al. 2010: 38, 39). After 1986, when a grand coalition between the Social Democrats and the People's Party came into office, the government opted for a strategy of compensation. The Social Democrats and the People's Party came closer together ideologically under the new Chancellor Franz Vranitzky, but still displayed differences. The grand coalition presented itself as a restructuring partnership that would solve new arising problems in consensus (Obinger et al. 2010: 41). After the election, the new Chancellor, Franz Vranitzky, stated, "*Josef Taus*[3] *and I have discussed matters for a long time, before there was even the slightest sign of a grand coalition, and we found middle ground*"[4] (Die Zeit 1987). The consequences resulted in a reform subject catalogue that both parties presented to the public at the beginning of their time in office (Müller 1994). The focus on cooperation was also fueled by an uprising from the Greens and the Freedom Party (Obinger et al. 2010: 43–45). Hence, the relatively balanced power between the parties, which would allow them to block each other, together with the threat from the political competition, resulted in a compensation strategy of the two ideologically divided but still pro-welfare state parties (Obinger 2002; Obinger et al. 2010: 67).

Several policy reforms were introduced in form of a bargaining exchange, for example the unemployment insurance reform law of 1989 in which the Social Democrats and the unions agreed to reduce the contribution rates coupled with a tightened use of sanctions against the upward homogenizations of net replacement rates (Tálos and Rossmann 1992: 52, 58–59).

Policy reform patterns between 1980 and 1990 support my argument that de-liberalizing policies are introduced to compensate voters or opposing parties for

---

[3]Josef Taus was the leader of the People's Party between 1975 and 1979 (Österreichisches Parlament 2017).

[4]This quote was translated from German. The original quote states: "*Über die Grundidee haben wir beide, Josef Taus und ich, aber schon lange, ehe von einer Großen Koalition überhaupt die Rede war, ziemlich oft diskutiert und uns auf einer gemeinsamen Linie gefunden*" (Die Zeit 1987).

the introduction of liberalization. Pressures to reform were not directly translated into far-reaching cuts in salient policy fields, but rather retrenching reforms were introduced incrementally and coupled with de-liberalization. Authors such as Rathgeb (2016), Tálos and Rossmann (1992: 51–52), and Tálos and Kittel (2001: 124) see the reason for the balanced reform outcome, despite deep convictions to reform, also in the cooperation strategy between two parties which were supporting both their electorate as well as associated interest groups.

In sum, the period between 1980 and 1989 marked Austria's first departure from its earlier, untroubled economic and political period in the post-war era. Austria was pressured by both exogenous and endogenous strains. The government reacted to the pressures by liberalizing the financial sector and the state-owned industry, while only gradually reforming welfare policies. Thus, the overall period demonstrates a policy path of incremental adjustment coupled with de-liberalizing policies. De-liberalization strategies clearly helped to compensate both coalitional partners and voters.

4.3 Liberalization and De-liberalization Between 1990 and 1999

Mounting pressure further emphasized liberalizing endeavors during the early 1990s. Austria experienced a labor supply shock at the beginning of the new decade (Unger and Heitzmann 2003). As a result, unemployment rose to 4.2% in 1993 (OECD 2017a), while the labor market was simultaneously pressured by a rise in long-term unemployment. Moreover, the country was stressed by a very costly pension system, which was stimulated by extensive labor hoardings. In 1994, Austria spent nearly 15% of its gross domestic product (GDP) on pension expenditures, making their pension system one of the most expensive in the world (IMF 1997; Obinger et al. 2010: 41; Busemeyer 2007). Alongside the labor market and the welfare state, the stress on Austria's budget grew due to a decrease in economic growth (Obinger et al. 2010: 41; Busemeyer 2007). The problems facing both the economy and the welfare state were particularly highlighted by the country's upcoming accession to the European Union and the concomitant fulfillment of the Maastricht criteria. Hence, there was a strong incentive to impose austerity policies (Obinger et al. 2010: 41, 42).

Faced with mounting expenditure problems, the grand coalition adopted a novel programmatic approach focusing on moderate supply-side economic modernization. While the Social Democratic Party opted for a mixed approach, including cuts and expenditure, the People's Party officially settled on economic neoliberalism by advocating for deregulation, flexibilization in the labor market, and expenditure cuts. Despite the newly proclaimed policy course, the period between 1990 and 1999 was one of balanced reforms. Even though the government moved away from Austro-Keynesian measures, it still did not engage in far-reaching liberalizing welfare state adjustments (Obinger et al. 2010: 42, 47). As the following policy reform analysis shows, the majority of liberalizing welfare state reforms were clearly paired with de-liberalizing compensation measures that targeted voters. The consequences were made clear through a rise in public debt which grew up to 69.2% the GDP in 1995 (Obinger et al. 2010: 47).

4.3.1 Liberalization Policies Between 1990 and 1999

At the start of the 1990s, the government still opted for a mixed reform approach in the labor market, introducing expansions and retrenchments. In terms of liberalizing policies, the government increased the pressure on the long-term unemployed who had received unemployment benefits for more than three years. From the mid-1990s on, the government intensified retrenchment and activation policies. Thus, the replacement rate was lowered to 57% and the qualifying conditions for unemployment benefits were made more strictly. Another important liberalization on the labor market concerned the change of governance within the organization responsible for running the employment service. In 1994, the government shifted the governance responsibility from the Austrian employment service (Arbeitsmarktservice—AMS) towards the social partners (bipartite for decisions and control, tripartite for the supervisory board of the federal AMS). The grand coalition also adopted a law to promote labor market flexibilization in 1997 (Obinger et al. 2010: 45, 48). The employers demanded this change of responsibility because they wanted to increase the efficiency with regards to the management of short- and long-term unemployment.

In the mid-1990s, efforts were made to introduce a budget consolidation package (*Strukturanpassungsgesetz I*) in order to prepare for EU membership and reduce the strain on the budget. In 1995, the government introduced the first package, which failed because the social partners did not give their consent. A second consolidation package (*Strukturanpassungsgesetz II*), prepared by the social partners, followed shortly afterwards in 1996. In the course of this package the accrual rate of pensions was made more linear, while the eligibility for early retirement and disability pensions was tightened. However, some eager aspirations of the People's Party were not realized and resulted in discontent between the parties and the interest groups (Obinger et al. 2010: 47–52).

The coalition also tried to offset mounting healthcare expenditures by cutting down on various reimbursements for medical services and raising the co-payment amounts on patient rehabilitation programs. Most importantly, the government introduced diagnosis-related budgeting into the healthcare system (Obinger et al. 2010: 46; 51, 52; Busemeyer 2007; Unger and Heitzmann 2003).

Throughout the 1990s, the government also intensified its privatization programs, specifically in the fields of banking, energy services, transportation, and in the metal industries, for instance with the privatization of Voestalpine, a steel-based technology and capital goods group (Braumann 2004; Belke and Schneider 2005). After 1995, when Austria joined the European Union, new policy approaches emerged and privatization slowly took over. This early privatization process was strongly influenced by EU deregulation and privatization initiatives in the field of telecommunications, gas, electricity, and other service markets. However, the privatization of state-owned companies mainly resulted in national takeovers (Belke and Schneider 2005; Braumann 2004; Hammerschmied and Meyer 2005).

4.3.2 De-liberalization Policies Between 1990 and 1999

Even though the grand coalition attempted to contain welfare state expenditures, the spending on social policies grew from 23.2% the GDP in 1990 up to 26% the GDP in 1995 (OECD 2017b). The rising expenditures were also mirrored by the introduction of comprehensive de-liberalization reform changes. Various factors led to these de-liberalization processes. On one side, the government compensated for some liberalizing measures with de-liberalizing measures. One the other, the 1990s marked the first period in which Austria had to abide by European law, and thus introduced some de-liberalizing policies in the labor market, which hinged on the European Union.

At the beginning of the 1990s, expansionary measures clearly outweighed liberalizing attempts on the labor market. The government abolished a discriminatory clause that precluded women from obtaining unemployment assistance if their partner or spouse was employed full-time. Further, based on a constitutional court ruling, foreigners were accepted into the unemployment assistance schemes. The government increased benefits for older unemployed workers with long insurance records and strengthened dismissal protection for older workers: if workers aged 50 or older were laid off, their employer would be required to submit justification in writing to the labor office and provide compulsory contributions for the retraining of the older worker. The coalition also made it easier for workers to receive part-time pensions. Additional de-liberalizing measures included the following changes: the unemployment benefits qualifying period for persons under 25 was reduced from 52 to 20 weeks (Obinger et al. 2010: 44; Armingeon et al. 2019). The government also increased its spending on active labor market policy and adopted training measures while bolstering protections for workers in the event of company takeovers. The employment contract adjustment law guaranteed that existing employment contracts would be taken over except if the company was sold due to bankruptcy. The administration also passed laws advancing the employment rights of atypical workers and the rights of work councils.

The coalition increased the eligibility for social insurance by including self-employed workers into the health, pension, and accident insurance scheme in 1996. Lastly, the government raised payroll taxes, and also raised the corporate tax rate from 30 to 34% (Obinger et al. 2010; Armingeon et al. 2019; Hofer and Weber 2006).

The social partners adjusted the vocational education system to meet the challenges of the lack of apprenticeships (Lehrstellen), the shortage of qualified personnel, and the increasing competition between school-based and dual-based training in 1997. Reform actions included the modernization of apprenticeship trades as well as the possibility for vocational trainees to take a university entrance exam (Trampusch 2009). Overall, the 1990s were a time of large-scale de-liberalizing reform efforts in the field of salient welfare state policies; in the early 1990s, de-liberalization processes even superseded liberalization processes.

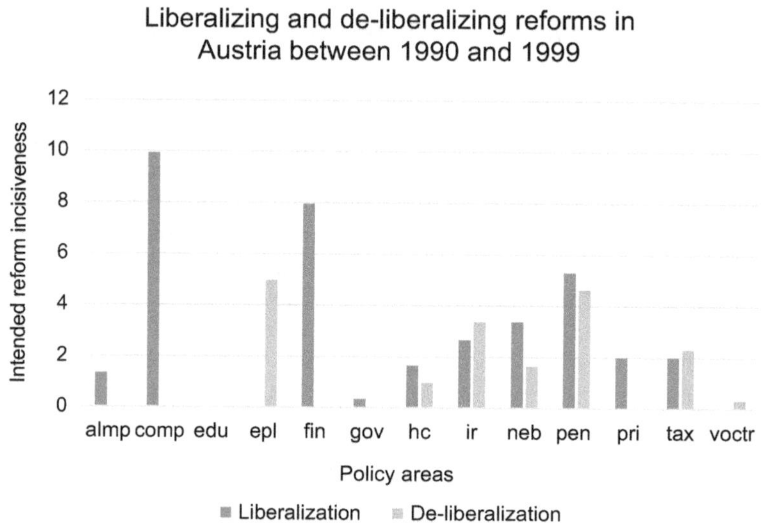

Fig. 4.3 Liberalizing and de-liberalizing reforms in Austria between 1990 and 1999 across all policy fields. Reforms are weighted according to the liberalization index (values: first-order changes: 0.33; second-order changes: 0.66; third-order and status quo changes: 1). Source: Liberalization Database (Armingeon et al. 2019)

4.3.3 Politics Between 1990 and 1999: Going European—On the Verge of Liberalization

Both parties in the grand coalition systematically shifted course towards moderate supply-side strategies. This new focus was the result of several influences: the Social Democrats were led by a new Chancellor, Franz Vranitzky, who was a former bank manager and opted for a pragmatic modernization approach. The People's Party adopted an approach of internationally inspired moral conservatism under their new ambitious and reform-minded leader, Wolfgang Schüssel. With these changes in consideration, these new approaches have also been fueled by the accession to the European Union and budgetary problems (Obinger et al. 2010: 42; Unger and Heitzmann 2003; Bischof and Plasser 2010).

Under their new programmatic course, the Social Democrats advocated revenue increases mixed with spending cuts, while the People's Party promoted far-reaching expenditure cuts. The social democratic approach focused also on the modernization of the welfare state emphasizing the feasibility of combining work and family (Tálos and Wörister 1998: 227; Mairhuber 2003). In the late 1980s until the mid-1990s, the government parties were close enough to find common ground and agree on compensation strategies. Looking at the following analysis of comprehensive de-liberalizing policies, one can see how both pro-welfare-state parties were able to agree on compromises whereby the Social Democrats were always a bit stronger and were able to demand more concessions. This underpinning was also confirmed from an employee of the BAK who said that when grand coalitions rule, there will always be talks and compensation politics, yet, the weaker party will have to give more concessions (Obinger et al. 2010; Interview BAK 2016b).

After the mid-1990s, however, the ideological gap between the two parties widened, leading to serious discontent and resulting in earlier elections. Judging from the outcome of the 1995 election, the Social Democrats' two-fold reform approach was more popular than the ÖVP's campaign for fiscal retrenchment (Wagschal and Wenzelburger 2008: 104). The Social Democrats increased their votes from 35.3% to 38.8% in a single year, while the People's Party came in second with 28.4% (Armingeon et al. 2016). Hence, the Social Democrats, being successful with their compensation strategy, tried to preserve a dual reform strategy for their voters that included both de-liberalizing and liberalizing approaches.

The discord between the two parties increased throughout the preparations for EU accession. Even though the parties in the grand coalition, employers, and unions favored entry into the European Union, the government had difficulties agreeing on appropriate measures to bring the budget in order (Unger and Heitzmann 2003; Heinisch 2001). The government finally opted for cuts across all welfare policy fields in order to accelerate fiscal consolidation, as evidently illustrated in their government program of 1994 (Rathgeb 2016). The reform attempts resulted in two austerity packages: one in 1995 and one in 1996 (Obinger et al. 2010: 47–49). The former was adopted against the will of the social partners and led to disagreement between the political parties, as well as between the government and the social partners. After the parties in the grand coalition were unable to agree on further reform measures, the social partners coordinated the second austerity package. Labor and capital served as reform brokers and influenced reform policies on the behalf of the grand parties (Heinisch 2000; Tálos and Badelt 1999). Even though the second austerity policy package was successfully implemented, the relationship between the grand parties deteriorated. Negotiations on how to divide the costs of fiscal consolidation emphasized the disharmony between the ideologically divided camps (Obinger 2002). Tensions over ideological differences on policymaking spilt also over on to the social partners (Obinger et al. 2010: 48).

The accession to the European Union marked a watershed in the political concerns of the Austrian electorate. In 1994, a majority of Austrians voted to join the European Union. When Austrians were asked in 1995 to state their main political concern, 56% said 'the budget deficit and taxes' while only 30% mentioned 'social justice and concern for the unemployed' and around 15% were worried about 'welfare abuses and scandals' (IMAS-poll quoted in die *Wirtschaftswoche* 20 November, 1995 cited in Heinisch 2001; Granell 1995). When we look at these figures, it is clear that the quest for de-liberalization had also abated amongst the electorate.

Against the backdrop of increasing economic pressures and the accession to the European Union, Austrian politics and reform approaches changed after the mid-1990s. The Social Democrats moved towards the center, while the People's Party adopted a neoliberal approach under their new leader, resulting in a political disagreement between the two parties. This change of heart was mirrored in the policy reform path, which had demonstrated both a de-liberalizing and liberalizing pattern up until 1995. After 1995, however, liberalizing reforms took over. Thus, the 1990s were a significant turning point in terms of the demand and implementation of de-liberalizing policies. It was not only the accession to the European Union, which emphasized budget problems and decreased the country's scope of action, that led to this new policy reform path; more importantly, it was the result of a new policy approach from politicians coupled with a shift in the voters' preferences that was picked up by the ÖVP in particular.

4.3.4 *Comprehensive De-liberalization Policies Between 1990 and 1999*

The Austrian government introduced several comprehensive de-liberalizing policy reforms between 1990 and 1999, which can be categorized as second-order policy changes according to Hall (1993). The government, however, was only responsible for two of these de-liberalizing policy reforms; the other two measures stemmed from European Union law. The first two measurers concerned the enactment of the Women's Package and the introduction of early retirement schemes (Tálos 2004). The other two comprehensive de-liberalizing reforms, instituted by the European Union, affected labor market policies.[5]

4.3.4.1 Women's Package

In 1992 and 1993, several new de-liberalizing measures were introduced as part of what was called the Women's Package. These comprehensive de-liberalizing measures accompanied a liberalizing pension reform measure ["*Begleitmaßnahmen zur Pensionsreform*" (BGBl 1992/832/833/837)].

As part of the Women's Package, the government initiated a new labor law ["*Arbeitsrechtliches Begleitgesetz*" (BGBl 1992/833)], which resulted in the following change: any parent, mother or father, was now allowed to pursue, if he or she wished to do so, one year of part-time employment (at least up to a minimum of 2/5

---

[5]These two policies were introduced due to external constraints and will not be discussed in this book.

of the earlier working time) after the first year of parental leave is over (even if he or she had a full-time contract before the child was born). Moreover, the *Equal Treatment Act*[6] [*"Berichte der Bundesregierung betreffend den Abbau von Benachteiligungen von Frauen"* (BGBl 1992/837)] aimed to equalize the conditions for men and women in the labor market through the creation of more child care institutions and attempts at equalizing wages.

Another adjustment contained in this package was a new law that was introduced in 1993 in the course of the pension reform and resulted in an adjustment of the pension reference period. After the enactment of the law, up to 48 months of childcare would be counted towards a woman's pension reference period, whether a woman chose to work during this period or not; if a woman worked during the first 48 months after her child was born, childcare and employment would be counted separately as two different forms of 'occupation activity for the pension reference period' (BGBl 1993/336).

All the above-mentioned reforms were second-order changes and came about over the course of the Women's Package, which was a compensatory measure for the liberalizing increase in the retirement age for women (Butschek 1992). The Women's Package contained additional de-liberalizing measures such as the expansion of the parental leave period.

While this de-liberalizing measure has officially been declared a compensatory measure for liberalizing reform, the question of its existence still remains. How can we explain this de-liberalizing policy?

As a Bismarckian welfare state, Austria followed a male breadwinner model with regard to family policy until the 1980s (Obinger and Tálos 2006). However, from the 1970s onward, a growing number of female workers were employed on Austria's labor market, a fact that highlighted the difficulties of reconciling family and employment in a traditional Christian Democratic welfare state (Unger and Heitzmann 2003; Mairhuber 2013). The rate of female employment rose from 44% in 1972 to 50% in 1984 and to 55% in 1991 (Prenner and Scheibelhofer 2001). Apart from the changing labor market situation, Austrian voters' policy preferences began to lean towards more leftist libertarian issues or feminist issues on the whole, including not only the promotion of equal opportunities for men and women, but also the redefinition of the relationship between a man and a woman (Kitschelt 1994: 11, 12).

The Austrian Social Democrats incorporated these new topics into their agenda by emphasizing feminist issues and making it easier for women to reconcile work and family. The female Social Democratic members of parliament lobbied in favor of women's concerns, resulting in a decade of 'equal opportunity politics' (Liebhart et al. 2003; Sauer 2007; Kitschelt 1994: 13).

The Social Democrats' demands to promote gender equality were strongly questioned when, in 1990, the constitutional court in Austria decided that the retirement age for women should be raised in accordance with that of men in order to ensure

---

[6]The Equal Treatment Act was also part of the Women's Package.

gender equality. In view of the upcoming pension reform, Social Democrats' representatives, trade union members, and women's advocates from other parties sought concession policies in return for this new liberalizing policy, demanding a Women's Package (Appelt 1995; Mairhuber 2003). The Social Democratic Minister for Women and Family Affairs, Johanna Dohnal, and the Vice President of the ÖGB, Irmgard Schmidtleitner, in particular argued forcefully for a gender equality package (Mairhuber 2003).

The parliamentary negotiations for the package were tough, but the parliament decided in favor of the de-liberalization measures. Though the main actors came from the Social Democratic camp and the trade unions, there were also female members of other parties (except the Freedom Party) who advocated for the Women's Package in parliament and made the introduction of the package possible (Mairhuber 2003, 2013). When the package was enacted, the Minister for Women and Family Affairs stated that, "[. . .] the following [Women's Package] compensates for the equalization of the retirement age between men and women"[7] (Österreichisches Parlament 1992).

The indices used offer strong evidence that these second-order de-liberalizing policy actions came about in order to compensate for liberalization measures, and were agreed upon as part of a bargaining strategy: Firstly, the women's package is officially declared as compensatory measure to a liberalizing reform (Tálos and Wörister 1998: 227; Butschek 1992). Secondly, the relevant political actors incorporated this new programmatic de-liberalizing focus into their platform as voters were changing their preferences (Kitschelt 1994). Thirdly, the de-liberalizing policies were part of a policy package that was decided on with the People's Party together with capital and labor (Butschek 1992).

4.3.4.2 Pension Reform

In 1993, the government introduced another pension reform that contained both liberalizing and de-liberalizing measures. The liberalizing measures concerned the indexation of benefits and a reduction in survivor's pensions in an effort to cut spending. The de-liberalizing measures contained a change in the reference period, a modification of the assessment period up to the best 15 years, the expansion of early retirement due to reduced ability to work, and the introduction of a part-time pension, which is *a de-liberalizing second-order change* (Obinger and Tálos 2006: 86; Obinger et al. 2010: 45). The part-time pension allowed male employees at age 60 and female employees at age 55 to transition into part-time work coupled with part-time pension, provided that they have accumulated a certain amount of

[7]Translated from German. The original quote states: "*Bundesministerin für Frauenangelegenheiten Johanna Dohnal sagte: „Herr Präsident! Sehr geehrte Damen und Herren Abgeordnete! Hohes Haus! Das heute zur Beschlußfassung vorliegende um-fangreiche Paket an Gesetzen und Novellen trägt, wie wir wissen und schon in vielen Wortmeldungen erwähnt wurde, einer Aufgabe Rechnung, vor die die Bundesregierung und das Parlament vom Verfassungsgerichtshof durch sein Erkenntnis von 1990 über das ungleiche Pensionsalter von Frauen und Männern gestellt wurden*"! (Österreichisches Parlament 1992).

insurance coverage and obtained their employers' consent (BGBl. No. 189/1955; BGBl. No. 335/1993).

While the pension reform was explicitly designed to consolidate the rising budget costs of the pension system, the adjustments introduced to tackle this problem were rather small, and the reform package also contained de-liberalizing measures (Tálos 2004; Obinger et al. 2010: 45; Schludi 2005: 167). Thus, this modification was anything but a radical liberalizing break with the system. The reform was debated without any serious conflicts. While all parties agreed to the overall liberalizing goal of fiscal consolidation, the parties had varying opinions on the exact use of policy mix. The conservative party and the employer's association pleaded for expenditure cuts, while the Social Democrats and the unions advocated for adjustments on the revenue side (Tálos and Kittel 1999; Schludi 2005: 167). These discrepancies were resolved though intense, compromise-oriented negotiations between the parties. The social partners composed the main proposal that was submitted to the parliament (Schludi 2005: 167).

The main de-liberalizing policy was a part-time pension policy. Pension policies have always been an integral part of the social democratic and trade union policy realm. In particular, at the onset of welfare state retrenchments, social democratic parties wanted to influence state expenditures and redistribution in order to provide equalizing goods and services to the population (Huber et al. 1993). Unions, on the other hand, were interested in influencing pension reforms to avoid severe welfare retrenchment and maintain a de-commoditization policy for their members (Ebbinghaus 2011: 215). In Austria, the influence and interest of social democratic parties and unions in reforming pension policies was even stronger, since the same people performed key functions in both organizations, thus influencing the policy outcome on several levels (e.g., until the 1990s, over one-third of Social Democratic deputies were also trade union functionaries). By pushing for a part-time pension, the Social Democrats were not only able to ease pension policies for their constituency, but were also able to offset upcoming labor market problems by allowing for early part-time retirement, hence reducing the overall number of workers.

The pension reform therefore shows that the government tried to preserve low unemployment without transforming the system in a radical way (Schludi 2005: 168; Tálos and Kittel 2001: 84–85, 95–97). The outcome of this reform can be traced back to a compromise-based solution that exhibits both liberalizing and de-liberalizing consequences. Even though the stated goal was clearly to economize the pension system, the final changes included transformations in both liberalizing and de-liberalizing directions but no grave interruptions. Hence, these reform policies can be considered compensation-based de-liberalizing reforms introduced to help pass liberalization reforms.

In conclusion, the period between 1990 and 1999 in Austria was a time in which both liberalizing and de-liberalizing policies were introduced. Comprehensive de-liberalizing policies were enacted as compensation for liberalization in order to appease political parties, interest groups, and voters, and were coupled with the European Union's minimum standards setting policy. Thus, the reform policies did not mark a fundamental departure from Austria's balanced and incremental reform path. However, the extent and the speed of reforms were accelerated in comparison to the early reform period. Throughout the 1990s, budgetary pressure increased and the scope of action was narrowed due to the accession to the European Union. At the same time, the discontent between the two main parties and the affiliated interest groups increased. Even though the two grand coalition parties moved systematically towards liberalizing strategies, they still exhibited major ideological differences. The Social Democrats opted for a compensatory approach, mixing spending cuts with expansionary measures, while the People's Party advocated neoliberal reforms. Also, according to the poles, the voters' focus moved to supply-side policies. At the onset of these altered circumstances, the push for de-liberalizing reforms fizzled out. Thus, the period between 1990 and 1999 marked the beginning of a shift towards liberalization.

4.4 Liberalization and De-liberalization Between 2000 and 2006

At the end of the 1990s, the disagreement between the two grand parties grew significantly. The reform-minded party leader of the ÖVP, Wolfgang Schüssel, and his chief strategist, Andreas Khol, were convinced that the Social Democrats and the unions were a hindrance to their liberal reform vision (Bischof and Plasser 2010; Khol 2001: 209–2010). Consequentially, the conservative party increasingly opted for a collision course in the policymaking process (Bischof and Plasser 2010). At the end of the 1990s, the conservative People's Party desired to pursue neoliberal reforms strategies in Austria. However, several political reform proposals, such as the plan to significantly liberalize the pension system, were not accepted by the Social Democratic Party and the trade unions.

The national parliament election of 1999 offered the conservative People's Party an opportunity to depart from the grand coalition. While the SPÖ and the ÖVP suffered losses during the election, the Austrian Freedom Party was able to greatly increase its share. The outcome of the election presented a slightly weakened, albeit still leading, SPÖ with 33.2% of the vote (−4.9%), a battered ÖVP with 26.9% (−2.6) and rising third party—the FPÖ—with 26.9% of the vote, which was 415 votes more than the ÖVP (Müller 2000; Obinger and Tálos 2006: 23). After negotiations between the ÖVP and the SPÖ fell apart and a minority government by the SPÖ failed, the ÖVP and the FPÖ formed a coalition (Afonso 2014; Müller 2000). Even though the FPÖ had condemned the austerity plans of the former grand coalition, the party was quickly open to new policy plans when presented with the possibility of getting into office (Heinisch 2003).

The coalition aimed for a paradigm shift towards liberalization, an alleviation of the social partnership, and a balanced budget. Their most significant reform targets were pension policies, privatization, competition policies, social policies, and family policies (Müller 2000; Luther 2009; Bischof and Plasser 2010).

4.4.1 Liberalization Policies Between 2000 and 2006

The new government coalition's liberalizing reform endeavors marked a clear break with earlier periods and demonstrated an unprecedented focus on welfare state retrenchment.

The new government enacted several far-reaching pension reforms throughout their time in power. The pension reforms introduced in 2000 resulted in substantial changes, including an increase in the eligible age for early retirement schemes, a cut in widowers' pension schemes, and new punitive measures for going into early retirement (Schulze and Schludi 2009; Unger and Heitzmann 2003; Busemeyer 2007). In 2003, the government scheduled another pension reform with severe adjustments plans that resulted in massive strikes organized by the trade unions, and candid objections from the opposition. Even some ÖVP and FPÖ party members met these plans with disapproval. Thus, the bill was amended in the parliamentary stage, and subsequently included only a third of the initial demands (Schulze and Schludi 2009). Finally, the reform ended in the abolishment of part-time pensions, early retirement (in the case of unemployment), and early retirement for people with long contribution records. Moreover, early retirement benefits were curtailed and deductions for taking out early pensions were raised.

The calculation base for pension benefits was adjusted to 40 years (from 2028 on), which altered the base for assessment of a lifetime work record. Additionally, the number of years required to qualify for a maximum pension was extended from 40 to 45 (Obinger et al. 2010: 55, 56). In 2005, more pension alterations followed. In this phase, some of the omitted statutes from the 2003 reform were included such as the pension harmonization law, which adjusted but did not fully equalize the pension claims of public sector workers, farmers, and private sector workers.[8] Furthermore, the yearly pension benefit adjustment was no longer pegged to the net wages, but to the consumer price index (CPI). Additionally, the coalition paved the way for a three-pillar pension model by extending the options for a second and third pillar. The pension reforms in 2003 and 2005 deviated strongly from earlier reforms and included drastic adjustments (Schulze and Schludi 2009; Obinger et al. 2010: 55–57).

The government also liberalized other areas of the welfare state such as the labor market. The coalition introduced labor market reforms that they claimed would '*combat fraud and end malpractice in the field of unemployment insurance programs*' (Obinger and Tálos 2006: 124). Henceforth, the ÖVP-FPÖ coalition emphasized expenditure cuts and strict activation measures (Nijboer and Vliet 2012; Hofer and Weber 2006). The reforms resulted in a variety of cuts such as a reduction in the net income replacement rate resulting in 55% for regular unemployed persons, while the net replacement rate for long-term unemployed persons was scaled down to 52%

[8]The pension law of 2005 applies to people born after 1954 and foresees some exceptions in the case of civil servants employed by the Austrian Federal States (*Länder*) (Obinger et al. 2010: 55).

in 2002 (OECD 2017c; Hofer and Weber 2006). The government also abolished unemployment benefits for recipients of subsistence benefits.

The second part of the labor market program concerned activation policy. Thus, the criteria for taking on work, such as prior qualification or commutes to new possible places of employment, were made stricter. The government also increased the punishment in the event of non-compliance with the active labor market measure, resulting in a loss of benefits. Moreover, the coalition aimed to expand new jobs in the low wage sector with its *Employment Promotion Act*, which promoted service jobs in the private sector by lowering the required social security costs and benefits for employees to a minimum (Obinger and Tálos 2006: 126, 127; Obinger et al. 2010: 57, 58). The government liberalized working time regulations for night shifts. Many of these new laws were enacted without consulting the social partners and in spite of opposition from the Social Democrats and the trade unions (Obinger and Tálos 2006: 151, 152).

The government also targeted healthcare and education policies during its attempts at retrenchment. In the field of healthcare, the government raised out-of-pocket payments in cases of hospitalization or increased prescription medicine costs, and introduced an electronic healthcare card. The coalition also raised the surcharge on healthcare and the contribution rate for white collar workers. Furthermore, the government introduced university fees that were met with great disapproval from the public (Jonke 2011; Obinger et al. 2010: 60, 61; Armingeon et al. 2019).

At the same time, the government accelerated public sector reform by restructuring and partly privatizing the following fields: transportation (including the setup of the private state-held company for the Austrian Federal railways), electricity, telecommunications, the postal service, the metal industry, federally-owned property, and universities. Afterwards, the government initiated several tax reforms which led to tax cuts for personal income and corporation taxation (Ditz 2010; Armingeon et al. 2019). The liberalizing reforms included several second- and third-order changes. The reforms occurred across all policy fields, both politically salient and non-salient.

4.4.2 De-liberalization Policies Between 2000 and 2006

Despite these stark liberalizing reforms, the government still enacted some small-scale de-liberalizing reforms. It demonstrated a turnaround in family policy towards conservatism, e.g. through increasing the benefits for women who chose to stay at home. Additionally, the government introduced some compensatory measures for older workers and reformed the vocational education system.

The issue of family policies experienced a revival because the conservative People's Party and the Freedom Party both wanted to strengthen conservative family values. Hence, the government raised the amount and the duration of childcare benefits while cutting down the parental leave allowance. However, the government changed its course slightly in its second term and introduced measures to reconcile family and work for women, expanding part-time opportunities for women and providing special retraining labor market measures for women.

The government introduced de-liberalizing measures for older workers in order to offset the effects of curtailing early retirement schemes. This measure made it easier for employees to contest their dismissal in court and required companies to report any dismissal of an employee over the age of 50. In addition, the duration of unemployment benefits had temporarily been extended for unemployed people aged 60 and older, and the government relaxed the eligibility criteria for obtaining sick pay (Armingeon et al. 2019). In the field of vocational education, the government increased the number of young people allowed to attend qualification courses and provided more financial support. The severance payment system was also reformed in a package that included both de-liberalizing and liberalizing changes (Obinger et al. 2010; Armingeon et al. 2019).

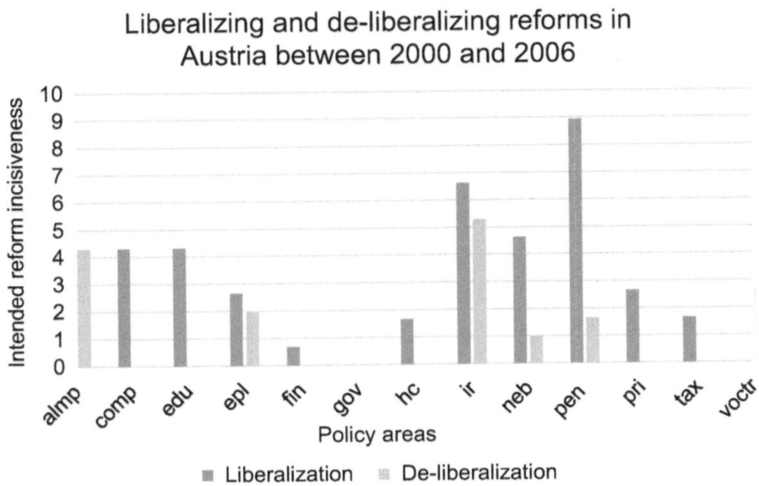

Fig. 4.4 Liberalizing and de-liberalizing reforms in Austria between 2000 and 2006 across all policy fields. Reforms are weighted according to the liberalization index (values: first-order changes: 0.33; second-order changes: 0.66; third-order and status quo changes: 1). Source: Liberalization Database (Armingeon et al. 2018)

4.4.3 Politics Between 2000 and 2006: A Major Shift Towards Liberalization

The politics between the 2000 and 2005 marked a shift away from Austria's earlier compromise-based, corporatist policymaking. Albeit being the strongest party in the 1999 elections, the Social Democrats found themselves in the oppositional minority role for the first time in 30 years, while the coalition between the People's Party and the Freedom Party formed the majority. Despite European sanctions that isolated Austria from foreign politics, the reform-minded Chancellor Schüssel continued with his ambitious liberalization plans, accepting political clashes both in Austria and abroad (Bischof and Plasser 2010). The beginning of what was referred to in Austria as the 'black-blue' term of office was characterized by a rejection of Austria's consociational democracy and corporatist policymaking (Wineroither 2010: 58, 59). The new coalition also departed from old economic policies, emphasizing a small state, zero-deficit budget, and a rejection of the 'social partnership and its spending manners'. The government aggressively sold its new liberalizing agenda to the public and blamed the Social Democrats for problems and reform blockages in the earlier coalition. In this way, the government was able not only to distance itself from the earlier legislation period, which had been received negatively by the public, but also to discredit the Social Democrats' ability to solve problems. This resulted in strong approval numbers for the People's Party and a clear loss for the Social Democrats in national polls (Wineroither 2010: 58–60; Obinger et al. 2010: 52, 53; Karlhofer 2010: 107,108).

Under the motto 'speed kills', the government developed a new policymaking approach in which policies were enacted in a very short time without consulting the social partners (Bischof and Plasser 2010; Belke and Schneider 2005; Hinterseer 2011). Henceforth, the coalition simply broke with existing practices of corporatism and negotiation-based adjustment; even delicate issues, such as pension reforms, were implemented while bypassing the traditional channels of the social partners (Hamann and Kelly 2007; Belke and Schneider 2005). Some of these reforms were legislated in 'cloak-and-dagger-operations' and overruled by the constitutional court due to the poor quality of the bills (Obinger et al. 2010: 54; Interview BAK 2016a).

The policymaking strategies in this period reveal a great deal about the coalition's policy course. The ÖVP had wanted to increase the speed and the extent of liberalization for a long time; however, in earlier periods, the SPÖ and ÖGB-BAK, demanded significant concessions for liberalization. Now that the ÖVP finally held the reins, it simply excluded the social partners in order to implement liberalization reforms. Hence, there was no longer a need for compensation since the ÖVP had the upper hand and did not have to offer any compromises to the SPÖ or the ÖGB-BAK. The coalition's reform capacity was very high at the beginning of the black-blue coalition period. Interviews with members of the Chamber of Labor, the ÖVP, the Economic Chamber, and the Austrian Federation of Industries showed that the increase in liberalization and the retreat of de-liberalization can be traced back to the ÖVP's new agenda under the ambitious and reform-minded Chancellor Schüssel. In order to implement his agenda, Schüssel risked consequences such as internal disputes within his party and their coalition partner (Interview BAK 2016a, b; Interview IV 2016; Interview WKÖ 2016).

Thus, in 2002, an interim election was held due to internal conflicts between the ÖVP and the FPÖ, which wanted to challenge the liberalizing course (Obinger et al. 2010: 55). The ÖVP became the strongest party by winning an additional 15.4

percentage points, culminating in a total of 42.3% of the votes, the SPÖ came in second with 36.51% (+3.36%), while the FPÖ came in at a distant third place with 10.01%, experiencing a loss of 16.9%. Despite the earlier conflict, the black-blue coalition continued on in order to be able to 'finish the job of restructuring the country' (Fallend 2003).

From the beginning of the black-blue period, the Social Democrats and the unions opposed a number of liberalizing reforms. However, the government simply excluded the trade unions from the reform process, while the Economic Chamber and the Federation of Industry still enjoyed access to policymakers. Moreover, the government tried to actively weaken the unions by changing the composition of the Federation of Austrian social insurance, which used to be predominantly administered by a majority of labor representatives, leading to a shared responsibility of capital and labor (Obinger et al. 2010: 54). More importantly, the government also cut the mandatory payments to the Chamber of Labor in order to limit the resources for negotiating collective agreements and consultation on social and economic legislation (Obinger et al. 2010: 51–56; Karlhofer 2010: 111). In particular, at the beginning of the black-blue coalition, the SPÖ and the ÖGB-BAK were no longer able to give their electorate's demands a voice within the government. A representative of the Labor Chamber commented on this period by saying that "*the ÖVP-FPÖ coalition was so presumptuous at the beginning of their reign that they believed they could abolish the system of social partnership completely*" (Interview BAK 2016a). Since both the SPÖ and their affiliated interest group organizations were completely shut out of the governing process, there was no longer a need to compensate the Social Democratic voters anymore, and the consequence was a clear cut process of liberalization.

However, the unions undertook public action and cast a ballot vote in 2001 that resulted in 90% of participants demanding more militant actions from the unions (Karlhofer 2010: 112). Politicians and employers were impressed by the results, the social partnership experienced a slight revival, and the cooperation between the social partners improved from 2003 onwards. At the end of 2003, the zeal for the black-blue coalition and their liberalizing agenda subsided. ÖVP and FPÖ lost votes in several elections in the federal states (*Länder*) and experienced ongoing tensions within their own coalition, resulting in a split within the Freedom Party and the establishment of a new party: The Alliance for Austria's Future (BZÖ). The majority of the electorate voted against a continuation of the ÖVP-FPÖ coalition, which provided an upsurge for the SPÖ and the Greens (Obinger et al. 2010: 61–63; Karlhofer 2010; Bischof and Plasser 2010; Interview BAK 2016a; Duncan 2007).

Consequentially, the People's Party experienced major losses in the 2006 election, while the Social Democrats came out as the strongest party. According to the SORA institute (Ogris et al. 2006), the Social Democrats won the election based on their campaign that focused on social justice, education, healthcare, and unemployment. The Social Democrats were not only able to mobilize their own voters, but took over the majority of ÖVP defectors. The election resulted yet in another grand coalition between the Social Democrats and the People's Party.

4.4.4 Comprehensive De-liberalization Policies Between 2000 and 2006

4.4.4.1 Reforming the Severance Pay System

The only comprehensive de-liberalization reform carried out in this period was the adjustment of the severance pay system. In the early 1990s, the deficiencies of the old severance scheme became more and more apparent, and the social partners began to criticize the system. When workers were dismissed, the old system required employers to disburse their severance payments in a lump sum. The payments were based on the total years of employment and the last gross monthly salary. Consequentially, if small employers had to minimize their labor force in an economic downturn, their finances would be additionally stressed by to the lump sum severance pay (Klec 2007). However, workers who left voluntarily were only eligible for payment after having worked for at least 10 years at the same company. In the event of redundancies, employees usually became eligible after three years of employment; the severance pay increased with the duration of the job up to a maximum value of one year's income after 25 years (Hofer 2007). Thus, the system harmed small- and medium-sized businesses, but it was also affecting the severance payment of workers who decided to change jobs prior to having worked 10 years at the same company.

Against this background, discussions on both sides of the social partners started in the 1990s. However, the social partners were not immediately able to produce a proper reform proposal, which finally brought the topic to the parliament under the black-blue coalition. Internal disagreements between the parties on possible modifications returned the reform topic back to the social partners (Koman et al. 2005). After lengthy negotiations, the social partners were able to agree on a reform scheme that contained 14 specific points and resulted in an overall decrease in employment protection legislation regulations for core workers and an increase for irregular workers (Hinterseer 2011). The old severance pay scheme was replaced by a new system of individual saving accounts. Instead of giving the employee a lump sum at the end of the employment relationship, employers would now pay monthly contributions of 1.53% of the employees' gross salary into a newly created employee provisions fund. All employees would be entitled to take the accumulated capital from their individual accounts; in the case of dismissals, the employee would be able to receive his severance pay or leave the money in the account and transfer it to the next employer, indirectly strengthening the second pension pillar (Nijboer and Vliet 2012). The de-liberalization concerns the possibility for the employee to transfer his severance payment and not lose it to an employer should he or she decide to leave his or her job.

While the government proved unable to solve this deficiency, the social partners adjusted this institution by finding a compromise for the problems. The ÖGB as well as the WKÖ claimed this reform as 'success' for each side.

The de-liberalization was brought about throughout corporatist action and can therefore be considered a *quid pro quo* exchange between liberalizing and de-liberalizing policies. The timing of the reform also acts as an indicator for a compensating measure: the institution was reformed in both directions at the same time (Hinterseer 2011). Looking at the policy process of this reform, one can see that it followed the old structures of compensation. The social partners struck a compromise-based deal that included both liberalizing and de-liberalizing changes that would benefit both parties. The timing of this reform stands out because it points to compensating measures rather than liberalizing measures throughout the period of strict liberalization. However, the topic was traditionally rooted in the social partnership and the coalition parties were lacking the expertise needed to solve this problem. Hence, it was delegated to the social partners, who arranging for compensating reform which benefited both workers and employers (Hinterseer 2011; Koman et al. 2005). Thus, this de-liberalization is still a case in which a de-liberalizing policy was enacted in return for a liberalizing one. This policy process therefore mirrors the compensation strategy of the argument.

In sum, the policy period between 2000 and 2006 marks a genuine departure from the earlier reform paths towards liberalization. The government fully adhered to liberalizing policies and generally avoided de-liberalizing policies. Throughout this distinct period, the government broke with existing rules of policymaking and actively tried to discredit the Social Democrats and weaken the left. Judging from the second election outcome in 2002, the majority of the voters supported the reform course; however, at the end of 2003 they experienced a change of heart. At the end of the legislation period, the popularity for the government and its policy course abated, while the left, through strong mobilization of the unions, experienced a recovery. In the 2006 election, the majority of the electorate voted for the Social Democrats based on their campaign around social topics, making them strongest party. Overall, this period demonstrates far-reaching liberalization proceedings in Austria's welfare state and a clear break with corporatist policies.

4.5 Liberalization and De-liberalization Between 2007 and 2013

In 2006, a new grand coalition of the Social Democratic Party and the conservative People's Party was voted into office. This new government marked not only the end of Austria's liberalization period, but also the beginning of a new era of de-liberalizing policy reforms. The Social Democrats continued their programmatic approach to social justice, which they had advertised throughout their election campaign and which contributed to their electoral victory in 2006. After promising de-liberalizing reforms on several salient topics that were raised as topics throughout the election campaign, the new coalition kept their promises and introduced several comprehensive de-liberalizing reform packages. By introducing these new reforms, the coalition was able to take credit for their introduction. Despite internal problems and interim elections, the grand coalition maintained its expansionary course throughout both government administrations.

4.5.1 Liberalization Policies Between 2007 and 2013

Even though this coalition government emphasized a de-liberalizing policy course throughout its time in office, it still introduced some liberalizing reforms. The grand coalition wanted to advance the 'flexicurity' scheme in consensus with the social partners. Thus, it opted to increase flexibility on the labor market by deregulating working time somewhat. Other reforms on the labor market concentrated on activation programs for the long-term unemployed and reducing employment protection for the disabled. Additional welfare reforms heightened the eligibility criteria for early retirement and diagnosis-based healthcare financing. The government liberalized the field of tax policy by cutting the personal income and corporation tax rates and increasing the amount of annual tax-free income (Obinger et al. 2010; Armingeon et al. 2019). The liberalizing reforms consisted of just two second-order changes; the extent of the liberalization is therefore much less than the earlier reform period.

4.5.2 De-liberalization Policies Between 2007 and 2013

In line with their new focus, this administration introduced a variety of de-liberalizing reforms. Some of these reforms were reversals of earlier liberalizing reforms, while others created new minimum standards or adjusted institutions in response to liberalization. All of the policies were introduced in the realm of politically salient policy fields.

In 2008, the social partners were anchored into Austria's constitution (BGBl. I No. 2/2008). Financial support for the tasks of the social partnership was also stipulated in the same law (BGBl. I No. 2/2008, Art. 120c). As a result, the chambers are now legally integrated into Austrian policymaking and the chamber system received immunity against changing parliamentary majorities (Karlhofer 2008).

The government established a kind of means-tested basic income scheme (*Bedarfsorientierte Mindestsicherung*) that was supplemented by the introduction of a minimum wage of EUR 1000 per month and a general increase in unemployment benefits for low-income groups. The government also changed the unemployment insurance in view of rising price inflation in order to stabilize national consumption. In addition, employees who only earned up to EUR 1100 were exempted from unemployment contribution payments and the unemployment contributions for people earning between EUR 1100 and EUR 1350 were lowered. Moreover, self-employed persons were entitled to take out voluntary unemployment insurance, and social protection for atypical workers was improved by incorporating them into the compulsory insurance system.

As part of their anti-poverty program, the grand coalition increased the monthly minimum pension to EUR 726 (for single persons) and EUR 1091 (for couples). Furthermore, the government chose to exempt early-retired persons from deductions if they had a long-standing insurance record. In view of the ongoing poverty crisis, the government (in consensus with the social partners) passed a package: the most important labor market measures included an extension of short-time work for up to 24 months, a modification of partial retirement, the introduction of new combined wage model, training programs for unemployed youth, and wage subsidies for small businesses (Obinger et al. 2010; Armingeon et al. 2019).

The coalition also wanted to change course in the area of family policy and introduced more childcare facilities and adapted the existing childcare benefits, securing higher benefits, albeit with a shorter duration. In 2009, after the second grand coalition under Chancellor Faymann came into power, the government passed a law introducing a free mandatory first year of kindergarten for five-year-old children. The government later repealed university fees, which were introduced under the black-blue coalition (Obinger et al. 2010; Armingeon et al. 2019).

In 2011, the government, in conjunction with the social partners, legislated an *Anti-Wage- and Social-Dumping Act*. The act was pushed forward in particular by the trade unions and the Chamber of Labor in order to protect Austrian workers from falling wages during the accession of Eastern European countries into the EU. The act was strengthened several times between 2011 and 2017 (Eurofund 2017a; Obinger et al. 2010; Ogris et al. 2006; Armingeon et al. 2019; Hinterseer 2011).

Among these de-liberalization policies, there were several far-reaching policy changes that were either a reversal of earlier liberalization policies or newly legislated de-liberalizing policies. A number of strong expository measures were introduced in the period between 2006 and 2013. Moreover, this period was characterized by a return to corporatist and consociational policymaking compared to the previous coalition (Obinger et al. 2010; Armingeon et al. 2019; Hinterseer 2011).

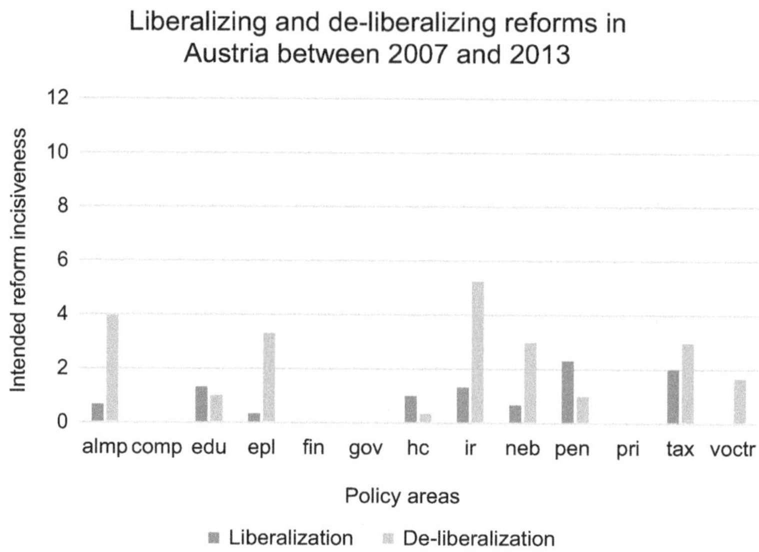

Fig. 4.5 Liberalizing and de-liberalizing reforms in Austria between 2007 and 2013 across all policy fields. Reforms are weighted according to the liberalization index (values: first-order changes: 0.33; second-order changes: 0.66; third-order and status quo changes: 1). Source: Liberalization Database (Armingeon et al. 2019)

4.5.3 Politics Between 2007 and 2013: Taking Credit Among Voters

The era between 2007 and 2013 constituted a deviation from the liberalization course and a return to traditional Austrian post-war politics. The grand coalition, despite their ongoing struggles, was back in office co-governing with the social partners, while corporatism experienced a revival (Hinterseer 2011; Obinger et al. 2010: 62–63). As in earlier periods, the coalition partners were unable to reach a consensus on how to govern, and consequently dissolved the coalition in mid-2008. After the election, another grand coalition was formed and the Social Democrats again appointed a Chancellor. There were, however, some personnel changes in both parties' leadership positions. The Social Democrats elected Werner Faymann as their party leader and Chancellor, while the People's Party opted for Michael Spindelegger as leader and Vice Chancellor. Despite the elections and the change in leadership, the grand coalition continued its expansionary course in politics. During the campaign, both parties tried to outperform the other by proposing new expansionary measures, particularly for families (Obinger et al. 2010: 62, 63).

However, there was a difference in comparison to earlier periods: while the government continued to introduce de-liberalizing measures, they did so without linking them to liberalization; on the contrary, the government split from the liberalization course by promising de-liberalizing policies, introduced these de-liberalizing policies, and then advertised these policies as new social programs for the electorate. How can we explain this change in behavior? According to representatives from the WKÖ and the IV, the government's main goal was to introduce counterpoints to the earlier government period under the black-blue coalition (Interview IV 2016; Interview WKÖ 2016). In an interview, the chief economist of the Austrian Federation of Industries stated that the government increased the benefit provisions in order to win over voters (Interview IV 2016). Moreover, both the IV chief economist and a representative of the WKÖ said that the SPÖ-led government did not want to fully reverse all of the former coalition's reform, but to visibly reduce the amount of liberalization in the welfare state in order to appease the electorate (Interview IV 2016; Interview WKÖ 2016). The governor of the Austrian National Bank, Dr. Ewald Nowotny, also supported this claim; he predicted no restrictive reforms in Austria's near future. He believes that the grand coalition will continue with its expensive reform policies for their voters in order to avoid electoral losses '*à la* Schröder' and to compensate for the welfare state problems that have arisen due to Eastern European countries joining the EU (Interview ÖNB 2016). These interviews appear to validate the claim that politicians introduce de-liberalizing policies in order to take credit for de-liberalization with the electorate. Hence, the government did not introduce de-liberalizing reforms to compensate for liberalizing reforms, but to respond to earlier liberalization and take credit for new de-liberalization. In particular the Social Democrats, who appointed the Chancellor throughout both administrations, advertised these de-liberalization policies.

4.5.4 *Comprehensive De-liberalization Policies Between 2007 and 2013*

The period between 2007 and 2013 was defined by multiple comprehensive de-liberalization processes; for that reason, we will only analyze the most important ones in this section.

4.5.4.1 Repeal of University Fees

In 2002, the coalition between the Austrian People's Party and the Freedom Party liberalized the governing *university law*, altering the universities' freedom and budget rules. On the one hand, universities became legal, personified entities, while on the other hand they received less money and could introduce university fees (BGBl. I No. 120/2002; Leidenfrost 2010).

Thus, in 2002, Austrian universities began introducing university fees of EUR 363.36, despite vehement protests from the Austrian Students' Union. Several high-leading Social Democrats and representatives of universities as well as the general public all criticized the law and mobilized against it; the Social Democrats even filed an official complaint with the Austrian Constitutional Court regarding several basic points of the law (Leidenfrost 2010). The issue became highly politically salient and was one of the major topics in the national election campaign in 2006 between the Social Democrats and the People's Party. The Social Democrats promised to repeal the university fees if they were able to appoint a Chancellor after the elections. According to the SORA Institute, some non-traditional Social Democratic voters elected the Social Democrats specifically based on their promise to repeal the university fees (Ogris et al. 2006; DiePresse 2010; Jonke 2011).

However, once the Social Democrats were back in power, they merely eased the eligibility for stipends while keeping the university fees in place. It was only after the second election in 2008 that the Social Democrats, against the will of the People's Party but supported by the Greens and the Freedom Party, finally abolished university fees (DiePresse 2010; Jonke 2011). The abolishment of the university fees is a clear reversal of an earlier liberalization reform. A large percentage of the voters favored this de-liberalization and the Social Democrats took credit for it after campaigning on the promise of free education in both of their elections (Ogris et al. 2006). This de-liberalization process supports my argument and presents a clear-cut case in which politicians introduced de-liberalization in order to distance themselves from earlier liberal reformers and take credit for the new de-liberalizing reform. Additional evidence from a governmental study states that the introduction of fees did not necessarily keep people with less financial resources from studying; hence, it seems that this de-liberalizing reform was introduced due to its high political saliency and not necessarily due to the societal risk of harming poorer students (Österreichische Parlamentsdirektion 2008).

4.5.4.2 Legalization of Working Arrangements

In 2006, a heated debate on the topic of illegal (at-home) caregiving surfaced in the run-up to the upcoming national election. The issue became salient after it was revealed that former Chancellor Schüssel had hired an illegal foreign nurse to care for his mother-in-law. While the interest in the Schüssel affair abated, the issue became salient against the context of rising costs for caregiving and illegal employment[9] (Lengauer 2010; Larsen et al. 2009).

The Social Democratic Party took up the topic during the election campaign and promised to handle this situation if they were voted into office. The issue was of high political saliency and played an important role in the national election of 2017 (Ogris et al. 2006). After the Social Democrats were back in office, the grand coalition introduced the *Home Care Act* (*Hausbetreuungsgesetz*) in 2007 to cope with the problem of at-home caregiving. The act provides the basis for private employment

[9]It was estimated that between 27,000 and 30,000 illegal, mostly Eastern European, caregivers were working in Austria in 2006. Caregivers would typically work for older people who were unable to care for themselves (Larsen et al. 2009).

of qualified nursing staff or caregivers for disabled and elderly people in private households (BGBI. I No. 33/2007). The government supported 'home caregiving by providing public grants under certain circumstances. Additionally, the government enabled further financial help through a special fund for disabled persons. The new law also incorporated a temporary amnesty for illegally employed caregivers up until the June 30, 2008 (Larsen et al. 2009).

This de-liberalization came about after the issue of illegal caregivers became a politically salient topic. Similar to the university fees, the Social Democrats had focused on the topic throughout the election and kept their promise after the election was over. By adopting this de-liberalization, the Social Democrats were able to take credit for the newly enacted reform. The Social Democrats claimed that this solution was their way of successfully making Austrian society more socially just (Weninger 2017). The Social Democrats capitalized on the mistakes of former Chancellor Schüssel and advertised this topic as part of their anti-poverty program (Prochazkova et al. 2008; Larsen et al. 2009; Schmidt 2010; Obinger 2008). However, the policymaking process was clearly a common effort between the government, the social partners and the various interest groups such as the Austrian Association for Elderly People, trade unions, and trade unions for nurses and caregivers, and is an example of a classic corporatist policymaking process (Prochazkova et al. 2008; Larsen et al. 2009). This topic's high degree of saliency throughout the election campaign and the active selling of the program after implementation support my argument that politicians de-liberalize to take credit for these changes.

4.5.4.3 Introduction of a Means-Tested Minimum Income Scheme

In 2010, the newly elected government introduced a uniform, means-tested minimum income scheme (*Bedarfsorientierte Mindestsicherung*) as part of their anti-poverty-package. The means-tested minimum income scheme consisted of several measures in the areas of social security, unemployment benefits, healthcare, and pensions. The main goal of the law was to set a common, harmonized, minimum standard for the Austrian federal states (*Länder*) and to introduce an effective tool to help fight poverty in Austria. The amount for minimum income scheme was set at EUR 733 per month disbursed at least 12 times a year (it is up to the federal states whether they want to include a thirteenth and 14th contribution). The new federal threshold resulted in an increase in generosity on the part of the federal states; however, it never undercut any of the prior income schemes. The minimum income scheme has also an influence on Austrian wage politics, leading to higher gross minimum wages of EUR 1000 a month for full-time employees (about EUR 820 net, 14 times a year) (RIS 2017; Obinger et al. 2010: 62; Tálos 2008b).

Even though poverty reduction and minimum income schemes are long-debated topics in Austria, the main initiative came about after the Social Democrats and People's Party returned to office. In 2007, the newly elected government took up the debate and introduced the means-tested minimum income scheme under the auspices of their novel programmatic anti-poverty approach. The Social Democrats once again sold the introduction of the minimum income scheme to the public as a new way of fighting of poverty (Obinger et al. 2010: 62; Leibetseder 2012; Woltran 2008). In 2007, when the Social Democratic Minister for Social Affairs at the time, Erwin Buchinger, presented the proposal to the public he said that, "*Austria does not want to create a second Hartz IV, but an appropriate minimum income scheme*" (Tálos 2008b). The SPÖ advertised this new scheme by clearly contrasting it against the 'negative associations of a liberalized labor market *à la* Germany'. The Social Minister therefore demonstrated once more that the SPÖ presented their de-liberalizing policies against the context of liberalization. While the policy evidently has a de-liberalizing effect, several interview partners emphasized the importance of the homogenization of the minimum income scheme, which previously had been in place in the federal states in different forms and to varying extents (Interview BAK 2016a, b).

The introduction of the minimum income scheme is another case in which the government introduced a de-liberalization as part of their new programmatic approach without a corresponding earlier liberalization. As in other instances, the topic had already been debated for a long time, but the Social Democrats adopted it, took it up in their de-liberalizing reform approach, and advertised it under the umbrella of their new justice-focused policy approach. Taking this into account, it is clear that this policy supports my claim that politicians introduce de-liberalization in order to take credit and target voters.

4.5.4.4 Introduction of an Anti-Wage-Dumping Act

In 2011, the government introduced a new *Anti-Wage-Dumping Act* (*Lohn- und Sozialdumping-bekämpfungsgesetze*) that included penalties in the case of employers paying less than minimum wage (as provided for in the collective agreements), whereby employees and companies had to provide formal evidence to Austrian authorities in German (Eurofund 2014, 2017b). In 2014, the act was expanded, resulting in a greater scope of action for the authorities, which were then able to take legal action even if the affected worker does not want to do so. Moreover, the expansion allows administrative courts to sue employers should they disobey the law, and force them to pay higher fees to the workers as well as increased penalty payments. Notably, the penalty for presenting wrongful documentation or no documents at all was raised from EUR 5000 to EUR 10,000 (Eurofund 2017b).

The first law came about because the transitional period for workers from the eight new Eastern and Central European member states of the European Union was ending (Eurofund 2014, 2017b). At the beginning of this policy process, not all political actors agreed on introducing this de-liberalizing measure. The employers did not share the concern of the unions with regards to opening up the labor markets for Eastern European workers. However, after a corporatist negotiation, the social partners agreed to introduce *the Anti-Wage-Dumping Act* as well as to extend labor market access to highly-skilled persons from third countries through the newly established "*rot-weiss-rot* (English: red-white-red) card". Both policy processes were articulated as a common effort in the form of social partner packages (Krings 2013).

It was only after 2011, when the employers faced actual problems due to rising competition from Eastern European firms, that they themselves wanted to strengthen the law. Between 2011 and 2015, the number of Eastern European firms requesting permission to work in Austria rose from 15,000 to 27,000. At the same time, due to the increase of posted foreign workers, infringements against Austrian labor law rose dramatically, which led employers to change their positions (DiePresse 2016; WKÖ 2017; Interview WKÖ 2016). From the beginning, the unions had a clearly conflicting position regarding the liberalization process of the labor market access and had demanded security measures for the Austrian labor market throughout the negotiations of the European Eastern accessions (Krings 2013). The Austrian unions always demanded a regulated and legal system to control, and if necessary, correct labor migration. When the Eastern European countries joined the EU, the peak trade union and the Chamber of Labor voiced their concerns on labor migration and wage dumping; however, the government and the WKÖ welcomed the accessions and an open labor market. At this period in time, the unions had difficulty getting their voices heard within the government, which was made up of a coalition of the People's Party and the Freedom Party (Krings 2013; Hinterseer 2011).

In 2008, however, after the new government was instated, the unions were able to successfully lobby for and promote this de-liberalization with the newly elected government. The new government began to request research studies on the possible effects of the labor migration and also anticipated possible difficulties in terms of the liberalization of the labor market (Krings 2013).

As in other cases, this de-liberalization came about undoubtedly as a response to earlier liberalizing reforms. The (European) liberalization of the Austrian labor market to include Eastern European workers posed a threat to Austrian workers, affecting the institution of wage in particular. However, while the black-blue government was not willing to address these labor issues, the grand coalition, and in particular the SPÖ, which is closely linked to the labor unions, were open to this change. Even though this liberalization of the labor market clearly brought about institutional problems, it was only after a Social Democratic government was in place that these threats were taken seriously and de-liberalization was introduced. In sum, this law came about in response to an earlier liberalizing reform. Secondly, the unions, the Ministry of Social Affairs, and the Social Democrats were able to advertise this law as success for their constituency, offering them protection against the threat of foreign workers (BMASK 2017). Thus, this law also confirms my claim that de-liberalizing strategies come about in response to earlier liberalizing reforms and in order to allow political actors to take credit for these new measures.

In conclusion, when compared to the period from 2000 to 2006, the period from 2007 to 2013 exhibits a notable different pattern of reforms. The newly elected government, under Social Democratic leadership, clearly chose to return to pre-2000 politics. However, there was one significant difference: the government introduced a number of de-liberalizing reforms without liberalizing reforms. In some cases, the de-liberalization reforms came about in response to earlier liberalization reforms under the black-blue coalition, while in other cases, the government simply introduced new de-liberalizing policies and advertised them as part of their new focus. The period was characterized by the introduction of several far-reaching de-liberalizations and a decrease in liberalizing policies.

4.6 Conclusion: The Austrian Case Study

The Austrian case study illuminates two points about reform politics: political actors use de-liberalizing policies strategically, however the strategies vary over time. Hence, there have been different periods of de-liberalizing policy in Austria.

The first period is characterized by the politics of compensation. As demonstrated by my analysis above, comprehensive de-liberalizing reforms were introduced in order to compensate for liberalizing policy reforms until the early 2000s. This claim is supported by Obinger, who states, "*overall, the social policy reforms launched by the Grand Coalition in the new millennium are remarkably consistent. [...] The bulk of measures adopted [...] led to welfare state expansion rather than retrenchment. [...] In contrast, the reform proposals involving elements of cost containment such as healthcare reform failed.*" (Obinger et al. 2010: 66). The grand parties, which are basically two pro-welfare-state parties, and the closely affiliated labor and capital organizations, wanted to continue their old style of policymaking against rising economic pressures (Obinger et al. 2010: 67). The introduction of compensatory measures despite fiscal constraints and the clear goal of both parties to contain the budget in the 1990s supports my claim that governments introduce de-liberalizing policies to accompany liberalizing policies in order to avoid blame and increase popularity with voters. Contrary to *power resource* (Korpi 1983) and *producer group theories* (Hall and Soskice 2001), the two comprehensive de-liberalizing policies introduced in the mid-1990s were clearly enacted and organized by the government, which further supports my argument.

However, this case also demonstrated the fact that policies and preferences change over time. At the end of the first period, the pressure to liberalize became greater during the in the onset of the accession to the European Union, and both parties, as well as the voters, moved towards greater liberalization ideologically. The People's Party, fully committed to liberalization, took this opportunity to form a new political coalition with the Freedom Party in 1999, broke with the old methods of policymaking, and introduced far-reaching liberalizing reforms. The fact that the majority of these reforms were introduced without compensating measures argues against the *compensation hypothesis* (Rodrik 1998).

Judging from the outcome of the 2002 elections, voters supported the aggressively advertised liberalization program at the outset; however, by the end of the black-blue coalition, the government had become greatly unpopular and the majority of the voters were looking for a change. The Social Democrats and the unions launched a determined election campaign that emphasized de-liberalizing policies and social justice causes. While the unions organized strikes, the Social Democrats campaigned around de-liberalizing reforms and promised to reverse some of the severe liberalizing reforms. The zeal for liberalization and the popularity of the black-blue coalition abated, and the Social Democrats won the election in 2006, appointed a Chancellor, and formed a coalition with the People's Party. Even though the two parties were not able to govern in harmony, the coalition began introducing many comprehensive de-liberalizing reforms after 2007.

When we look at the post-liberalization period, two points in particular support the claim of this book. Firstly, many of these de-liberalizing policies had already been debated for a long time; however, it was only once these topics became publicly salient during the 2006 election campaign that they were taken up by political actors and acted upon. Hence, the timing of several reforms throughout this case highlights the fact that many of these reforms were not de-liberalized due to institutional pressures or new social risks, but mainly to target voters. Furthermore, several interviewees stated that after 2006, political actors mainly wanted to set ideological counterpoints to the earlier period, while also providing benefits to win over voters (Interview IV 2016; Interview WKÖ 2016). Thus, as soon as the public turned its back on liberalization in welfare states, the political actors changed their strategy. Additionally, my findings are supported by the fact that all of the comprehensive de-liberalizing measures across all periods were only applied to politically salient issues (Culpepper 2011).

One factor that deserves special attention in the Austrian case is the distinctive entanglement between parties and organized interests. Social Democrats and unions are so closely interconnected and share so many common members that both will act in the other's interest when it comes to the voters. Thus, in many cases, their close ties resulted in a common strategy that empowered de-liberalizing policies.

Overall, the Austrian case clearly supports the argument that governments use de-liberalizing policies to compensate for liberalizing reforms, to mitigate blame for liberalizing reforms that receive negative feedback, and to take credit for the introduction of new de-liberalizing policies.

Table 4.1 Overview of the different policy reform periods in Austria

Policy period	Government and period	Share of lib.	Share of de-lib.	Social expend. (as a percentage of GDP)
Compensation period: De-liberalizing policies are introduced in order to avoid blame during periods of liberalization	1980–1983: SPÖ	62%	38%	1985: 23.3%
	1983–1986: SPÖ-FPÖ			1990: 23.2%
	1987–1999: SPÖ-ÖVP			1995: 26%
Liberalization period: Economic pressure and new political strategies lead to full-fledged liberalization	2000–2006: ÖVP-FPÖ	65%	35%	2000: 25.5%
				2005: 25.9%
Post-liberalization period: After liberalization proceedings are negative associated by the public, governments introduce de-liberalization policies to set ideological counterpoints and take credit	2007–2013: SPÖ-ÖVP	33%	67%	2010: 27.6%
				2013: 27.6%

Source: Liberalization Database (Armingeon et al. 2019; Obinger et al. 2010; OECD 2017d)

References

Afonso A (2012) Employer strategies, cross-class coalitions and the free movement of labour in the enlarged European Union. Soc Econ Rev 10(4):705–730

Afonso A (2014) Choosing whom to betray: populist right-wing parties, welfare state reforms and the trade–off between office and votes. Eur Polit Sci Rev 7(2):271–292

Appelt E (1995) Gleichstellungspolitik in Östererich." L'Homme. Zeitrischt for feministische Geschichtswissenschaft 3. https://www.degruyter.com/view/j/lhomme.1995.6.issue-2/issue-files/lhomme.1995.6.issue-2.xml. Accessed 8 Mar 2017

Armingeon K, Fill A (2016) Trajectories of liberalization and de-liberalization: actors matter. The cases of Austria, Germany, and Switzerland. Working paper presented at the annual conference of the Swiss Political Science Association on 22 Jan 2016

Armingeon K, Isler C, Knöpfel L, Weisstanner D, Engler S (2016) Comparative political data set 1960–2014. Institute of Political Science, University of Bern, Bern

Armingeon K, Baccaro L, Fill A, Galindo J, Heeb S, Labanino R (2019) Liberalization database 1973–2013 (20170619). Available Online Jul 2019

Belke A, Schneider F (2005) Privatisation in Austria: response to internal and external pressures. CESifo DICE report 1/2005. http://core.ac.uk/download/pdf/6630953.pdf. Accessed 8 Mar 2017

BGBl 120/2002 (2002) Bundesgesetzblatt für die Republik Österreich. https://www.ris.bka.gv.at/GeltendeFassung.wxe?Abfrage=Bundesnormen&Gesetzesnummer=20002128. Accessed 1 Jul 2017

BGBl 1992/832/833 (1992) Bundesgesetzblatt für die Republik Österreich. https://www.ris.bka.gv.at/Dokumente/BgblPdf/1992_833_0/1992_833_0.pdf. Accessed 1 Jul 2017

BGBl 1992/833 (1992) Bundesgesetzblatt für die Republik Österreich. https://www.ris.bka.gv.at/Dokumente/BgblPdf/1992_833_0/1992_833_0.pdf. Accessed 1 Jul 2017

BGBl 1992/837 (1992) Bundesgesetzblatt für die Republik Österreich. https://www.ris.bka.gv.at/Dokumente/Bundesnormen/NOR11001158/NOR11001158.pdf. Accessed 1 Jul 2017

BGBl 1993/336 (1993) Bundesgesetzblatt für die Republik Österreich. https://www.ris.bka.gv.at/Dokumente/BgblPdf/1993_917_0/1993_917_0.pdf. Accessed 1 Jul 2017

BGBl. I No. 2/2008 (2008) Bundesgesetzblatt für die Republik Österreich. https://www.ris.bka.gv.at/Dokument.wxe?Abfrage=Bundesnormen&Dokumentnummer=NOR40094632. Accessed 1 Jul 2017

BGBl. I No. 2/2008, Art. 120c (2008) Bundesgesetzblatt für die Republik Österreich. https://www.ris.bka.gv.at/Dokument.wxe?Abfrage=Bundesnormen&Dokumentnummer=NOR40094634. Accessed 1 Jul 2017

BGBl. No. 189/1955 (2018) Bundesgesetzblatt für die Republik Österreich. https://www.ris.bka.gv.at/GeltendeFassung.wxe?Abfrage=Bundesnormen&Gesetzesnummer=10008147. Accessed 1 Jun 2018

BGBl. No. 33/2007 (2007) Bundesgesetzblatt für die Republik Österreich. https://www.ris.bka.gv.at/Dokumente/BgblAuth/BGBLA_2007_I_33/BGBLA_2007_I_33.pdf. Accessed 1 Jul 2017

BGBl. No. 335/1993 (2018) Bundesgesetzblatt für die Republik Österreich. https://www.google.com/url?sa=t&rct=j&q=&esrc=s&source=web&cd=2&cad=rja&uact=8&ved=0ahUKEwjJjrSB79zbAhUEdCwKHY3xDqsQFggzMAE&url=https%3A%2F%2Fwww.ris.bka.gv.at%2FDokumente%2FBgblPdf%2F1993_335_0%2F1993_335_0.pdf&usg=AOvVaw1wRri-nq55teZLHa2tN-5s. Accessed 1 Jun 2018

Bischof G, Plasser F (2010) Rollercoaster: Schüssels' electoral (Mis)fortunes and the dynamics of public approval. In: Bischof G, Plasser F (eds) The Schüssel Era in Austria. Innsbruck University Press, Innsbruck, pp 21–37

BMASK—Bundesministerium für Arbeit, Soziales, Gesundheit und Konsumentenschutz (2017) SOZIALBERICHT 2013–2014. Ressortaktivitäten und sozialpolitische Analysen https://www.sozialministerium.at/cms/site/attachments/8/8/2/CH3582/CMS1448291544364/sozialbericht_2013-2014_gesamtausgabe.pdf. Accessed 1 Mar 2017

Braumann B (2004) Tu Felix Austria: evidence for a decelerator in financial reform. IEEP 1:53–73

Busemeyer M (2007) Pension reform in Germany and Austria: system change vs. quantitative retrenchment. West Eur Polit 28(3):569–591

Butschek F (1992) Wirtschaftschronik, IV. Quartal 1992 http://www.wifo.ac.at/bibliothek/archiv/MOBE/1993Heft01_017_018.pdf. Accessed 1 Jun 2017

Culpepper P (2011) Quiet politics and business power—corporate control in Europe and Japan. Cambridge University Press, Cambridge

DiePresse (2010) Chronologie: Die Geschichte der Studiengebühren. DiePresse, 7 Dec 2010. http://diepresse.com/home/bildung/universitaet/618306/Chronologie_Die-Geschichte-der-Studiengebuehren. Accessed 1 Feb 2017

DiePresse (2016) Lohndumping durch Firmen aus Osteuropa. DiePresse, 21 Jun 2016. http://diepresse.com/home/wirtschaft/economist/5031896/Lohndumping-durch-Firmen-aus-Osteuropa. Accessed 1 Jan 2017

DieZeit (1987) Am Ziel geschlagen und geschwächt. DieZeit, 05/1987, 23 Jan 1987, Updated 21 Nov 2012. https://www.zeit.de/1987/05/am-ziel-geschlagen-und-geschwaecht/seite-2. Accessed 1 Feb 2017

Ditz J (2010) Economic policies and economic change. In: Bischof G, Plasser F (eds) The Schüssel Era in Austria. Innsbruck University Press, Innsbruck, pp 235–262

Duncan F (2007) The end of the Wende? The 2006 Austrian parliamentary election. Perspect Eur Polit Soc 8(7):13–30. https://doi.org/10.1080/15705850701204061

Ebbinghaus B (2011) The role of trade unions in European pension reforms: from 'old' to 'new' politics? Eur J Ind Relat 17(4):315–331. https://doi.org/10.1177/0959680111420208

Ennser-Jedenastik L (2016) Die personelle Verflechtung zwischen Sozialpartnern und Bundesregierung in Österreich, 1945–2015. Österreichische Zeitschrift für Politikwissenschaft. http://homepage.univie.ac.at/laurenz.ennser/Verflechtung_ÖZP.pdf. Accessed 1 Mar 2017

Esping-Andersen G (ed) (1996) Welfare states in transition: national Adaptations in global economies. Sage, London

Eurofund (2014) Austria: anti-wage dumping and social dumping law updated. https://www.eurofound.europa.eu/news/news-articles/working-conditions-labour-market-industrial-relations-law-and-regulation/austria-anti-wage-dumping-and-social-dumping-law-updated. Accessed 1 Feb 2017

Eurofund (2017a) Austria: working life country profile. https://www.eurofound.europa.eu/country/austria. Accessed 1 Feb 2017

Eurofund (2017b) Austria: updated law against wage and social dumping comes into force. https://www.eurofound.europa.eu/observatories/eurwork/articles/austria-updated-law-against-wage-and-social-dumping-comes-into-force. Accessed 1 Oct 2017

Fallend F (2003) Austria. Eur J Polit Res 42:887–899

Granell F (1995) The European Union's enlargement negotiations with Austria, Finland, Norway and Sweden. J Common Mark Stud 33(1):117–141. https://doi.org/10.1111/j.1468-5965.1995.tb00520.x

Hall P (1993) Policy paradigms, social learning and the state. Comp Polit 25:275–296

Hall P, Soskice D (eds) (2001) Varieties of capitalism: the institutional foundations of comparative advantage. Oxford University Press, Oxford

Hamann K, Kelly J (2007) Party politics and the re-emergence of social pacts in Western Europe. Comp Pol Stud 40(8):971–994

Hammerschmied G, Meyer R (2005) New public management in Austria: local variation on a global theme? Public Adm 83(3):709–733

Häusermann S (2010) The politics of welfare state reform in continental Europe. Modernization in hard times. Cambridge University Press, Cambridge

Heinisch R (2000) Coping with economic integration: corporatist strategies in Germany and Austria in the 1990s. West Eur Polit 23(3):67–96. https://doi.org/10.1080/01402380008425384

Heinisch R (2001) Defying neoliberal convergence: Austria's successful supply-side corporatism in the 1990s. Environ Plan Gov Policy 19(1):29–44

Heinisch R (2003) Success in opposition—failure in government: exploring the performance of the Austrian freedom party and other European right-wing populist parties in public office. West Eur Polit 26(3):91–130
Hinterseer T (2011) Flexicurity in Österreich—Sozialpartner just renamed. Zentrum für Zukunftsstudien, Fachhochschule Salzburg https://zfzsalzburg.files.wordpress.com/2011/08/03_hinterseer_flexicurity_neu.pdf. Accessed 1 Mar 2017
Hofer H (2007) Austrian severance pay reform. CESifo DICE Rep 5(4):41–47
Hofer H, Weber A (2006) Active labour market policy in Austria: practice and evaluation results. Vierteljahrshefte zur Wirtschaftsforschung 75(3):155–167
Huber E, Ragin C, Stephens J (1993) Social democracy, Christian democracy, constitutional structure, and the welfare state. Am J Sociol 99(3):711–749
IMF (1997) From generosity to sustainability: the Austrian pension system and options for its reform. http://www.imf.org/external/pubs/ft/wp/wp9710.pdf. Accessed 16 Sept 2017
Interview, BAK (2016a) Employee of the Federal Chamber of Labor: Arbeiterkammer Wien, Vienna, 6 Apr 2016
Interview, BAK (2016b) Josef Wallner: Arbeiterkammer Wien, Vienna 7 Apr 2016
Interview, IV (2016) Dr. Christian Helmenstein: Österreichische Industriellenvereinigung, Vienna, 6 Apr 2016
Interview, ÖNB (2016) Dr. Ewald Nowotny: Österreichische Nationalbank, Vienna, 8 Apr 2016
Interview, WKÖ (2016) Dr. Rolf Gleißner: Wirtschaftskammer Österreich, Vienna, 8 Apr 2016
Investopia (2017) Accrual rate. http://www.investopedia.com/terms/a/accrual-rate.asp. Accessed 1 Mar 2017
Jonke A (2011) Neoliberalisierung der Bildung im Kontext des Bologna Prozesses am Beispiel Österreichs. Diplomarbeit, Universität Wien http://othes.univie.ac.at/16278/1/2011-08-30_9707376.pdf. Accessed 1 Mar 2017
Karlhofer F (2008) Krise—Reform—Vertrauen. Die Arbeiterkammern nach den Turbulenzen der 90er-Jahre. 60 Jahre AKNÖ: 15–23. Wien
Karlhofer F (2010) The politics of asymmetry: (non) corporatist policy making, 2000-2006. In: Bischof G, Plasser F (eds) The Schüssel Era in Austria. Innsbruck University Press, Innsbruck, pp 104–119
Katzenstein P (1985) Small states in world markets industrial policy in Europe. Cornell University Press, Ithaca
Khol A (2001) Die Wende ist geglückt der schwarz-blaue Marsch durch die Wüste Gobi. Molden, Wien
Kitschelt H (1994) Austrian and Swedish social democrats in crisis party strategy and organization in corporatist regimes. Comp Pol Stud 27(1):3–39
Klec G (2007) Flexicurity and the reform of the Austrian severance-pay system. ETUI-REHS European Economic and Employment Policy Brief no 4. European Trade Union Institute, pp 1–10. https://www.google.ch/url?sa=t&rct=j&q=&esrc=s&source=web&cd=1&ved=0ahUKEwj4pdmsy-HWAhVMF8AKHeaGAZcQFggoMAA&url=https%3A%2F%2Fwww.etui.org%2Fcontent%2Fdownload%2F3059%2F35645%2Ffile%2F07%2BEEEPB%2B09%2B2007.pdf&usg=AOvVaw0TxVPg0HR1t3d6vPnMfwi7. Accessed 9 Jan 2014
Koman R, Schuh U, Weber A (2005) The Austrian severance pay reform: toward a funded pension pillar. Empirica 32:255–274
Korpi W (1983) The democratic class struggle. Routledge & Kegan Paul, Boston
Krings T (2013) Von der "Ausländerbeschäftigung" zur Rot-Weiß-Rot-Karte: Sozialpartnerschaft und Migrationspolitik in Österreich. Österr Z Polit 42(3):263–278
Larsen C, Joost A, Heid S (2009) Illegale Beschäftigung in Europa: die Situation in Privathaushalten älterer Personen. Hampp, München
Leibetseder B (2012) Spaltung oder gesellschaftliche Stratifizierung durch Sozialpolitik? Kurswechsel 3:21–29. http://www.beigewum.at/wordpress/wp-content/uploads/Spaltung-oder-gesellschaftliche-Stratifizierung-durch-Sozialpolitik.pdf. Accessed 1 Mar 2017

Leidenfrost J (2010) The demise of "Minoritenplatz-Schleicherei" eighty-four months of Wende higher education policy in Austria. In: Bischof G, Plasser F (eds) The Schüssel Era in Austria. Innsbruck University Press, Innsbruck, pp 283–320

Lengauer G (2010) Schüssel and the media: an ambivalent relationship. In: Bischof G, Plasser F (eds) The Schüssel Era in Austria. Innsbruck University Press, Innsbruck, pp 37–56

Liebhart K, Peto A, Schiffbänker A, Stoilova R (2003) Familienpolitische Maßnahmen in Österreich, Bulgarien und Ungarn. Österreichische Zeitschrift für Politikwissenschaften 32 (4):417–417. https://webapp.uibk.ac.at/ojs2/index.php/OEZP/article/view/1131/826. Accessed 1 Mar 2017

Luther K (2009) Governing with right-wing populists and managing the consequences: Schüssel and the FPÖ. KEPRU working papers. https://www.google.com/url?sa=t&rct=j&q=&esrc=s&source=web&cd=1&ved=0ahUKEwiz1M3Z_fXbAhVkYZoKHcV6AugQFggsMAA&url=https%3A%2F%2Fwww.keele.ac.uk%2Fmedia%2Fkeeleuniversity%2Fgroup%2Fkepru%2FKEPRU%2520WP%252030.pdf&usg=AOvVaw3vJeW0oQqB64JNy1fo2JL1. Accessed 12 Apr 2016

Mairhuber I (2003) Pensionsreform in Österreich: Akteure und Inhalte (1980–2003). FORBA Forschungsbericht 12/2003. http://www.forschungsnetzwerk.at/downloadpub/fb%2012-2003.pdf. Accessed 1 Mar 2017

Mairhuber I (2013) Sozialpolitik als Frauenpolitik—das „schwere" Erbe von Johanna Dohnal. In: Mesner M, Niederkofler H (eds) Johanna Dohnal. Ein politisches Lesebuch. Mandelbaum, Wien, pp 113–132. https://www.google.com/url?sa=t&rct=j&q=&esrc=s&source=web&cd=1&ved=0ahUKEwj_iLCK_vXbAhXTyKYKHRxeAzcQFggpMAA&url=https%3A%2F%2Frenner-institut.spooe.at%2Fwp-content%2Fuploads%2Fsites%2F202%2F2015%2F05%2FMairhuber_Sozialpolitik_als_Frauenpolitik.pdf&usg=AOvVaw1Gst9JGL5Sn5tJqg5PQn8C. Accessed 1 Mar 2017

Mares I (2003) The politics of social risk: business and welfare state development. Cambridge University Press, Cambridge

Müller W (1994) Koalitionsabkommen in der österreichischen Politik. Zeitschrift für Parlamentsfragen 25(3):346–353. http://www.jstor.org/stable/24226682

Müller W (2000) The Austrian general elections of 1999: a shift to the right. West Eur Polit 23:191–200

Nijboer H, Vliet O (2012) Flexicurity in the European Union, flexibility for outsiders, security for insiders. University of Leiden, Department of Research of Economics. http://papers.ssrn.com/sol3/papers.cfm?abstract_id=2013295. Accessed 15 Jun 2016

Nowotny E (1996) Privatisation in Austria: causes and consequences. Ann Publ Cooper Econ 67 (3):387–401

Obinger H (2002) Veto players, political parties and welfare state retrenchment. Int J Polit Econ 32 (2):44–66

Obinger H (2008) Sozialpolitische Bilanz Der Großen Koalition in Österreich. Drei-Ländertagung von DVPW, SVPW, OGPW 2008 in Osnabruck, Germany. https://www.researchgate.net/profile/Herbert_Obinger/publication/266333362_Sozialpolitische_Bilanz_der_Grossen_Koaliti-_on_in_Osterreich/links/5730611c08ae3736095cd5af.pdf. Accessed 8 Mar 2017

Obinger H, Tálos E (2006) Sozialstaat Österreich zwischen Kontinuität und Umbau. Eine Bilanz der ÖVP/FPÖ/BZÖ-Regierung. Verlag für Sozialwissenschaften, Wiesbaden

Obinger H, Castles F, Leibfried S (2005) Introduction: federalism and the welfare state. In: Obinger H, Leibfried S, Castles FG (eds) Federalism and the welfare state. New World and European experiences. Cambridge University Press, Cambridge, pp 1–46

Obinger H, Starke P, Moser J, Bogedan C, Gindulis E, Leibfried S (2010) Transformations of the welfare state. In: Small states, big lessons. Oxford University Press, Oxford

OECD (2017a) Employment database, 2017. http://stats.oecd.org/Index.aspx?QueryId=64196#. Accessed 27 Mar 2017

OECD (2017b) Real GDP forecast, 2017. https://data.oecd.org/gdp/real-gdp-forecast.htm#indicator-chart. Accessed 27 Mar 2017

OECD (2017c) Benefits and wages. http://www.oecd.org/els/benefits-and-wages-statistics.htm. Accessed 8 Sept 2017

OECD (2017d) Social expenditure: aggregated data. OECD Social Expenditure Statistics (database). http://www.oecd.org/social/expenditure.htm. Accessed 8 Sept 2017

Ogris G, Hofinder C, Zeglovits E, Nisch S (2006) Analysen zur Nationalratswahl 2006. SORA—Institute for Social Research and Analysis. http://www.sora.at/themen/wahlverhalten/wahlanalysen/nrw06.html. Accessed 8 Jul 2017

Österreichische Parlamentsdirektion (2008) Parlamentskorrespondenz No. 771 vom 25.09.2008. Studienbeiträge mit S-F-G-Mehrheit abgeschafft. https://www.parlament.gv.at/PAKT/PR/JAHR_2008/PK0771/index.shtml. Accessed 1 Mar 2017

Österreichisches Parlament (1992) Stenographische Protokoll der 90. Sitzung des Nationalrats. Österreichisches Parlament. https://www.parlament.gv.at/PAKT/VHG/XVIII/NRSITZ/NRSITZ_00090/imfname_142119.pdf. Accessed 8 Jul 2017

Österreichisches Parlament (2017) Dr. Josef Taus. Österreichisches Parlament. https://www.parlament.gv.at/WWER/PAD_01323/index.shtml. Accessed 1 Sept 2017

Pastor T (2014) Why did Austrian business oppose welfare cuts? How the organization of interests shapes business attitudes toward social partnership. Comp Pol Stud 47(7):966–992

Pierson P (1996) The new politics of the welfare state. World Polit 48(2):143–179. https://doi.org/10.1353/wp.1996.0004

Pontusson J (2011) Once again a model: Nordic social democracy in a globalized world. In: Cronin J, Ross G, Shoch J (eds) What's left of the left? Futures of the left. Duke University Press, Durham, pp 89–115

Prenner P, Scheibelhofer E (2001) Qualifikation und Erwerbsarbeit von Frauen von 1970–2000 in Österreich. Institut für HÖhere Studien (IHS) (Reihe Soziologie/Institut für HÖhere Studien, Abt. Soziologie 49). Institut für HÖhere Studien, Wien. http://nbn-resolving.de/urn:nbn:de:0168-ssoar-220771. Accessed 1 Mar 2017

Prochazkova L, Rupp B, Schmid T (2008) Evaluierung der 24-Stunden-Betreuung. Sozialökonomische Forschungstelle, Wien. http://www.sfs-research.at/projekte/P66-Evaluierung-24-h-Betreuung/Bericht_neu_August.pdf. Accessed 1 Mar 2017

Rathgeb P (2016) Strong governments, precarious workers: labour market policy-making in the era of liberalization. EUI PhD theses. Department of Political and Social Sciences. http://hdl.handle.net/1814/43276. Accessed 1 Sept 2017

Rathgeb P (2017) Relying on weak governments: Austrian trade unions and the politics of smoothed dualization. Aust J Polit Sci 45(3):45–55. https://doi.org/10.15203/ozp.1371.vol45iss3

RIS (2017) Landesrecht konsolidiert Wien: Gesamte Rechtsvorschrift für Verordnung zur Bedarfsorientierten Mindestsicherung in Wien 2016, Fassung vom 06.10.2017. https://www.ris.bka.gv.at/GeltendeFassung.wxe?Abfrage=LrW&Gesetzesnummer=20000503. Accessed 1 Oct 2017

Rodrik D (1998) Why do more open economies have bigger government? J Polit Econ 106:997–1032

Sauer B (2007) What happened to the model student? Austrian state feminism since the 1990s. In: Outshoorn J, Kantola J (eds) Changing state feminism. Palgrave Macmillan, London, pp 41–61

Scharpf F (1987) Sozialdemokratische Krisenpolitik in Europa. Campus, Frankfurt A.M

Schludi M (2005) The reform of Bismarckian pension systems a comparison of pension politics in Austria, France, Germany, Italy and Sweden. Amsterdam University Press, Amsterdam

Schmidt T (2010) Hausbetreuung in Österreich—zwischen Legalisierung und Lösung? In: Scheiwe K, Krawietz J (eds) Transnationale Sorgearbeit, ihre Regulierung und die Praxis der Akteure—eine Einleitung. Springer Verlag für Sozialwissenschaften, Heidelberg, pp 171–198

Schulze I, Schludi M (2009) Austria: from electoral cartels to competitive coalition-building. In: Immergut EM, Anderson K, Schulze I (eds) The handbook of west European pension politics. Oxford University Press, Oxford, pp 555–593

Tálos E (2004) Umbau des Sozialstaates? Österreich und Deutschland im Vergleich. Politische Vierteljahresschrift 45(2):213–236

Tálos E (2008a) Sozialpartnerschaft. Ein zentraler Gestaltungsfaktor der zweiten Republik. Studienverlag, Innsbruck

Tálos E (2008b) Armutspolitik am Beispiel Österreichs: Bedarfsorientierte Mindestsicherung. WSI-Mitteilungen. https://www.boeckler.de/wsimit_2008_03_talos.pdf. Accessed 1 Mar 2017

Tálos E, Badelt C (1999) The welfare state between new stimuli and new pressures: Austrian social policy and the EU. J Eur Soc Policy 9(4):351–361

Tálos E, Kittel B (1999) Austria in the 1990s: the routine of social partnership in question? In: Berger S, Compston H (eds) Social partnership in Europe. Berghahn Books, Oxford

Tálos E, Kittel B (2001) Gesetzgebung in Österreich. Netzwerke, Akteure und Interaktionen im politischen Entscheidungsprozess. Fakultas, Wien

Tálos E, Rossmann B (1992) Materielle Sicherung im Wohlfahrtsstaat. Am Beispiel der pensions- und Arbeitslosenversicherung. In: Tálos E (ed) Der geforderte Wohlfahrtsstaat. Traditionen—Herausforderungen—Perspektiven. Löcker, Wien, pp 17–59

Tálos E, Wörister K (1998) Soziale Sicherung in Österreich. In: Tálos E (ed) Soziale Sicherung im Wandel. Böhlau, Wien, pp 209–288

Thelen K (2014) Varieties of liberalization: the new politics of social solidarity. Cambridge University Press, New York

Trading Economics (2017) Österreich Arbeitslosenquote. https://de.tradingeconomics.com/austria/unemployment-rate. Accessed 1 Dec 2016

Trampusch C (2009) Europeanization and institutional change in vocational education and training in Austria and Germany. Gov Int J Policy Admin Inst 22(3):369–395

Unger B, Heitzmann K (2003) The adjustment path of the Austrian welfare state: back to Bismarck? J Eur Soc Policy 13(4):371–387

Wagschal U, Wenzelburger G (2008) Haushaltskonsolidierung. VS Verlag für Sozialwissenschaften, Wiesbaden

Weninger, H. (2017). "Positive SPÖ-Bilanz in Parlament und Regierung." http://www.hannesweninger.at/artikel/positive-spo-bilanz-parlament-und-regierung. Accessed 1 Mar 2017

Wineroither D (2010) Making Omelets and breaking eggs? Schüssel's leadership in government and party. In: Bischof G, Plasser F (eds) The Schüssel Era in Austria. Innsbruck University Press, Innsbruck, pp 56–59

WKÖ (2017) Lehrlingsstatistik: Hauptergebnisse der WKO-Lehrlingsstatistik. https://www.wko.at/Content.Node/Interessenvertretung/ZahlenDatenFakten/Daten_zum_Thema_Lehrlinge.html. Accessed 1 Mar 2017

Woltran I (2008) Bedarfsorientierte Mindestsicherung—ein gemeinsames Ziel der Bundesregierung, Auswirkungen Der Bedarfsorientierten Mindestsicherung Auf Armut Und Soziale Ausgrenzung In Österreich. Auszug aus WISO 1/2008, Institut für Sozial- und Wirtschaftswissenschaften. http://www.isw-linz.at/themen/dbdocs/LF_Woltran_01_08.pdf. Accessed 1 Mar 2017

Chapter 5
Germany: Attempts to Compensate the Electorate

Germany's liberalizing and de-liberalizing reform path has been heavily debated in the comparative literature on the welfare state and capitalism. Opinions on Germany's reform development vary greatly: while some authors argue that Germany managed to preserve continuity, broadly refraining from liberalization processes (Hall and Soskice 2001; Hall and Thelen 2008), others claim that Germany's development process demonstrates an in-depth transformation towards liberalization (Streeck and Thelen 2005; Baccaro and Howell 2017). A third opinion is that Germany steered a middle course between continuity and liberalization (Schmidt 2012).

In the area of salient policies, however, this chapter shows that Germany did not necessarily pursue continuity, but rather a strategy of both liberalization and de-liberalization, whereby liberalization always had the upper hand. Germany experienced a fair amount of de-liberalization between 1995 and 2000, and from 2010 to the present. In comparison to Austria and Switzerland, however, Germany enacted fewer de-liberalizing reforms. In contrast to the other cases, Germany implemented the most de-liberalizing reforms in fields such as pensions and non-employment benefits, while liberalizing reforms centered on the labor market, particularly on active labor market policies and employment protection legislation (Armingeon et al. 2019).

© Springer Nature Switzerland AG 2019

A. Fill, *The Political Economy of De-liberalization*, Contributions to Political Science, https://doi.org/10.1007/978-3-030-01066-9_5

Fig. 5.1 Liberalization and de-liberalization processes in Germany across all policy fields. Source: Liberalization Database

How do we explain the distinct path of Germany's reform policies? A *convergence approach* would highlight Germany's liberalization proceedings in the welfare state and on the labor market throughout the 1990s and the 2000s (McKenzie and Lee 1991). However, a convergence-focused explanation cannot account for de-liberalization proceedings in the same period. The German case also brings the *compensation hypothesis* into question (Rodrik 1998). Even though the *compensation hypothesis* allows for liberalization and de-liberalization reforms, it links the occurrence of those two together. Yet, in the early 2000s, when Germany's most far-reaching liberalization reforms were introduced across all policy fields, there were almost no compensatory de-liberalizing measures (Armingeon et al. 2019).

The same liberalization period also tests the conventional political explanations. A *classical partisan approach* (Häusermann 2010; Häusermann et al. 2013) attributes Germany's de-liberalization period to the rise of the German Social Democratic Party (Sozialdemokratische Partei Deutschlands) and, while it is true that the Social Democrats helped bring about some de-liberalization reforms such as the statutory minimum wage, they were also responsible for the intense liberalizing reform proceedings in the 2000s. The flexibilization of the labor market, in particular the introduction of the *Hartz* reforms, clearly broke with social democratic traditions and permanently damaged the German Social Democratic Party (Paterson and Sloam 2006; Egle 2017; Weishaupt 2010). A *power resource approach* is also somewhat unsuited to explaining the occurrence of de-liberalization. German trade unions are very heterogeneous and have supported different sides in the battle for de-liberalization at different times (Mabbett 2016). The introduction of the statutory minimum wage

(SMW) in particular divided the unions, leading to a pro and a contra group and revealing that not all German unions favor de-liberalization (Die Welt 2008).

VOC-based explanations encounter difficulties when confronted with Germany's reform reality (Hall and Soskice 2001). A *producer group account* would link German employers to the introduction of de-liberalizing policies. Generous welfare state policies organized through cross-class coordination are said to provide security for workers and their skill investment in the industry, leading to a comparative advantage in terms of the coordination of the economy (Hall and Soskice 2001; Thelen 2014). Yet, German employers have long favored liberalization over de-liberalization, taking a strong stance against the introduction of a statutory minimum wage and advocating for liberalization in the manufacturing sector (Mabbett 2016; Baccaro and Howell 2017).

In quest for explanations, this case explores how Germany's distinct path of liberalization and de-liberalization came into existence. This chapter demonstrates how far-reaching liberalization led to the adoption of de-liberalizing policies. Moreover, this section will reveal why a far-reaching, de-liberalizing process similar to Austria's was not possible.

This case study will start out by providing a brief overview of Germany's post-war development in order to set the starting point for Germany's liberalization and de-liberalization processes. Subsequently, I will analyze different reform periods according to the legislative governmental periods. As with the Austrian case study, I will provide a detailed overview of the liberalizing and de-liberalizing policy reforms in each period, the politics behind them, and an analysis of Germany's de-liberalizing second-order, third-order, and status quo policy changes. The analyses will include process tracing and interviews.

5.1 Germany's De-liberalization Processes: The Beginnings

Germany's first short-lived de-liberalization period started in the early 1980s after liberalization processes had commenced. Despite preceding cost-cutting reforms in the fields of pensions and unemployment benefits, Germany was a fully matured welfare state with strong 'conservative-corporatist' Bismarckian traits, such as a male-bread-winner model, in which income maintenance was secured but benefits were primarily linked to contribution records (Esping-Andersen 1990; Starke 2008).

The political economy of post-war Germany was based on a corporatist consensus involving the government, the unions, and employers (Manow 2001: 31, 42). This consensus was reflected in socially regulated markets and social insurance systems that were widely excluded from market principles. Thus, the German model evolved around a capitalist market economy, which was highly organized and regulated but did not entirely commit to full employment, social-democratic hegemony, or an active macroeconomic management. Instead the German model allowed for embedded liberalism and a decentralized compromise of labor and capital jointly governing the labor market and the field of industrial relations, while the *Bundesbank* regulated monetary stability (Streeck 1995: 9–12, 2009).

The emphasis on both a social market economy and sound fiscal policies was an important aspect of post-war Germany and found its origins in the commitment to ordoliberalism (Goldschmidt and Wohlgemuth 2008).

The German industrial relation system has mainly been regulated by the *Collective Agreement Act* (*Tarifvertragsgesetz*, TVG) and the *Works Constitution Act* (*Betriebsverfassungsgesetzt*) of 1952, both of which were established after the Second World War (Eurofund 2015a). Collective wage agreements, which used to protect workers from harsh labor market competitions and created homogenous conditions for companies with regards to labor costs, have traditionally formed the core of this system. Another important part of the system of industrial relations is the co-determination practice, which allows for overseeing of plant-level consultations by elected work councils and consulting on the implementation of collective agreements (Hassel 1999). The most important labor organization is the German Confederation of Trade Unions (*Deutscher Gewerkschaftsbund*—DGB) which unites eight different trade unions from various economic sectors under one umbrella organization. The most important of these trade unions are the *Industriegewerkschaft Metall* (IG-Metall), which is comprised of workers in the metal industry, including automobile and machine building, electronics, steel, textiles, wood, and synthetics, and the *Vereinte Dienstleistungsgewerkschaft* (Ver.di), which covers service industry professions (Hassel 1999). The most important employers' association in terms of membership is the Confederation of German Employers' Associations (*Bundesvereinigung der Deutschen Arbeitgeberverbände*—BDA), which mainly concentrates on labor market issues. The second most important employer's organization is the Chamber of Commerce and Industry (*Deutscher Industrie und Handelkammertag*—DIHK). Germany has a broad and heterogeneous landscape of business organizations representing firms according to size and policy interest (Grote et al. 2007: 154–165). Historically, the cooperation between parties and interest groups has not been as strongly pronounced as in Austria.

5.2 Liberalization and De-liberalization Between 1982 and 1989

The early 1980s marked the beginning of a new era in Western Germany. On one hand, the new decade started with a new government, and on the other, the German budget went into deficit, triggering the first small-scale liberalization reforms (Streeck 2009; Zohlnhöfer 2003). In 1982, a new government under Chancellor Helmut Kohl's Christian Democratic Party (*Christlich demokratische Union*—CDU) was voted into office in a coalition with the Free Democratic Party (*Freie Demokratische Partei*—FDP). The newly elected government announced a turnaround in economic policy towards a more liberal course. At his inauguration, Chancellor Kohl announced that he would promote a smaller state focusing on its core tasks, yet this new focus on liberalization cannot be compared with the liberal turnaround introduced by Margaret Thatcher (Zohlnhöfer 2001, 2003).

5.2.1 Liberalization Policies Between 1982 and 1989

In order to cope with the rising welfare state expenditures, the state mandated welfare cuts in a number of areas. The most important retrenchments took place in the realm of social assistance benefits, sick pay, unemployment benefits, social assistance for refugees, and pension policies (Schulze and Jochem 2009; Leibfried and Obinger 2003). In 1983, the government cut unemployment benefits and lowered the benefits for the transitional period between labor and unemployment. In 1984, the government reduced unemployment and short-term work benefits as well as remuneration for workers who lose income due to inclement weather (Zohlnhöfer 2001). Alongside restrictive reforms, the government actively attempted to flexibilize the labor market. In 1985, the government introduced the *Employment Promotion Act (Beschäftigungsförderungsgesetz)*, which established the usage of fixed-term work contracts and prolonged the deployment period for temporary agency workers from three to 6 months. Moreover, the law included a slight deregulation for employment contracts for disabled and young workers. Despite these changes, the existing employment protection legislation remained widely untouched (Zohlnhöfer 2001; Streeck and Hassel 2003; Jackson and Sorge 2012; Armingeon et al. 2019).

The government also decided to introduce a pension reform in 1989 in an attempt to reduce costs. The reform, implemented in 1992, included both liberalizing and de-liberalizing elements—the most important liberalizing components were a switch from gross to net wage indexation, actuarial reductions[1] in the case of early retirement, and curtailing of non-contributory benefits (with the exception of improved credits for parents) (Schludi 2005: 132). Additionally, the government increased the co-payment for drugs and hospital stays for patients and put a cap on social-assistance-inflation-linked increases between 1983 and 1984 (Armingeon et al. 2019; Schludi 2005: 129,130). In 1988, the government introduced legislation to curtail the power of unions and work councils in private factories (Hassel 1999; Streeck and Hassel 2003).

The government introduced privatization processes in the fields of postal services, telecommunications, and rail transportation, and gave away national monopoly positions while promoting financial markets (Starke 2008; Schmidt 2012; Zohlnhöfer 2003). In course of these reforms, new financial instruments such as zero-coupon bonds, floating rate bonds, dual currency bonds, and bonds linked to interest and currency swaps were introduced, as was a new law *regulating the Admission of Securities to the Stock Exchange* and advancing stock exchange instruments. The most important sale of state-owned shares included the sale of shares in the *Volkswagen Group* and the *Industrieverwaltungsgesellschaft* (Armingeon et al. 2019). *Deutsche Telekom* and the *Deutsche Bundespost* (German Federal Post Office), which included postal, telegraph, and telephone service, were split into three different public entities. Additionally, the coalition established a commission

[1]The amount of benefit loss each pension member receives was calculated based on actuarial assumptions in the event of early retirement (OECD 2013).

on the prospective processes of privatization. The government also liberalized shopping hours, allowing for two more shopping hours per week (Zohlnhöfer 2003).

5.2.2 *De-liberalization Policies Between 1982 and 1989*

There was not a great deal of de-liberalization in the period between the early 1980s and 1990; however, the government introduced a few noteworthy de-liberalizing reforms. Some were aimed at increasing the state's revenues, while others focused on new arising social needs (Armingeon et al. 2019). After coming to office, the CDU-FDP government introduced a tax reform that increased VAT and various social insurance contributions such as unemployment insurance fund contributions (Zohlnhöfer 2003). The coalition also increased pension benefits for early retirees. Additionally, the government enacted a law facilitating early retirement for workers at age 58, given that an appropriate collective agreement had been reached (Armingeon et al. 2019). The maximum period for unemployment benefits for older employees (unemployed persons age 49 and older) was extended from 12 to 18 months between 1985 and 1989. Unemployed persons age 59 and older were made eligible for unemployment benefits even if they had already exhausted the maximum period of unemployment benefits. The government also passed a bill that introduced a parental leave scheme, including dismissal protection for a period of 12 months after the child has been born (Armingeon et al. 2019; Zohlnhöfer 2001).

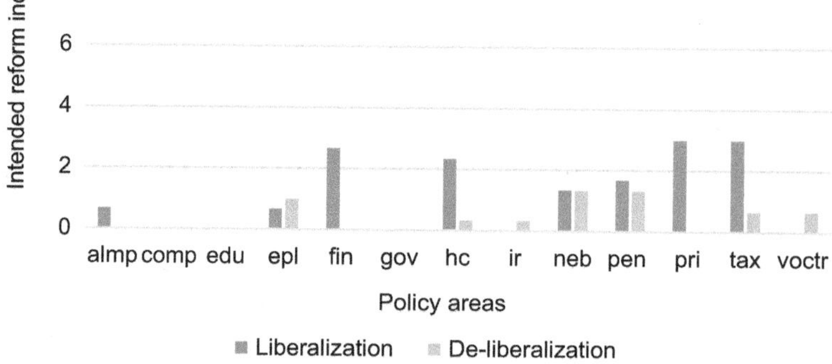

Fig. 5.2 Liberalizing and de-liberalizing reforms in Germany between 1982 and 1989 across all policy fields. Reforms are weighted according to the liberalization index (values: first-order changes: 0.33; second-order changes: 0.66; third-order and status quo changes: 1). Source: Liberalization Database (Armingeon et al. 2019)

5.2.3 *Politics Between 1982 and 1989: Compensation Within the Political Party*

Despite advertising major welfare state changes, the Kohl administration only undertook balanced reforms. Nevertheless, the period between 1982 and 1989 marked the beginning of a course of liberalization and was also an era in which the first fissures in the industrial relations system began to show.

As in other Western European countries, the German government was strained by rising social security expenditures, and introduced a cautious consolidation program. The government avoided far-reaching retrenchment and instead banked on strategies of reducing the labor pool, introducing slight cuts, increasing contributions, and inducing soft flexibilization on the labor market. The administration also increased various social benefits (Streeck and Hassel 2003; Zohlnhöfer 2001; Armingeon et al. 2019). How can we best explain this mild reform approach in the face of rising functional pressures and a lack of strong opposition from the Federal Assembly? It stands to reason that Germany introduced de-liberalizing reforms between 1982 and 1989 to avoid blame and compensate for the liberalizing reforms introduced during this period. Zohlnhöfer (2001, 2003) and Winter (1989, 1990) are also convinced that the politics of cautious liberalization, including de-liberalization, can be explained through strategies of compensation and blame avoidance.

The coalition between the Christian Democratic Union and the Free Democratic Party incorporated two ideological directions: on the one hand, there was the labor camp, predominantly represented by the Christian Democratic Employees' Association (also often called the CDU social committee), and on the other, there was the business camp within the CDU and the FDP. While the latter advocated for market-oriented reforms, the CDU social committee attempted to preserve the status quo or amend reforms towards moderation (Zohlnhöfer 2001). Both camps have clearly taken different positions over time depending on the topic. One noteworthy example of the internal disagreement within the government at that time were the negotiations surrounding the introduction of Paragraph 116 of the *Employment Promotion Act*, which aimed to deregulate the labor market. This example clearly demonstrates the compensation politics of this time and will therefore be briefly discussed (Winter 1989).

When the CDU business camp presented a liberalizing proposal in 1985 to cut unemployment and short-term work benefits for employees directly or indirectly affected by strikes, the Minister of Labor at the time, Norbert Blüm, tried to stop further friction with the unions by discounting the proposal and referring to the parties in the collective agreements as being responsible for the labor market. However, as complaints from both sides became louder, Blüm agreed to an amendment of the article. After the lawmaking process started, the top-ranking CDU members attempted to find a balance between the different interests of the preservation of the status quo (the unions), no curtailment of the unions (the CDA), and the initial demands of the business wing. The final amendment resulted in a compromise which included the deprivation of benefits if workers were directly affected and also profited from this strike. Furthermore, the employer had to demonstrate that the employee was clearly involved in the strike (BGBL 1986; for an in-depth case study, compare Winter 1989). The CDA attempted not only to curtail liberalizing action, but also to introduce de-liberalizing policies such as the expenditure program in 1987 and the extension of the passive labor market programs in the mid-1980s, which the FDP argued should have been reduced.

The strength of the CDA is best explained by its constituency, which represented a considerable amount of the Christian Democratic Party's voters. Thus, the policy reform path between 1982 and 1990 can be described as one of balanced reforms leaning towards liberalization without structural changes; others referred to this reform path as consolidation with expansion (Jochem 1999). The politics are a strategy of compensation and blame avoidance. However, comparing this era in Germany to the same period in Austrian, one can see that the German government did not adhere to the unions' demands, but only to those of the left camp within the CDU. Additionally, the German policy path shows less de-liberalization than the Austrian one, and instead rather cautious liberalization.

5.2.4 Comprehensive De-liberalization Policies Between 1982 and 1989

5.2.4.1 Parental Leave

The period between 1982 and 1990 was not characterized by many comprehensive de-liberalization policies; however, the adoption of the parental leave scheme marks an important de-liberalization in this period. In 1986, the coalition between the Christian Democratic Union and the Free Democratic Party introduced a new law for parental leave and child-raising allowances (*Bundeserziehungsgeldgesetz—BerzGG*) (BGBl. I S. 2154 1985). This new law allowed one parent to take parental leave as long as their child is below the age of three. If the parents' employers agreed, it would also be possible to split the parental leave period between both parents. One could also take a part-time leave if their workplace had more than 15 employees. Most importantly, someone taking parental leave was shielded from dismissal in the first 12 months (BGBl. I S. 2154 1985). Despite implementing parental-leave reforms in 1987, the Family Minister at the time, Heiner Geissler, had already advocated this new parental-leave law to the public in 1985.

How can we explain this de-liberalization? Several theoretical accounts indicate that the earlier introduction of this law can be traced back to negatively associated effects of prior cuts in the parental leave allowances (Pabst 1999; Seeleib-Kaiser 2002; Münch 1990). Münch (1990) stated, "*the circumstance that, in the end, the Minister of Finance, Gerhard Stoltenberg, did in fact yield to the family politicians of the CDU can be attributed to earlier cuts in the parental leave allowance scheme that they wanted the public to forget as quickly as possible*[2]" (Münch 1990: 58–59). The Family Minister' hasty actions reinforced ongoing discrepancies between the

[2]Translated from German. Original quote: "*Die Tatsache, dass Bundesfinanzminister Gerhard Stoltenberg damit dem Drängen der Familienpolitiker der Union doch noch nachgab, ist mit darauf zurückzuführen, dass die Einsparungen beim Mutterschaftsurlaubsgeld in der Öffentlichkeit möglichst schnell vergessen werden sollten*" (Münch 1990: 58–59).

conservative business wing of the CDU and the left-leaning labor wing of the government, including the CDA, various women's organizations, the trade unions, and the SPD. While earlier disputes concentrated on the cuts to child benefits, the main topic of this conflict was the 'dismissal protection' that was announced by the Family Minister. The liberal business camp of the CDU and FDP rejected the guaranteed claim of employment protection. After ongoing debates, the actors agreed to a compromise: the wording, which can be translated to 'employment protection' had to be changed to 'job protection', meaning that a person would be guaranteed to have a position at his or her company (after taking parental leave), but it would not necessarily be the same job they had before. Additionally, the FDP was able to push for an exception clause for small companies. Therefore, the law only applied to companies that had more than 15 employees (Münch 1990: 58–59).

The introduction of the parental leave scheme supports the claim that de-liberalization reforms are introduced in order to compensate and avoid blame for liberalization. Firstly, the law was introduced earlier than planned to distract the public from prior cuts in the parental leave allowance. Secondly, the law was the result of an ongoing dispute on the spending politics for family policies and resulted in an internal compromise.

In sum, the period between the 1980s and the 1990s paved the way for a new era of liberalization. Even though the changes in the field of salient welfare policies were rather minor, the debates and proposals for policy amendments signified a new reform course towards liberalization. The changes on the labor market, and the extension of fixed-term contracts and temporary agency working contracts in particular, foreshadowed the liberalization to come.

This period supports the claim that de-liberalization policies can be explained by the politics of compensation and blame avoidance. However, in comparison to Austria, the extent of de-liberalization seems less significant. The fact that unions in Germany were not as closely connected to the government as in Austria might account for the lower extent.

5.3 Liberalization and De-liberalization Between 1990 and 1998

When the Berlin Wall fell on November 9, 1989, the traditional policy course was interrupted and the policymakers in power were faced with significant unforeseeable challenges. The extent of the impact of reunification was unprecedented and forced German policymakers to react much more rapidly than usual. While the overall adjustment process of reunification catalyzed a number of liberalizing and de-liberalizing policy processes, the immediate reaction to reunification was not a liberal one.

The essence of the reunification process was the expansion of all political-economic Western German institutions to the five new federal states of the former (East) German Democratic Republic (GDR) (Streeck 2009: 209–211). The challenges of reunification temporarily reinvigorated co-operation between the government, business, and labor—all parties agreed on the institutional transplantation (Jochem 1999). The strategy of reunification, however, came at a high cost and put a heavy strain on German competitiveness, the industrial relation system, and the social security system (Baccaro and Howell 2017; Jochem 1999).

5.3.1 Liberalization Policies Between 1990 and 1998

As described above, the initial post-reunification reforms were predominantly de-liberalizing in nature. The immediate reform actions greatly added to the German budget deficit, while unemployment continued to rise. Consequentially, the overall reform pressure grew enormously (Streeck 2009; Hassel 2011). The government introduced several liberalizing policies to counteract the increasing social policy expenditures. In 1993, the government started to reform the healthcare system by introducing global budget caps in various sectors such as expenditures for hospital treatment, outpatient medical care, outpatient dental care, and ambulatory healthcare; funding was also limited to prescription drugs. In 1996, the government introduced a quasi-market system between the sickness funds to steer competition (Kamke 1998).

In 1997, the government decided on comprehensive pension reform (*Pension Reform Act 1999*) to reduce the quickly rising pension costs, which had greatly increased due to labor hoarding strategies and the inclusion of the new Eastern federal states in the pension system. The key elements of this reform included the introduction of a demographic factor into the pension formula and stricter eligibility criteria for disability pensions (Schludi 2005: 139).

Throughout the 1990s, the government also began reforming the labor market. The government reduced unemployment benefits once in 1994 and again in 1996, resulting in a 60% replacement rate for a maximum period of 12 months. Additionally, the eligibility and the conditions for various social benefits were altered to make it more difficult to receive these benefits (Armingeon et al. 2019). Moreover, the coalition allowed for increased use of fixed-term and flexible contracts. In 1997, the maximum duration for temporary contracts was raised from 12 to 24 months (Armingeon et al. 2019). In the field of industrial relations, decentralization occurred at the level of collective bargaining and through deregulations in company- and plant-specific agreements. The answers to these problems were opening clauses for working-time arrangements and pay (Jochem 1999; Streeck and Hassel 2003). The government introduced tax reforms, including a decrease in corporate tax rates and the abolishment of the wealth tax (Armingeon et al. 2019).

Presented with increasing economic problems, the German Federal government and the governments of the federal states started to sell off state property such as public utilities and state holdings. In order to sell the telecommunications and postal services at advantageous conditions, Germany reformed its capital market through extensive reform legislation in the 1990s (Streeck 2009). The most important law to create a legal framework included the *Act to Remove Barriers to the Privatization of*

Companies and to Promote Investment (*Gesetz zur Beseitigung von Hemmnissen bei der Privatisierung von Untemehmen und zur Förderung von Investoren*). The most significant privatizations, apart from the telecommunications and postal services, occurred in the electricity industry and the transportation sector, including the federal railways (Armingeon et al. 2019).

Further reform measures included the contracting out of several public services, in particular hospitals, school, universities and government offices, as well as the purchase of a range of non-essential services from private firms. It is also important to note that the government encouraged competition in formerly public or semi-public sectors, including public banking, higher education, the railroads, healthcare, and health insurance.

5.3.2 De-liberalization Policies Between 1990 and 1998

Many de-liberalizing reforms between 1990 and 1998 were directly targeted at the aftermath of reunification. De-liberalizing reform efforts focused on increasing social security contributions, which were used to finance the reunification process, as well as on expanding benefits.

Hence, between 1993 and 1997, the government increased the pension contribution rate from 17.5% to 20.3%, while the contribution rate for unemployment benefits was raised from 4.3% to 6.8%. The combined social security contribution rose from 35.1% in 1990 to 42.1% in 1997, which in turn vastly increased the German non-wage labor cost. The government also established the German Unity Fund for the federal government. In the course of the reunification process, the government also introduced surcharges on corporate income tax and personal income tax (Armingeon et al. 2019; Schulze and Jochem 2009; Schludi 2005: 135, 136). Throughout the reunification proceedings, the government not only increased social security contributions, but also expanded various labor market programs and benefits; not only for Eastern but also for Western Germany. The most important increase in benefits was marked by the rising expansion of temporary work permits, which were granted to approximately 1.6 million people from Eastern Europe in 1990 (Zohlnhöfer 2001). The duration for short-term work benefits was extended up to 15 months in the case of work stoppage for cyclical reasons, and up to 24 months for structural reasons. The notice period for blue collar workers was extended in line with the notice periods in place for white collar workers (Armingeon et al. 2019).

The government introduced new labor market training programs and subsidized employment, particularly part-time employment of elderly workers who had previously been employed full-time. The public employment service also granted wage subsidies to employers, which in turn facilitated the employment of previously unemployed persons (Armingeon et al. 2019). Aside from benefits and active labor market programs, the government attempted to reduce the labor supply through the increased use of early retirement programs and transitory schemes; the government reduced the age limit for receiving transitory benefits from 57 to 55, and raised old age benefits by 3.86% in Western Germany and by 14.24% in Eastern Germany (Armingeon et al. 2019; Zohlnhöfer 2001).

In terms of industrial relations, de-liberalization only occurred in the early 1990s. Following a 1990 agreement, working hours in the metal industry were reduced to 35 hours per week. The German metal industry accepted a 5.45% nationwide increase in wages and salaries in April 1992, and a further 3% increase in April 1993 (Armingeon et al. 2019).

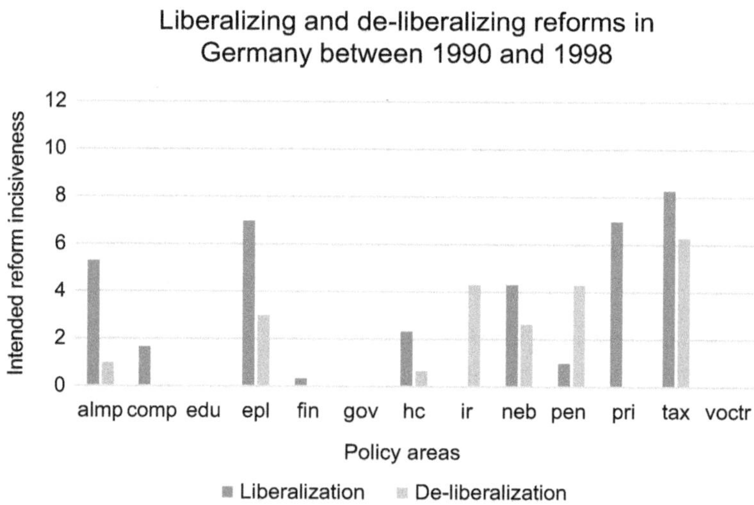

Fig. 5.3 Liberalizing and de-liberalizing reforms in Germany between 1990 and 1998. Reforms are weighted according to the liberalization index (values: first-order changes: 0.33; second-order changes: 0.66; third-order and status quo changes: 1). Source: Liberalization Database (Armingeon et al. 2019)

5.3.3 *Politics Between 1990 and 1998: Reunification and Its Effects*

The politics of the reunification process can be divided into two parts: the first part is characterized by political unity and resulted in comprehensive de-liberalizing policies, while the second part is exemplified by deteriorating political relationships, particularly in the field of industrial relations, and denoted the beginning of the liberalization period in Germany.

In 1990, there was an evident consensus between the government, capital, and labor that, as part of reunification, all social security and industrial institutions would be transferred from Western Germany to Eastern Germany. Thus, the direct response to reunification was a large expansion of the government sector. Germany was said to engage in *reunification Keynesianism*, denoting extensive de-liberalization (Zohlnhöfer 2001: 671). Presented with various options on how to finance reunification, the government believed it was best to increase government debt over the short-term and raise social security contributions. Additionally, the government opted for a consolidation program that mainly focused on non-salient political fields because this allowed the government to offset cuts in welfare state policies. The majority of de-liberalization policies arose due to the distinct financing strategy and the institutional expansion to Eastern Germany (Zohlnhöfer 1999, 2001; Jochem 1999). Several indicators point to the fact that de-liberalization was the result of compensation and credit taking. In its 1990 election campaign, the CDU promised to keep the costs of reunification low. Even though the CDU proved unable to keep the costs down, the strategy of increasing government debt and boosting contributions was less visible than starting far-reaching retrenchment reforms in the field of welfare policies. Additionally, the government was able to compensate voters through increased benefits for reunification efforts.

Zohlnhöfer (1999) and Czada (1995) also support the claim that the government opted for a de-liberalization course due to prior electoral promises and because of competition between parties or the struggle to attract and keep voters. Since the SPD remained an opposition party throughout the reunification proceedings and promoted a de-liberalizing strategy, it would have been risky to introduce welfare cuts. By opting for a de-liberalizing strategy of consolidation, the CDU was able to compensate for and balance its internal disagreements between the CDA and the business wing.

However, while there was a consensus from all political actors to opt for de-liberalization, this harmony faded soon after the consequences of this reform path became clear. The rise in unit labor costs undermined the competitiveness of Eastern and Western German firms. Thus, employers chose to leave or refused to comply with the collective agreements, resulting in an evasion of collective agreements (*stille Tarifflucht*) after 1993 in the East (Jochem 1999). Employers used hardship clauses[3] in particular to undercut wage agreements.

Rising unemployment and lagging growth plagued the German economy at this time. The strategies chosen to combat employment problems reinforced government debt. In an attempt to reduce unemployment, the government tried to use early retirement and transitory benefits to diminish the labor supply, thus reinforcing the pressure on the social security budget and social insurance carriers (Jochem 1999). The chosen reform path led not only to major economic difficulties, but also to criticism from various expert commissions, high-minded economists, and even several German newspapers (Baccaro and Howell 2017; Hassel and Schiller 2010: 103–105). In view of the arising challenges, the government, the unions, and employers had trouble agreeing on new strategies. The contentious topic of labor market reforms in particular hardened the fronts between and within the different groups (Streeck and Hassel 2003; Zohlnhöfer 1999). In 1993, the government started

[3]Hardship clauses were originally intended to avoid bankruptcy and high unemployment through lower wages than agreed upon in collective agreements. The hardship clauses had to be agreed upon by special arbitration boards that included representatives of capital and labor (Jochem 1999).

to adopt soft retrenchment measures; the extent and direction of these measures led to increased discrepancies between the various political actors (Jochem 1999; Peffekoven 1997).

In order to bridge the divides, midway throughout the 1990s IG Metall proposed a tripartite agreement—the *Alliance for Jobs* (*Bündnis für Arbeit*). In the proposed agreement, IG Metall would link its wage increases to inflation rather than productivity, which would allow them to offer lower wages to the long-term unemployed, while employers would provide employment guarantees and new job programs. The government was asked to increase its financial and political commitment and reduce social security contributions (Baccaro and Howell 2017: 109). However, while the Kohl administration was very open to this new idea at the beginning, approval quickly faded when the different parties were unable to agree on concrete terms (Schludi 2005: 136, 137). The unions found themselves in a weak position after reunification. Union density was falling and employers were pushing for decentralization (Streeck and Hassel 2003; Hassel 2011; OECD 2017b). As a result, the rift within the government and between unions and employers persisted until the end of the governmental period. Thus, the Social Democrats and the trade unions loudly emphasized the demands of de-liberalizing labor market policies before the 1998 elections (Zohlnhöfer 1999).

5.3.4 Comprehensive De-liberalization Policies Between 1990 and 1998

While several comprehensive de-liberalization policies were introduced in the period following reunification, the most important one was the tax surcharge.

5.3.4.1 Introduction of Tax Surcharge

The aftermath of reunification was extremely challenging, both politically and economically. However, despite the mounting problems, Chancellor Kohl promised '*reunification without sacrifices*'. At the beginning of the 1990s, German politicians did not know what reunification would cost, but it soon became clear that reunification proceedings would cost more than expected. Thus it was Chancellor Kohl himself in spring 1991 who pushed for the introduction of a 7.5% solidarity surcharge on income, capital gains, and corporate tax (Zohlnhöfer 1999; Neckermann 1992). Initially, the Gulf War was named as the reason for this increase, and the introduction of the tax surcharge was a result of the changing state of the world ("*Veränderungen in der Weltlage; insbesondere der Finanzierung des Golfkrieges*"). However, this was only partly true because more than half of the money gained through this tax went to the treasury and was used for reunification (Zohlnhöfer 1999). Some authors argued that the government merely used the Gulf War as a pretense to minimize possible public resentment over the new tax policy (Renzsch 1998).

The introduction of the solidarity surcharge mirrors the financing strategies of reunification. The government decided from the beginning to increase contributions and taxes, including the solidarity surcharge, rather than introducing welfare cuts. Also, in the early 1990s, the government opted once again for the reintroduction of the solidarity surcharge instead of focusing on cuts in consolidation negotiations (Zohlnhöfer 1999). How can we explain this strategy of de-liberalization?

It stands to reason that the government focused increasing taxes and contributions over cuts in order to reach consensus in politics and avoid blame from the voters: by focusing on increased contributions rather than cuts, the Kohl administration was able to reach a consensus between the CDU and the opposition party (Zohlnhöfer 1999). In the first discussion on how to approach reunification, the FDP and the business wing of the CDU advocated for liberalizing reforms, while the CDA opposed. Heiner Geissler, one of the parliamentary leaders of the CDU (CDA) wrote a letter to his colleagues stating that "a cut to social security benefits would be an unacceptable injustice for millions of people. To cut benefits from those who are already dependent on social benefits would be a bitterly unrighteous act"[4] (Frankfurter Rundschau 21.1.1993 cited in Feldengut 1993). The CDA opinion was clearly shared by the SPD, which was strongly against cuts. By focusing on increased contributions, the government was able to introduce fiscal consolidation without cuts. In addition to creating a political consensus, the focus on increased contributions over cuts also helped to make consolidation less visible (Zohlnhöfer 1999). Several authors agree that the policy choice of de-liberalization is best explained by the government's desire to reach consensus within the government and to mitigate blame from voters (Peffekoven 1997; Czada 1995; Zohlnhöfer 1999). Thus, despite the extraordinary circumstances surrounding the introduction of this policy, the main reason for choosing a fiscal strategy of increased contributions rather than cuts corresponds to the main argument of this book.

In sum, the period between 1990 and 1998 was shaped by reunification. Throughout this entire period, the government was unable to decide on a continuous strategy for reform. Hence, the early period is marked by de-liberalization in the welfare state, while the later period featured more liberalization processes. De-liberalization strategies happened in consensus, while liberalization was introduced during times of disagreement. Politically, this period was very important because it marked the beginning of the disharmony between capital and labor.

---

[4]Translation from German. Original quote: „*Eine pauschale Kürzung der Sozialhilfe z. B. wäre aber ein nicht hinnehmbares Unrecht für Millionen von Menschen, die ausschließlich von der Sozialhilfe leben müssen, vor allem für Millionen von Behinderten, Pflegebedürftigen, aber auch z. B. von alleinstehenden Müttern, für die eine solche Kürzung eine bittere Ungerechtigkeit wäre. Einer alten Frau, die zusätzlich zu ihrer kleinen Rente noch einen Sozialhilfeanspruch hat, 15 oder 20 DM wegzunehmen, wäre eine Schande*" (Frankfurter Rundschau 21.1.1993 cited in Feldengut 1993).

5.4 Liberalization and De-liberalization Between 1999 and 2005

In 1998, a new government was voted into office. The new coalition was made up of the Social Democrats and Alliance 90/the Green Party under Chancellor Gerhard Schröder. At the start of this administration, the government delivered on its electoral promises to refrain from liberalization and social policy cutbacks, despite a heavy economic recession and an all-time high in unemployment which surpassed 12.7% in 1997 (OECD 2017a; Egle and Henkes 2004). However, throughout this government period, the 'red-green' coalition as it was known introduced far-reaching liberalization policies. Confronted with major economic difficulties in its second government term, the Schröder administration made a U-turn in its policy course towards liberalization (Seeleib-Kaiser and Fleckenstein 2007).

5.4.1 Liberalization Policies Between 1999 and 2005

As part of Agenda 2010, several far-reaching reforms were implemented, including the *Hartz I–IV* reforms, which concentrated on the labor market. The majority of these reforms were approved between 2003 and 2005 and had a substantial impact on the welfare state and the labor market. *Hartz I* and *Hartz II* focused primarily on the deregulation of atypical work. Hence, the *Hartz I* reforms set up joint agencies between Public Employment Services (PES) and staffing agencies. Agency work was deregulated and promoted through simple employment without a guaranteed job afterwards, and also by lowering wages in comparison to regular workers by waiving collective agreements. Additionally, the duration of employment for agency workers was prolonged and dismissal protection was lowered (Kemmerling and Bruttel 2006; Baccaro and Howell 2017).

As part of *Hartz II*, mini- and midi-jobs were introduced. These jobs came with reduced social security contributions and tax rates and involved an income between EUR 400 and EUR 800. This system was introduced in order to reduce the tax burden of low-wage jobs; the most important programs were the *Ich-AG*, which made it easier for people to move from unemployment to launching their own business, and the establishment of mini-jobs, which aimed to facilitate jobs for low-wage earners. *Hartz III* merged local PESs and social welfare offices into job centers, aiming to enhance efficiency (Kemmerling and Bruttel 2006; Konle-Seidl et al. 2007). *Hartz IV* merged unemployment benefits and social assistance benefits. Moreover, benefits were not only reduced in terms of generosity and duration, but eligibility was also made more contingent on asset availability and active job searches (Baccaro and Howell 2017).

Another part of the Agenda 2010 reforms involved changing the pension formula in 2004 and introducing a sustainability factor that reflected the ratio between pensioners and contributors. Other reforms included an increase in the retirement age for part-time workers or unemployed pensioners from 60 to 63, a change in the limit of the contingency reserve[5] resulting in a downgrade, and the introduction of taxation of pension benefits (Schulze and Jochem 2009). Further reforms aimed to disburden the first pillar by granting tax subsidies and tax exemptions for private pensions. The reforms triggered very limited reductions in spending, but there was also a shift in the public-private mix focusing on a greater involvement of the private sector (Börsch-Supan and Wilke 2005; Schulze and Jochem 2009; Busemeyer 2007).

In 2000, Germany induced a diagnosis-related group-based hospital reimbursement system in order to cut costs (Altenstetter and Busse 2005). Amidst these reforms, privatization was also promoted and eased through several EU-directives in various service fields (Streeck 2009).

5.4.2 *De-Liberalization Policies Between 1999 and 2005*

The majority of de-liberalization policies were introduced at the beginning of the first red-green coalition administration before the government took a liberal turn. Early reforms focused particularly on the labor market and signaled a friendly course towards workers and unions. The reform approach in social and labor market policy focused on keeping election promises and reversing the retrenchment measures that had been introduced by the Kohl government (Baccaro and Howell 2017; Leibfried and Obinger 2003).

The government started out by introducing an action program to reduce youth unemployment through different qualification and employment programs as well as grants for labor costs. The government also strengthened job creation schemes. Moreover, the government reintroduced dismissal protection for companies employing six to ten employees. In addition to job protection and creation, the government also increased benefits. In 1999, the government loosened the eligibility regulations for receiving unemployment benefits for recipients who have children or dependent relatives. In 2001, the red-green coalition decided to entitle disabled workers to personal assistance funding between EUR 250 and EUR 1000 per month. The government also included the self-employed and marginally employed into the pension scheme and the social insurance scheme. Further, the government opted to treat temporary workers and other employees equally in 2003 (Armingeon et al. 2019; Leibfried and Obinger 2003).

In 1998, the government introduced new legislation to reverse higher patient co-payments and restrictions on the provision of health services that were introduced by the previous government. Moreover, short-term sickness benefits were returned to 100% and the chronically ill were excluded from co-payments for drugs, transportation, and other treatment-related costs. From 2002 onwards, health insurance

[5]An amount of money established from retained earnings to allow for unforeseen losses in business (Dictionary 2017).

premium contributions were raised (Armingeon et al. 2019). In the field of pensions, the government suspended the demographic factor in the pension computations which the Kohl government had planned for the year 1999. Additionally, the government reversed all foreseen cuts in the field of eligibility pensions, and also placed the emphasis on new social risks by introducing pension claims during contribution-free periods for child raising (Leibfried and Obinger 2003).

Furthermore, the government reformed the parental unemployment scheme by making it possible to receive benefits while working up to 30 hours, and by increasing the generosity of these benefits. The red-green coalition also introduced childcare tax allowances in 2001 (Fleckenstein and Lee 2012; Leibfried and Obinger 2003).

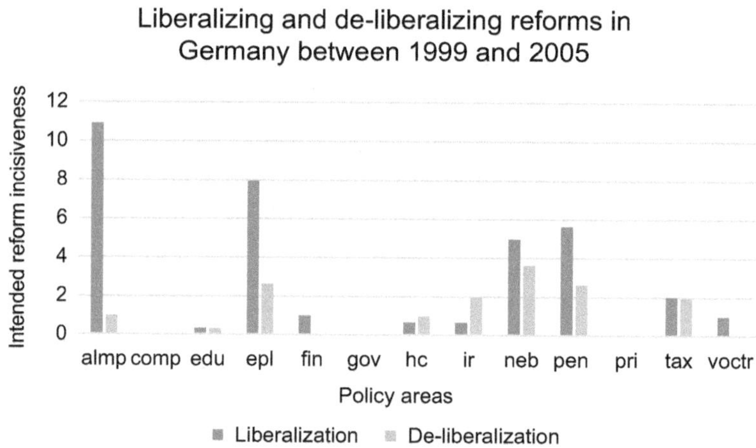

Fig. 5.4 Liberalizing and de-liberalizing reforms in Germany between 1999 and 2005 across all policy fields. Reforms are weighted according to the liberalization index (values: first-order changes: 0.33; second-order changes: 0.66; third-order and status quo changes: 1). Source: Liberalization Database (Armingeon et al. 2019)

5.4.3 Politics Between 1999 and 2005: From Credit Taking to Far-Reaching Liberalization

In 1998, a new coalition government between the Social Democratic Party (SPD) and Alliance 90/the Green Party came into office. The two heads of the Social Democrats were two ideologically disparate leaders: Gerhard Schröder and Oscar Lafontaine. While Schröder, who served as Chancellor, was known to be market-friendly, Lafontaine, who was appointed Minister of Finance, was a traditionally left-leaning Social Democrat with a close relationship to the trade unions (Egle and Henkes 2004). At the beginning of its administration, the government kept its election promises by reinstating the tripartite *Alliance for Jobs, Education, and*

Competitiveness, reversing some of the liberalizing reforms that had been introduced under Kohl and promoting de-liberalization in the fields of social and labor market policies (Egle and Henkes 2004; Streeck and Hassel 2003). After Kohl failed to coordinate labor market and social policy reforms with capital and labor, the Social Democrats aimed to solve this problem by providing concessions to the unions in order to get them on board for further reforms. Similar to the Kohl administration, Schröder intended to implement 'far-reaching reforms to foster employment' by introducing a 'fundamental reform in the social security system' according to the 1998 Declaration of Alliances for Jobs. While, the left wing of the Social Democrats was adamant that the government needed to reverse Kohl's reforms and keep its election promises to the unions and the voters, the unions in turn were not so eager to engage in this tripartite agreement, fearing that the government would centralize relations with capital and labor (Streeck and Hassel 2003).

The de-liberalizing strategies described above were owed to the left faction of the Social Democrats who wanted to work with the unions, which had helped bring the Social Democrats to power in 1998. The Social Democrats made an election pledge to their core constituency and to the unions, stating that they would withdraw from fiscal tightening. It stands to reason that the Social Democrats would have disenfranchised their core constituency if they had not followed up on their election promises. Aside from being able to take credit for their election claims, the Social Democrats needed the unions' consent in order to pass liberalizing reforms (Egle and Henkes 2004). The government hoped that by agreeing to some de-liberalizing reforms, the unions would agree to some liberalizing concessions in the *Alliance for Jobs, Education, and Competitiveness* (Streeck and Hassel 2003). Hence, this strategy of de-liberalization also intended to compensate the unions for potential liberalizing reforms.

However, in 1999, the circumstances surrounding de-liberalization policies changed greatly when Oscar Lafontaine resigned from his post due to irreconcilable ideological differences with the SPD stemming from a tax reform proposal. Afterwards, the market-friendly faction of the SPD gained the upper hand in the party, and the left wing of the SPD was weakened. As a result, the government had difficulties reaching an agreement on the *Alliance* with the unions, who were displaying more and more fissures between their various sub-organizations (Hassel and Schiller 2010: 131–133; Egle and Henkes 2004). In 2000, the Schröder government found itself in the same situation the Kohl government had been in: facing little progress in the *Alliance for Jobs, Education, and Competitiveness,* a very difficult economic situation, and upcoming elections. After a scandal concerning the PES went public, Chancellor Schröder switched to unilateral action. Looking for a new strategy, he stopped negotiations on the *Alliance* (Starke 2008; Streeck and Hassel 2003; Baccaro and Howell 2017: 109–112).

Thus, in the early 2000s, the Schröder administration started its liberal course after appointing the *Hartz* Commission under the Personnel Director of Volkswagen at that time, Peter Hartz. The aim of the commission was to propose solutions for the socio-economic problems that Germany was facing at that time. The trade unions and the employers were not directly involved in the *Hartz* Commission, but each interest group was able to send one representative (Streeck and Hassel 2003;

Zohlnhöfner 2003; Starke 2008). The *Hartz* Commission recommended a strong liberalization course for welfare state and labor market reforms. Despite fierce criticism from the unions, the government adopted many of the proposed changes in the course of the *Agenda 2010* reforms (Streeck and Hassel 2003; Zohlnhöfer 2003). How can we explain this sudden about-face?

By promoting the *Hartz* reforms, the SPÖ tried to adopt a new path of policy reform in Germany in order to alter the economic situation. However, while the SPD was able to break with earlier reform politics, they were not able to internalize this new course and collectively back up these reforms as a party. Furthermore, many SPD voters and various trade unions strongly disagreed with this new policy course. The SPD experienced significant losses in various Federal State elections after 2003. Additionally, the party lost more than one-fifth of its members, and the party's ideology has suffered from the *Hartz* reforms to this day. The *Hartz* reforms also complicated the interrelationship between the government, employers, and unions (while the DGB opposed all reforms, other unions such as the Industriegewerkschaft Bergbau, Chemie, Energie (IG BCE) opted for a moderation of the *Hartz* reforms but not a total abandonment). The *Hartz* reforms had serious consequences for politics and policies, and marked a significant shift towards liberalization in terms of the welfare state and labor market policies (Hassel and Schiller 2010: 50–53, 265–270).

After 1998, the government attempted to introduce de-liberalizing strategies to compensate the unions for potential liberalizations and to deliver on their election promises. However, after the government and the unions showed internal fissures and were not able to agree on a common strategy, coupled with growing functional pressures, the government adopted a liberalizing strategy.

5.4.4 Comprehensive De-liberalization Policies Between 1999 and 2005

The government introduced a number of comprehensive de-liberalizing reforms between 1999 and 2005. The early de-liberalizing policies in this period were the result of election promises, and followed the logic of de-liberalizing strategies. Comprehensive de-liberalizing policies after 2000 were dependent on the European Union and will not be discussed in this section.

5.4.4.1 Marginal Employment Is Covered by Social Insurance

Throughout the 1998 election campaign, the SPD refrained from advocating for liberalizing labor market reforms. On the contrary, the SPD pledged to introduce traditional Social Democratic labor market reforms. The promised de-liberalizing reform actions included the pledge to include the so called 'false' self-employed into the pension insurance system, and include the marginally employed (the so called

630-DM-Jobs) in the social insurance system (Egle and Henkes 2004). Chancellor Schröder reinforced this promise in his government policy statement on November 10, 1998, in which he said, "*that is why we are not going abolish the so-called 620 DM jobs, but we will ensure that they are covered by social insurance contributions. [. . .] the German government recognizes the importance of these forms of employment. [. . .] together with employers and unions, we will prevent the fraudulent use of this employment regulation*[6]" (Schröder 1998). In comparison to other promises, the expansion of social insurance to this group was not merely symbolic, but rather had a strong de-liberalizing character. The law allowed for people who are marginally employed, meaning they earn up to DM 630 / EUR 325 a month, and what are known as 'false' freelancers (freelancers who earn more than 80% of their annual income from a single employer) to be covered by social insurance contributions (Zohlnhöfer 2004). Consequentially, regular forms of employment and marginal forms of employment were treated equally regardless of whether this job was a person's main source of income or a source of side income. Hence, after the change in legislation, small job holders and their employers had to pay the minimum amount of payroll taxes and employees were also eligible for minimum welfare benefits (Rudolph 1999). Employers met this policy with strong resistance because it put an end to one of the few areas of flexibility within the German labor market and actively increased contributions from both employers and workers. Also, the CDU objected this law, making it a politically salient topic (Egle and Henkes 2004; Butterwegge 2012: 157–158).

How did this law come about? Marginal employment had been on the rise since the 1980s. It was particularly appealing to employers because they only had to pay a low lump-sum tax for marginally employed workers. As a result, some industries such as cleaners, discount grocery stores, and restaurants primarily offered marginal employment and no longer offered regular, full-time positions. Throughout Kohl's government in particular, many regular, full-time positions were split into several marginal employment positions. As a result, the German welfare state, which was already under a great deal of strain, was missing out on social security contributions. In their election campaigns, the SPD and Alliance 90/the Green Party pledged to fight against these forms of employment (Butterwegge 2012: 157–158). However, in 1998, after Schröder's government declaration, it took the government several

[6]Translation from German. Original quote: "*Haushaltshilfe und Altenbetreuung, Einpack- oder Einpark-Service sind Dienstleistungen an der Allgemeinheit, deren sich niemand schämen muß. Diejenigen, die diese Dienstleistungen in Anspruch nehmen wollen und sie angemessen zu bezahlen in der Lage sind, werden in unserer Gesellschaft immer mehr. Auch deshalb werden wir die sogenannten 620-Mark-Jobs nicht einfach abschaffen. Aber wir werden sie angemessen in die Sozialversicherungspflicht einbeziehen. Die Grenze werden wir auf 300 D-Mark festlegen. Da wir gleichzeitig die Pauschalbesteuerung aufheben, werden diese Tätigkeiten nicht unzumutbar verteuert. Man sieht daran: Die Bundesregierung erkennt ausdrücklich die Notwendigkeit und Berechtigung solcher Beschäftigungsverhältnisse an: sowohl für die Arbeitgeber als auch für die betroffenen Arbeitnehmerinnen und Arbeitnehmer und für die Verbraucher. Aber wir wollen gemeinsam mit Arbeitgebern und Gewerkschaften den Mißbrauch, der mitdieser Regelung betrieben worden ist, ernsthaft bekämpfen* " (Schröder 1998).

weeks to decide on an appropriate response to regulate this form of employment. While some SPD party members, such as Chancellor Schröder and Labor Minister Riester, pushed for a liberal regulation, other SPD members advocated an abolishment of this kind of employment. Aside from internal disagreements on appropriate measures, the SPD was also pressured by the industry and the employers. The government finally settled on a middle ground within the party, opting not for an abolishment but focusing on the original option, which sought to include marginal jobs into social insurance contributions (Butterwegge 2012: 157, 158). In 2003, most of the law's provisions were revoked to strengthen labor market flexibility and job creation (Ebbinghaus and Eichhorst 2006).

Several authors agree that this de-liberalizing reform came about in order for the politicians involved to take political credit for living up to their election promises and handling things differently than the Kohl government did. The government wanted to demonstrate that it could solve problems in a Social Democratic way (Leibfried and Obinger 2003; Egle and Henkes 2004). However, the introduction of this law helped also to increase social security contributions, which was not an irrelevant side effect at this time (Egle and Henkes 2004; Butterwegge 2012: 157, 158).

In conclusion, the period between 1998 and 2005 was an intense, colorful time when it comes to liberalization and de-liberalization. At the beginning of this period, the government sought to reposition itself and set itself apart from the earlier Kohl government by following a traditional Social Democratic reform path. The government hoped to use de-liberalizing policies to compensate voters and unions for potential future reforms, such as labor market reforms through the *Alliance for Jobs, Education, and Competitiveness*. However, internal disagreements within the SPD, which was torn between a traditional Social Democratic reform path and a modernizing 'third-way' reform path, aggravated negotiations. Presented with economic and political obstacles, the government opted for a unilateral reform course aiming for liberalization, which resulted in upset voters, disgruntled unions, and a highly conflicted SPD that was searching for its ideology.

5.5 Liberalization and De-liberalization Between 2006 and 2015

In 2005, a new coalition made up of the conservative party (CDU/CSU) under Chancellor Angela Merkel together with the Social Democratic Party was voted into office. Both parties experienced significant losses in the election, while the Free Democratic Party and *Die Linke*, or the Left, gained electoral votes. The losses were attributed to a lack of focus on social matters in the parties' programs. Despite these circumstances, both parties opted to continue on the same political course, meaning the *Hartz* reforms were not abolished but merely regulated or adjusted. It was only under a new coalition between the CDU/CSU and the Free Democratic Party in 2009 that the political tone towards liberalization changed. The government attempted to signal a new policy course by advocating that there would be no need for new liberalizing reforms (Butterwegge 2012: 229–234, 289–294). Thus, Germany entered into a period of marginal liberalization and re-regulation policies. Some reforms even brought about de-liberalization, particularly in the area of salient welfare state policies such as pensions, the labor market, and industrial relations. Germany has followed this path of marginal liberalization until recently. Moreover, the current government, a coalition between the CDU/CSU and the SPD, has actually intensified its de-liberalization efforts in the past few years (2013–present) (Walwei 2015; Armingeon et al. 2019). Above all, the conservative party and the Social Democrats have been very cautious when it comes to implementing radical liberal reforms after seeing how the Schröder administration was punished for their reforms (Fleckenstein 2011).

5.5.1 Liberalization Policies Between 2006 and 2015

The liberalization processes of the mid-2000s were still characterized by legislation that had been passed by the earlier government following the *Hartz* proposal. Past reforms also dominated the labor market. As a result, in 2005, the labor market was further decentralized. The full responsibility for labor market policies at the regional level was passed down to job centers, including financial budgeting and administration. Furthermore, the government introduced rapid offers in the labor market, which meant unemployed persons were immediately tested for their willingness to accept work, which also determined the amount of unemployment benefits they would receive (if unemployed persons rejected more than two job offers a year, they would lose up to 60% of their benefits). Additionally, the government focused on the employability of older workers through wage subsidies and improved conditions for employers who hired older persons on a temporary basis (allowing for up to 5 years with the same employer) (Armingeon et al. 2019).

The government raised the statutory retirement age from 65 to 67, while the retirement age for disabled persons was increased to 65. The government also strengthened the second-pillar capital-based supplementary pension schemes by lowering the minimum age for vesting entitlements to employer-financed occupational pensions from 30 to 25 years. The government also cut costs and increased competition in the field of healthcare (Armingeon et al. 2019). The government increased competitiveness in the retail sector by prohibiting location clauses. Furthermore, the government also implemented its first railway package following the EU directive 2004/51/EC on railway transportation. This package involved non-discriminatory access to railway infrastructure and promoted increased competition.

The Merkel administration also allowed for greater freedom in the field of insurance companies in terms of insured persons' contractual relations with providers. This allowed insurance providers to compete on the quality and efficiency of their products and made it easier for people to switch insurance companies. The government lowered the administrative hurdles to establishing corporations by introducing a simplified version of a limited liability corporation. Additionally, competition was strengthened in the education sector. In particular, the government increased the autonomy of universities and linked some forms of funding closer to performance (Armingeon et al. 2019).

Lastly, the coalition introduced a liberalizing tax reform that reduced income taxes in 2008. The corporate tax rate was reduced from 25% to 15% in January 2008, and the basic rate for local business tax (*Gewerbesteuermesszahl*) was cut from 5 to 3.5% (Armingeon et al. 2019).

5.5.2 De-liberalization Policies Between 2006 and 2015

The government introduced a number of de-liberalizing policies, with an uptick after 2009. In 2007, the government expanded on-the-job training, and in 2013, they extended the duration of legally guaranteed temporary employment benefits (*Kurzarbeitergeld*) from 6 to 12 months. The government adjusted the agenda reforms by raising the monthly tax-free pay threshold for mini-jobs—which had remained unchanged since 2003—from EUR 400 to EUR 450. The monthly threshold for midi-jobs was also increased from EUR 800 to EUR 850 (Jackson and Sorge 2012; Armingeon et al. 2019; Chung and Thewissen 2011; Walwei 2015). Most importantly, a statutory minimum wage of EUR 8.50 per hour was agreed on and has remained in place since January 2015. In the field of pensions, the government extended early retirement schemes for older employees (a gradual transition into retirement for employees over 55) and lowered the retirement age to 63 for special groups. In terms of industrial relations, the new federal government strengthened collective bargaining amongst the major trade unions by amending the *Law to Reinforce Collective Bargaining Autonomy* (*Tarifeinheitsgesetz*) (Walwei 2015).

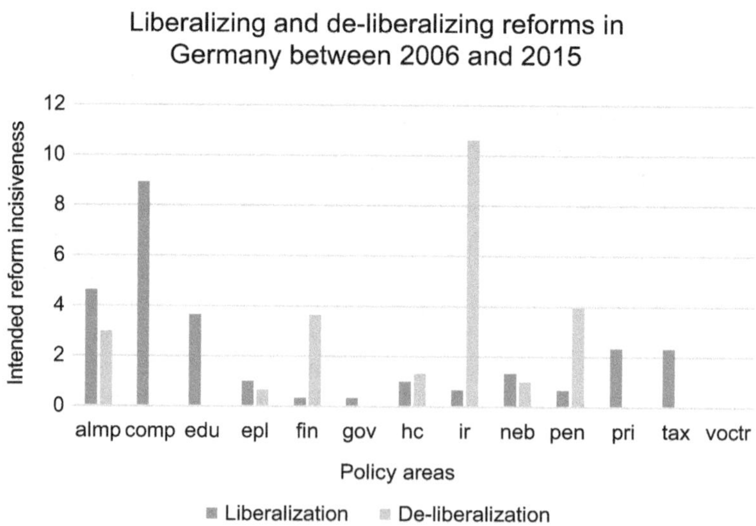

Fig. 5.5 Liberalizing and de-liberalizing reforms in Germany between 2006 and 2015 across all policy fields. Reforms are weighted according to the liberalization index (values: first-order changes: 0.33; second-order changes: 0.66; third-order and status quo changes: 1). Source: Liberalization Database (Armingeon et al. 2019)

5.5.3 Politics Between 2006 and 2015: Support for Liberalization Withers

The period between 2006 and 2015 was marked by shifting party formations, starting with a grand coalition,[7] transitioning to a coalition of the Free Democrats and the CDU/CSU,[8] and ending again in a grand coalition.[9] While the first government continued on an ideologically liberal course without applying many reforms, the recent period caused a stir with the introduction of markedly de-liberalizing laws; de-liberalizing policy reforms have significantly increased since 2009 in particular. Before the election in 2009, representatives of the CDU/CSU had already attempted to appease voters who were afraid of further cuts (Butterwegge 2012: 286–293). Thus, in 2009, the parliamentary leader of the CDU, Volker Kauder, said, "There is absolutely no reason for social welfare cuts. [. . .] particularly during times of crisis, the social welfare systems must prove itself successfully[10]" (Taz 2009). Similar statements were also made by the CDU Social Minister, who said that the new coalition "would not be a coalition of social imposition.[11]" The first common initiative of the new coalition was a de-liberalizing adjustment of the *Hartz* reforms that was greatly highlighted by politicians and resulted in the increase of the old-age provisions contained in *Hartz IV* from EUR 250 to EUR 750. However, even though the CDU/CSU insisted that they would not make welfare cuts, their coalition with the FDP pursued a mixed approach of retrenchment and expansion. A debate on the principles of liberalizing and de-liberalizing policy reforms arose only in 2010 when the Federal Constitutional Court declared the standard rate of *Hartz IV* incompatible with the German constitution (Butterwegge 2012: 293–302). In an attempt to reconcile matters, the government planned to renegotiate the standard rate of the *Hartz* reforms; however, the government and the opposition parties were not able to agree on appropriate measures. The SPD, which attempted to reposition itself as a traditional Social Democratic Party after its catastrophic losses in 2009, demanded higher adjustment rates than the CDU and FDP. In 2011, the government and the SPD agreed on new rates following the recommendation of the conservative liberal faction (Butterwegge 2012: 303–317).

---

[7]CDU-SPD coalition under Chancellor Angela Merkel between Nov. 2005 and Sep. 2009 (Armingeon et al. 2016).

[8]CDU-FDP coalition under Chancellor Angela Merkel between Oct. 2009 and Sep. 2013 (Armingeon et al. 2016).

[9]CDU-SPD coalition under Chancellor Angela Merkel between Dec. 2013 and Sep. 2017 (Armingeon et al. 2016).

[10]Translation from German. Original quote: "*Für Sozialkürzungen sehe ich überhaupt keinen Anlass. Das würden die Menschen zu Recht nicht verstehen. Für die Banken werden Milliarden ausgegeben, für die normalen Leute hat man nichts? So wird es nicht laufen. Gerade in der Krise müssen sich die sozialen Sicherungssysteme bewähren*" (Taz 2009).

[11]Translation from German. Original quote: "*Keine Koalition der sozialen Zumutungen*" (Kölner Stadt Anzeiger September 29, 2009 cited in Butterwegge 2012: 290).

After this setback, the SPD continued to publicly push for de-liberalization and began endorsing the introduction of a statutory minimum wage and the increase of pension benefits. The SPD issued a public statement in which it declared its ideological departure from the *Hartz* reforms and its return to traditional Social Democratic values, "*The Hartz reforms had a single-minded focus on the goal of activation [of the unemployed,] but they were not in line with the justice and moral expectations of our working culture*" (SPD Präsidium 2010: 1 cited in Dostal 2012b). The SPD further demanded the 'reintroduction of orderly structures in the labor market' and advocated for the unions' demands for a minimum wage of EUR 8.50 (SPD Präsidium 2010: 2–3 cited in Dostal 2012b). The CDU/CSU in turn also shifted towards the center and away from hard neoliberalism (Dostal 2012b; Blätte 2010: 276).

It stands to reason that both parties adopted a de-liberalizing course in order to attract voters and distance themselves from earlier liberal reforms. The *Hartz* reforms have been an ongoing topic in the German public debate since they have been enacted; the reforms permanently altered labor market policies and German politics. The SPD suffered greatly in terms of loss of voters and members based on their decision to introduce the Agenda 2010 reforms (Dostal 2012a, b; Mabbett 2016). The issue of liberalization became a very politically salient topic. After the *Hartz* reforms, the public opinion towards liberalization reform became negative because Germans felt that unfair economic conditions were on the rise. Additionally, the public felt that politicians were most able to effectively change these unfair conditions.

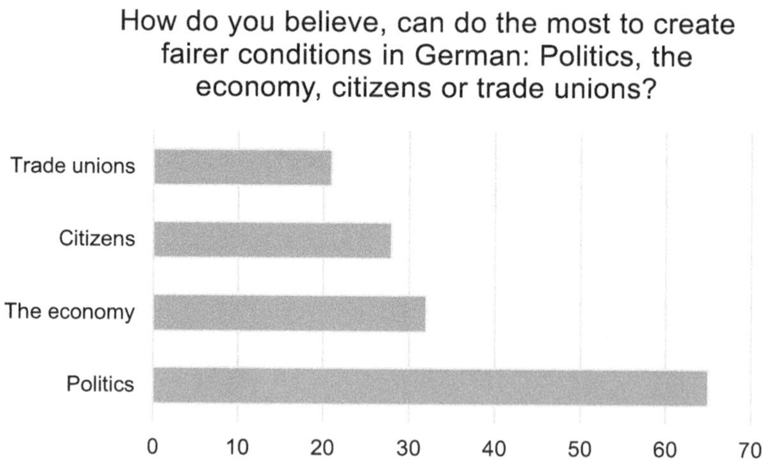

Fig. 5.6 Percentage of actors who can create fairer conditions in Germany. Source: Institut für Demoskopie Allensbach (2013a)

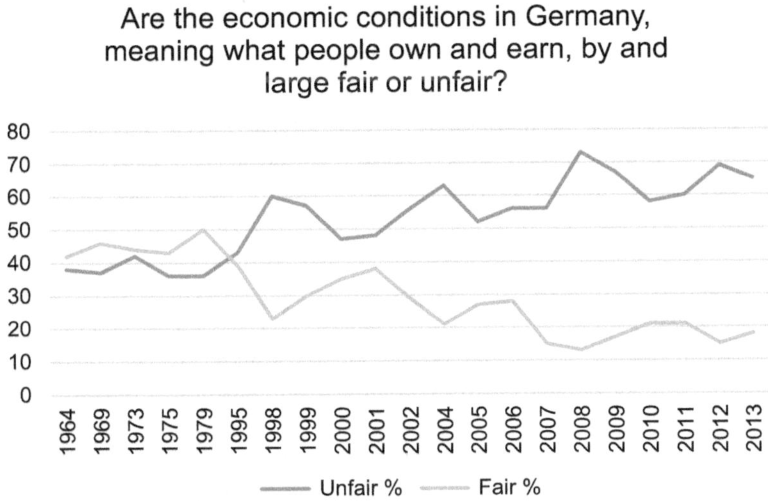

Fig. 5.7 Percentage of Germans who perceive the economic conditions as fair or unfair, 1964–2013 (until 1995 only West Germany). Source: Institut für Demoskopie Allensbach (2013b)

Hence, many authors agree that the Social Democrats—left with no other option—changed their policy course towards traditional Social Democratic values in order to mitigate blame for the Agenda 2010 reforms and respond to negative feedback from the voters. The party pushed for traditional Social Democratic policies in order to gain back the trust of lost voters and the support of the unions (Dostal 2012a, b; Mabbett 2016). The CDU/CSU also changed its course in an attempt to win the voters that the SPD had lost (Dostal 2012a; Blätte 2010: 288–292). One of our interviewees from the Confederation of German Employers' Association referred to similar circumstances, saying "*the Social Democrats have been the public whipping boy ever since the introduction of the Hartz reforms, and now they are attempting to shape their politics for the voters. Also the CDU, in particular the CDA, is trying to introduce various de-liberalizations*". When asked why, the representative of the BDA answered, "*both parties are trying to gain voters, and the economy is in good shape, which allows for de-liberalizing policy reforms at the moment*" (Interview Zenzen 2016).

The explanations for this new trend point towards an electorate-based reasoning, whereby both parties are trying to make policies that are attractive to their constituencies. In the case of the SPD, the new reforms were not only aimed at their constituency, but also at the trade unions, which were greatly unhappy after the Agenda 2010 reforms.

5.5.4 Comprehensive De-liberalization Policies Between 2006 and 2015

Several comprehensive de-liberalizing policy reforms were introduced between 2006 and 2015. The most important changes took place in the field of labor market policies, specifically industrial relations.

5.5.4.1 Introduction of Binding Minimum Wages in Several Sectors

From the mid-1990s on, the number of low-paid workers in Germany increased while the unions' power to negotiate collective agreements decreased. Against this background, debates on a binding minimum wage arose. The first step towards an industry-specific minimum wage occurred in 1996 after the *Posted Workers Directive 96/71/EC* was legislated. The *Posted Workers Directive* created a legal framework that enabled German employers and unions in the construction industry to conclude collective agreements that could then be extended to all workers and employers involved in construction projects on German soil (Hüttenhoff 2016; Mabbett 2016).

The employers in the construction industry and the unions recommended a universally applicable collective agreement in the construction industry that would have required the consent of the top labor and capital organizations. However, the BDA objected to the agreement, stating that the high wage standards in the construction industry could spill over to other branches and therefore possibly hamper employment and investment; the BDA agreed after a second round of bargaining in which the minimum wage was lowered. In 1998, after the coalition between the Social Democrats and Alliance 90/the Green Party came into power, the government changed the legislation procedures, extending the right to conclude these agreements to the Minister of Labor. Hence, in 1999, when the BDA blocked an extending agreement for the construction industry, the other bargaining party turned to the Minister of Labor, who extended the agreement. As a result, the state began to step in for capital and labor. Nevertheless, the state only focused on specific industries, while other low-wage sectors remained neglected. The Food, Beverage, and Restaurant Trade Union (Gewerkschaft Nahrung-Genuss-Gaststätten—NGG) and the United Service Union (Ver.di), whose members were particularly affected, started to campaign for an hourly minimum wage of EUR 7.50 (Mabbett 2016; Bosch 2015).

Around 2005, some members of the SPD also started to demand a statutory minimum wage as part of the *Hartz* reforms; however, it was only after 2006, when the SPD entered into a coalition with the CDU/CSU, that the two parties began debating the minimum wage in Germany (Mabbett 2016). The SPD, whose voters were increasingly turning away from the party after the *Hartz* reforms, pushed the topic (Bosch 2015). One wing of the SPD began to push for two legislative initiatives that aimed to generate a minimum wage at the sectoral employment level (Dostal 2012b). After controversial internal debates, the DGB also started to demand that the *Posted Workers Directive* should be expanded to various sectors that were not fully covered by the collective bargaining agreements (Bispinck and Dribbusch 2011; Bispinck and Schulten 2008).

The CDU, which was strongly against a statutory minimum wage at the beginning, finally agreed to the SPD's and the unions' demands after the statutory minimum wage became extremely popular, even among conservative voters (Mabbett 2016; Bosch 2015). Employers heavily criticized the decision, while the unions welcomed this step but demanded further action. The Minister of Labor at the time, Olaf Scholz (SPD), stated that this new law was "*a victory for workers*", while the Minister of the Economy, Michel Glos (CSU), said that this law would "*certainly not lead to a statutory minimum wage*" (BBP 2008).

Table 5.1 Approval for a statutory minimum wage in Germany in 2006

Approval for a statutory minimum wage in Germany in 2006; approval rate displayed as a percentage			
		Yes	No
All respondents		70	30
Income	Lowest quintile	75	25
	Highest quintile	57	43
Employment	Employed	73	27
	Self-employed	61	39
	Unemployed	84	16
	Long-term unemployed	89	11
Gender	Female	75	25
	Male	65	35
Education	Low	74	26
	High	66	34
Age	18–34	69	31
	35–59	76	24
	60 and older	63	37

Source: Sozialstaatssurvey (2008) and Nüchter et al. (2009) cited in Bieräugel et al. (2010)

In order to introduce the binding minimum wages in various sectors, the government extended the *Posted Workers Directive of 1996*, which was based on the *European Posted Workers Directive*, thus supporting and protecting national collective agreements. The preconditions for this law were national collective agreements on industry-wide minimum wages that were declared to be generally binding by the federal government (Bosch 2015).

The binding, industry-specific minimum wages were extended during a period in which the number of SPD voters had declined and public approval rate for the introduction of minimum wage agreements was growing. Despite the CDU/CSU's original concerns and against the wishes of the employers, the government agreed to the extension of collective agreements of industry-specific minimum wages. It stands to reason that the government, and the SPD in particular, pursued a de-liberalizing strategy in order to mitigate the effects of the negative feedback received from voters and unions, and to adjust to the changes in public opinion (Marx and Starke 2017). Both the loss of votes and the high public approval towards the introduction of a minimum wage indicate a strategy of credit taking and mitigation of blame due to earlier reforms.

5.5.4.2 Pension 63/Mothers' Pension

Over the past 20 years, Germany has introduced a number of liberalizing reforms in the area of pensions. In the 1990s, the possibilities for early retirement were curtailed, and in the 2000s the retirement age was increased from 65 to 67.

However, in July 2014, the grand coalition introduced a pension reform package that contained two specific de-liberalizing pension reform measures. The first part of the package allowed for early retirement at the age of 63 for long-term insured workers who had made pension contributions for more than 45 years (Börsch-Supan et al. 2015). The *Pension 63 (Rente 63)* reform is only accorded to persons born before January 1, 1953 who would go into retirement on or after July 1, 2014. (Before the reform, statutory pension benefits were cut down by 0.3% for every month a worker went into pension before reaching the statutory retirement age) (Eurofund 2015b). The second part of the package is called the *Mothers' Pension (Mütterrente),* which extended the pension claim for mothers or fathers from 1 to 2 years. This means that mothers and fathers of children who were born before 1992 were allowed to include not just one but 2 years of parenting towards their pension claim. As a result, pension benefits would increase by around EUR 343 annually per child in Western Germany and around EUR 317 in the new federal states (Eurofund 2015b; Butterwegge 2014).

The introduction of these de-liberalizing pension measures was strongly criticized by the media, and prompted questions about the reasons behind these new policies. Many commentators stated that both the SPD and the CDU/CSU only introduced the *Pension 63* and *Mothers' Pension* reforms to appease voters. While *Pension 63* benefits blue-collar workers, who are traditionally close to the SPD, the *Mothers' Pension* potentially benefits women who chose to stay at home for 2 years, which is more in line with the values of CDU voters.

Both parties countered the media's suspicions by linking the pension reform to the goal of reducing poverty among the elderly. Experts, however, doubt that either the *Pension 63* or the *Mother Pension* is a strong enough instrument to significantly reduce old-age poverty (Butterwegge 2016, 2014). These de-liberalizing pension reforms will not have a significant effect on poverty among the elderly in Germany because the main groups affected by the changes are not particularly prone to poverty in their old age, having worked for more than 45 years or having chosen to stay at home to raise their children (Feld et al. 2014).

So, what were the politics behind these de-liberalizations?

After the Agenda 2010 reforms were enacted, the SPD attempted to return to its traditional values in order to win back their voters. Hence, in its 2013 election campaign, the SPD focused on equality and social justice (Jun et al. 2017). In view of a possible grand coalition government, the SPD made their membership in the coalition contingent upon, among other things, the *Pension 63* reform; in return, the CDU/CSU demanded the *Mothers' Pension*. Why did the parties agree to this expansion given that many commentators and experts had determined that neither reform was a valid tool to fight old-age poverty?

Even though only a few birth cohorts are eligible for *Pension 63*, critical trade unions see this de-liberalizing policy as a partial reversal of the agenda reforms for blue-collar workers and celebrate this policy as a social democratic success story. *Pension 63* partly offsets the liberalizing agenda reforms that resulted in the increase of the retirement age to 67. Hence, this reform benefits the SPD's constituency and is welcomed by the unions (Butterwegge 2014). The CDU/CSU agreed to this expansion because pensioners are a very important voting bloc for these parties (Kauder et al. 2014). Looking at this case, two factors point clearly towards credit-taking and voter appeasement as reasons for this de-liberalization. Firstly, experts do not believe that these de-liberalizing pension reforms had a significant impact on reducing old-age poverty. Secondly, both reforms evidently targeted SPD and CDU/CSU voter groups (Häusermann 2010).

5.5.4.3 The Law to "Strengthen Collective Bargaining"/Introduction of Statutory Minimum Wage

After the *Hartz* reforms were introduced in the early 2000s, the topic of statutory minimum wage began to enter the public debate. In 2004, Franz Müntefering, Chairman of the Social Democrats, was the first to publicly announce his intentions to seek an agreement with the German trade unions on a statutory minimum wage. However, both the parties and the unions had diverging opinions on the introduction of a minimum wage. One faction of the SPD, which included the Federal Minister of Economics and Labor, Wolfgang Clement, believed that a general statutory minimum wage (SMW) was not necessary except in the construction industry, while other leading SPD figures endorsed Müntefering's idea. Alliance 90/the Green Party also had differing views on this topic. The CDU/CSU and the Free Democratic Party, who were the opposition parties at this time, were against the introduction of a statutory minimum wage, while *Die Linke* supported the idea. The unions either supported or rejected the idea, depending on their specific industries: the Food, Beverage, Tobacco, Hotel and Catering, and Allied Trades unions all welcomed this idea, having called for the introduction of a national minimum wage since the late 1990s. The second largest trade union in Germany, Ver.di, was also in favor of a national statutory minimum wage of around EUR 7.50 per hour, while IG Metall, Germany's largest union, was against a statutory minimum wage, fearing that it would interfere with collective bargaining. However, after ongoing discussion, the DGB endorsed the introduction of a statutory minimum wage of EUR 7.50 per hour at its 2006 congress (Eurofund 2009). The two largest trade unions supported this idea only sometime after the decision was made (Bosch 2015). Employers collectively rejected a statutory minimum wage (Eurofund 2009; Mabbett 2016). The CDU/CSU rejected the SMW during their coalition with the Social Democrats (2005–2009) and during their coalition with the Freedom Party (2009–2013); however, they changed their official stance sometime after 2013.

The SPD, conflicted and battered after the introduction of the *Hartz* reforms, took the opportunity to win back their voters. Under the pressure of loss of votes, the party vehemently campaigned for the introduction of a statutory minimum wage in 2009 (Mabbett 2016; Bosch 2015). The SPD went as far as to make their participation in a grand coalition government contingent on the CDU/CSU's endorsement of a SMW. The CDU/CSU agreed to accept the SMW and, in August 2014, the Minister of Labor, Andrea Nahles (SPD), introduced the *Act to Strengthen the Autonomy of Collective Bargaining* (Bosch 2015). The act included the introduction of a statutory minimum wage, the establishment of a minimum wage commission, mechanisms to simplify the extension of industry-based minimum wage agreements, and the active strengthening of collective bargaining (Eurofund 2015c). In January 2015, Germany introduced a national minimum wage of EUR 8.50 per hour (Bosch 2015).

Several developments led to the introduction of a SMW. On one hand, the system of collective bargaining had been effectively eroding since the 1990s. Companies had a number of loopholes, which not only made collective bargaining extremely heterogeneous, but essentially made the instrument of collective bargaining largely ineffective in terms of protecting workers protection from low wages, which led to a drop in wages across all areas of the economy (Bosch 2015). The public evidently perceived the effects of earlier liberalizing changes negatively, and public opinion shifted as a result (Marx and Starke 2017). The topic of low wages and the introduction of the SMW became highly politically salient. The majority of the public clearly favored the introduction of a SMW after 2009 (Bosch 2015). According to a study by the Hans-Böckler Stiftung, the vast majority of the German population also viewed the introduction of a statutory minimum wage as a step toward greater social equality for Germany—even those who were afraid that the introduction of a SMW might negatively affect the employment situation in the country (Bieräugel et al. 2010). Moreover, a study by the DGB concluded that around 86% of the German population supported the introduction of a SMW (DGB 2015). Hence, the government as a whole—primarily the ailing Social Democratic Party, but also the CDU/CSU—was able to benefit electorally from the introduction of a minimum wage, given that it found such broad approval among the public.

After 2009, the SPD was keen to restore their voters' confidence and regain the support of the unions, and so they strongly pushed for the introduction of a SMW. Together with the unions, the SPD zeroed in on the employers' strategy of using temporary contracts to push down wages and core workers, and the importance of offsetting this effect through a SMW. Furthermore, the unions were able to capitalize on the SMW by using it as a bargaining chip to deploy their resources for political campaigning (Mabbett 2016). Lastly, the introduction of the SMW showed that in an open political contest between the unions, government, and employers, de-liberalizing policies can be used to campaign for an issue and build alliances (Mabbett 2016).

In sum, this period marked a clear turn in Germany's reform politics. Once the electorate punished the SPD for its liberalizing reforms and the public showed strong approval of de-liberalizing reforms, such as the introduction of an SMW, both parties changed course in terms of labor market and pension policies. The SPD in particular clearly shifted its ideologies in order to mitigate blame for the Agenda 2010 reforms. In all of the aforementioned comprehensive de-liberalization policies, indicators point to a credit-taking/blame-mitigating strategy.

5.6 Conclusion: The German Case Study

Germany's policy reform path cannot be understood without recognizing the importance of political parties and their drive to get elected. In stark contrast to producer group accounts, the German case demonstrated that de-liberalization mainly depends on the individual parties' interests at different times, rather than on employers who have continuously opposed de-liberalization from the 1980s onwards.

Similar to Austria, Germany's early comprehensive de-liberalizing policies served as compensation in order to reach agreements within the government. Yet, in comparison with Austria, the compensating measures were not carried out by the other major party (the SPD and the CDU/CSU), but rather within each party itself, each of which have two ideological camps. The subsequent phase of post-re-unification reforms included de-liberalizing reform politics which aimed to compensate for re-unification and to take credit for de-liberalization among voters. Confronted with the politically delicate situation of re-unification, the government opted for a soft reform approach coupled with de-liberalization in order to implement consolidation measures. However, when the pressure became unbearable, the Social Democrats radically switched to a liberalization course without compensation, which eliminates any explanations based on *traditional partisanship theory* or *power resource approaches* (Häusermann et al. 2013; Korpi 1983) or the *compensation hypothesis* (Rodrik 1998). In contrast to Austria, radical liberalization was pursued by a Social Democratic Party in a coalition with Alliance 90/the Green Party and not as part of a liberal-conservative government. Another difference is that the Social Democrats took the risk of breaking with the unions.

The comprehensive liberalization reforms specified disturbed the traditional relationship between the Social Democratic Party, its voters, and the unions. Not only did the reforms result in significant losses for the party, but they also led to strikes and illuminated the political saliency of employment protection and benefits. Both major parties in Germany only began to adopt a de-liberalizing course after the public began to disapprove of the liberalization reforms and demanded measures towards de-liberalization.

Looking at the SPD and the CDU/CSU's political trajectories, it becomes obvious how much the scope for de-liberalizing policies depends on voter preferences. The SPD very clearly distanced itself from the Agenda 2010 reforms after it was confronted with a loss of votes and after the public demanded de-liberalizing actions. The CDU/CSU also altered their preferences towards the introduction of a SMW when the high public approval rates for the SMW became clear. Hence, both parties clearly demonstrate that liberalization is not a politically stable outcome, but can change over time depending on voters' interests.

All in all, this case demonstrated that political parties change their strategies when met with great resistance from the public due to earlier liberalizing reforms. My findings are supported by the fact that all of the comprehensive de-liberalizing measures across all periods only took place in the area of politically salient policies (Culpepper 2011). Unlike in Austria, de-liberalizing strategies in more recent periods have not only been the result of credit-taking strategies, but also of an attempt to mitigate blame. The main de-liberalizing reforms in Germany also occurred on the labor market and in the field of pensions, both of which became politically more salient after the *Hartz* reforms and therefore were the ideal areas in which to make de-liberalizing amends. These reforms happened against the interest of the employers, revealing that de-liberalization in Germany was not the result of a far-reaching compromise as we see in consociational democracies or in VOC-centered theories (Lijphart 1999).

However, one factor deserves special attention in the German case: in comparison to Austria, Germany clearly demonstrates less de-liberalization, and the de-liberalizing reforms were introduced in different policy fields. Claiming that de-liberalization is dependent on office-seeking political parties, it stands to reason that the extent and direction of de-liberalization is also dependent on these political parties. When compared to the major parties in Austria, the grand coalition parties in Germany serve a much broader constituency in terms of political ideology, and the German parties often contain both a labor and a business wing. Additionally, the grand coalition parties are less entangled with the interest groups. Hence, the increased conflict lines within the parties themselves as well as between the different unions and the different employer groups make coalition-building based on de-liberalization more difficult in contrast to Austria, where the grand parties can draw on an exclusive coalition with capital and labor, and thus strengthen their support for pro-de-liberalizing policies if those are favored. This also explains the puzzling fact that the Social Democrats in Germany are able to pursue reforms against the will of several unions, while the Social Democrats in Austria have widely refrained from radical liberalizing reforms.

Overall, the German case broadly supports my claim for why de-liberalization occurs. All of the de-liberalizing reforms introduced in Germany were clearly implemented by the government and were less often in agreement with capital and labor. These findings are in line with the main claim of this book.

Table 5.2 Overview of the different policy reform periods in Germany

Policy period	Government and period	Share of lib.	Share of de-lib.	Social expend. (as a percentage of GDP)
Compensation period: De-liberalizing policies are introduced in order to avoid blame during periods of liberalization	1980–1989: CDU/CSU-FDP	65%	35%	1985: 22.2%
				1990: 21.4%
	1990–1997: CDU/CSU-FDP			1995: 25.2%
	1998–2001: SPD-alliance 90/the green party			
Liberalization period: Economic pressure and new political strategies lead to full-fledged liberalization	2002–2005: SPD-alliance 90/ the green party	82%	18%	2000: 25.4%
				2005: 26.3%
Post-liberalization period: After the public has a negative association with liberalization proceedings, the government introduces de-liberalizing policies to set ideological counterpoints and take credit	2006–2009: Grand coalition: CDU/CSU-SPD 2009–2013: CDU/CSU-FDP 2013–2014: Grand coalition: CDU/CSU-SPD	57%	43%	2010: 25.9%
				2014: 24.9%

Source: Liberalization Database (Armingeon et al. 2019; OECD 2017b)

References

Altenstetter C, Busse R (2005) Health care reform in Germany: patchwork change within established governance structures. J Health Polit Policy Law 30(1):121–142

Armingeon K, Isler C, Knöpfel L, Weisstanner D, Engler S (2016) Comparative political data set 1960–2014. Institute of Political Science, University of Bern, Bern

Armingeon K, Baccaro L, Fill A, Galindo J, Heeb S, Labanino R (2019) Liberalization database 1973–2013 (20170619). Available Online Jul 2019

Baccaro L, Howell C (2017) Trajectories of neoliberal transformation. Cambridge University Press, Cambridge

BBP, Bundeszentrale für politische Bildung (2008) Kabinett beschließt Regelungen für Mindestlöhne. Bundeszentrale für politische Bildung. http://www.bpb.de/politik/hintergrund-aktuell/69639/mindestloehne-17-07-2008. Accessed 8 Mar 2017

BGBl. I S. 2154 (1985) Gesetz zum Erziehungsgeld und zur Elternzeit—Bundeserziehungsgeldgesetz—BerzGG. https://www.bgbl.de/xaver/bgbl/start.xav?startbk=Bundesanzeiger_BGBl&jumpTo=bgbl185s2154.pdf#__bgbl__%2F%2F*%5B%40attr_id%3D%27bgbl185s2154.pdf%27%5D__1504098925525. Accessed 1 Jul 2017

BGBL (1986) Gesetz zur Sicherung der Neutralität der Bundesanstalt für Arbeit bei Arbeitskämpfen. https://www.bgbl.de/xaver/bgbl/start.xav?start=//*%5B@attr_id=%27bgbl186s0740.pdf%27%5D#__bgbl__%2F%2F*%5B%40attr_id%3D%27bgbl186s0740.pdf%27%5D__1530176852015. Accessed 1 Jul 2017

Bieräugel R, Nüchter O, Schmid A (2010) FORSCHUNG AKTUELL: Einstellungen der Bevölkerung zu Mindestlöhnen in Deutschland. WSI Mitteilungen 1:50–57. https://www.boeckler.de/wsimit_2010_01_bieraeugel.pdf. Accessed 1 Mar 2017

Bispinck R, Dribbusch H (2011) Collective bargaining, decentralisation and crisis management in the German metalworking industries since 1990. WSI-Diskussionspapier 177. http://nbn-resolving.de/urn:nbn:de:0168-ssoar-309241. Accessed 8 Mar 2017

Bispinck R, Schulten T (2008) Aktuelle Mindestlohndebatte: Branchenlösungen oder gesetzlicher Mindestlohn? WSI Mitteilungen 3:151–158. https://www.boeckler.de/pdf/wsimit_2008_03_bispinck.pdf. Accessed 8 Mar 2017

Blätte A (2010) Reduzierter Parteienwettbewerb durch kalkulierte Demobilisierung. Bestimmungsgründe des Wahlkampfverhaltens im Bundestagswahlkampf 2009. In: Korte K (ed) Die Bundestagswahl 2009. Analysen der Wahl-, Parteien-, Kommunikations- und Regierungsforschung. VS Verlag für Sozialwissenschaften, Wiesbaden, pp 273–297

Börsch-Supan A, Wilke C (2005) Reforming the German Public Pension System. Research Paper—National Bureau of Economic Research (NBER), Cambridge, pp 1–33. http://www.rand.org/content/dam/rand/www/external/labor/aging/rsi/rsi_papers/2006_axel1.pdf. Accessed 8 Jan 2014

Börsch-Supan A, Coppola M, Rausch J (2015) Die "Rente mit 63": Wer sind die Begünstigten? Was sind die Auswirkungen auf die Gesetzliche Rentenversicherung?" Perspekt Wirtsch 16 (3):264–288

Bosch G (2015) Der holprige Weg zum gesetzlichen Mindestlohn in Deutschland. Sozialer Fortschritt Unabhängige Zeitschrift für Sozialpolitik 64:173–181. ISSN 0038-609X, ZDB-ID 20886

Busemeyer M (2007) Pension reform in Germany and Austria: system change vs. quantitative retrenchment. West Eur Polit 28(3):569–591

Butterwegge C (2012) Krise und Zukunft des Sozialstaates. Verlag für Sozialwissenschaften, Springer Fachmedien, Wiesbaden

Butterwegge C (2014) Altersarmut und Sozialpolitik—Warum das Rentenpaket der Großen Koalition wenig zur Armutsbekämpfung beiträgt. Vierteljahrshefte zur Wirtschaftsforschung, pp 69–81. https://www.diw.de/sixcms/detail.php?id=diw_01.c.489290.de. Accessed 8 Feb 2017

Butterwegge C (2016) Das großkoalitionäre Rentenpaket—ein Mittel gegen die Armut im Alter? In: Butterwegge C (ed) Reichtumsförderung statt Armutsbekämpfung. Eine sozial- und steuerpolitische Halbzeitbilanz der Großen Koalition. Springer Fachmedien Wiesbaden, Wiesbaden, pp 11–18

Chung H, Thewissen S (2011) Falling back on old habits? A comparison of the social and unemployment crisis reactive policy strategies in Germany, the UK and Sweden. Soc Policy Admin 45(4):354–370. https://doi.org/10.1111/j.1467-9515.2011.00779.x

Culpepper P (2011) Quiet politics and business power—corporate control in Europe and Japan. Cambridge University Press, Cambridge

Czada R (1995) Der Kampf um die Finanzierung der deutschen Einheit. In: Lehmbruch G (ed) Einigung und Zerfall. Opladen, Budrich, pp 73–102

DGB (2015) Umfrage: 86 Prozent der Deutschen unterstützen gesetzlichen Mindestlohn. http://www.dgb.de/themen/++co++02e12b02-c246-11e4-bfbe-52540023ef1a. Accessed 8 Apr 2017

Dictionary (2017) Contingency reserve. http://www.dictionary.com/browse/contingency-reserve. Accessed 8 Sept 2017

DieWelt (2008) Erste Gewerkschafter kritisieren Mindestlohn. DieWelt, 8 Jan 2008. https://www.welt.de/wirtschaft/article1529588/Erste-Gewerkschafter-kritisieren-Mindestlohn.html. Accessed 2 Feb 2017

Dostal J (2012a) Explaining the crisis and electoral decline of the German Social Democratic Party (SPD) in the era of welfare state retrenchment (2002-2012). J Korean-German Assoc Soc Sci/Zeitschrift der Koreanisch-Deutschen Gesellschaft für Sozialwissenschaften 22(4):271–310

Dostal J (2012b) The German political economy between deregulation and re-regulation: party discourses on minimum wage policies. Korean J Policy Stud 27(2):91–120

Ebbinghaus B, Eichhorst W (2006) Employment regulation and labor market policy in Germany, 1991–2005. IZA discussion paper no 2505. http://ssrn.com/abstract=955839. Accessed 2 Mar 2017

Egle C (2017) No escape from the long-term crisis? The social democrats' failure to devise a promising political strategy. German Polit Soc 35(4):9–27

Egle C, Henkes C (2004) In search of social democracy—explaining the politics and policies of the Schröder. Working paper, Universität München. http://www.gsi.uni-muenchen.de/personen/wiss_mitarbeiter/egle/publikationen/ehe_social_democracy.pdf. Accessed 2 Mar 2017

Esping-Andersen G (1990) The three worlds of welfare capitalism. Polity Press, Cambridge

Eurofund (2009) Germany: 'wage formation'. https://www.eurofound.europa.eu/observatories/eurwork/comparative-information/national-contributions/germany/germany-wage-formation. Accessed 2 Feb 2017

Eurofund (2015a) "Germany: working life country profile." https://www.eurofound.europa.eu/observatories/eurwork/comparative-information/national-contributions/germany/germany-working-life-country-profile. Accessed 2 Feb 2017

Eurofund (2015b) Germany: new retirement package. https://www.eurofound.europa.eu/observatories/eurwork/articles/working-conditions-industrial-relations/germany-new-retirement-package. Accessed 2 Feb 2017

Eurofund (2015c) Germany: new law promotes collective bargaining. https://www.eurofound.europa.eu/observatories/eurwork/articles/industrial-relations/germany-new-law-promotes-collective-bargaining. Accessed 2 Feb 2017

Feld L, Kohlmeier A, Schmidt C (2014) Rentenpaket: die Bundesregierung auf Irrwegen; Analysen und Berichte Rentenpolitik. ZBW—Leibniz-Informationszentrum, Wirtschaft, pp 553–559. https://doi.org/10.1007/s10273-014-1713-7

Feldengut K (1993) Wer nimmt—wer gibt? Kraftproben um den Solidarpakt. Gewerkschaftliche Monatshefte 44:178–189

Fleckenstein T (2011) Institutions, ideas and learning in welfare state change: labour market reforms in Germany. New perspectives in German political studies. Palgrave Macmillan, Basingstoke

Fleckenstein T, Lee S (2012) The politics of postindustrial social policy. Comp Pol Stud 47 (4):601–630. https://doi.org/10.1177/0010414012451564

Goldschmidt N, Wohlgemuth M (2008) Social market economy: origins, meanings and interpretations. Constit Polit Econ 19(3):261–276. https://doi.org/10.1007/s10602-008-9047-3

Grote J, Lang A, Traxler F (2007) Germany. In: Huemer G, Traxler F (eds) Handbook of business interest associations, firm size and governance. Routledge, Oxon, pp 141–176

Hall P, Soskice D (eds) (2001) Varieties of capitalism: the institutional foundations of comparative advantage. Oxford University Press, Oxford

Hall P, Thelen K (2008) Institutional change in varieties of capitalism. Soc Econ Rev 7(1):7–34. https://doi.org/10.1093/ser/mwn020

Hassel A (1999) The erosion of the German system of industrial relations. Br J Ind Relat 37 (3):483–505

Hassel A (2011) The paradox of liberalization—understanding dualism and the recovery of the German political economy. LSE 'Europe in Question' discussion paper series no 42/2011. http://eprints.lse.ac.uk/53212/. Accessed 1 Feb 2017

Hassel A, Schiller C (2010) Der Fall Hartz IV. Wie es zur Agenda 2010 kam und wie es weitergeht. Campus Verlag, New York

Häusermann S (2010) The politics of welfare state reform in continental Europe. Modernization in hard times. Cambridge University Press, Cambridge

Häusermann S, Picot G, Geering D (2013) Partisan politics and the welfare state. Recent advances in the literature. Br J Polit Sci 43(1):221–240

Hüttenhoff F (2016) Mindestlöhne in Deutschland 2017: Anhebung von zehn Branchenmindestlöhnen und des gesetzlichen Mindestlohns. Institut Arbeit und Qualifikation der Universität Duisburg-Essen, Monatsgrafik, Dec 2016. http://www.sozialpolitik-aktuell.de/tl_files/sozialpolitik-aktuell/_Politikfelder/Einkommen-Armut/Datensammlung/PDF-Datei-en/abbIII4a_Grafik_Monat_01_2017.pdf. Accessed 1 Mar 2017

Institut für Demoskopie Allensbach (2013a) Was ist gerecht: Gerechtigkeitsbegriff und Wahrnehmung der Bürger. http://www.insm.de/insm/kampagne/gerechtigkeit/was-denkt-deutschland-ueber-gerechtigkeit.html. Accessed 16 Sept 2017

Institut für Demoskopie Allensbach (2013b) Stille Liebe zur Planwirtschaft: Eine Dokumentation des Beitrags von Dr. Thomas Petersen in der Frankfurter Allgemeinen Zeitung Nr. 276 vom 27, Nov

2013. http://www.ifd-allensbach.de/uploads/tx_reportsndocs/November_Planwirtschaft.pdf. Accessed 16 Sept 2017

Interview, Zenzen (2016) Dr. Jupp Zenzen: Bundesvereinigung der Deutschen Arbeitgeberverbände, Berlin, 12 May 2016

Jackson G, Sorge A (2012) The trajectory of institutional change in Germany 1979–2009. J Eur Publ Policy 19(8):1146–1167. https://doi.org/10.1080/13501763.2012.709009

Jochem S (1999) Sozialpolitik in der Ära Kohl: Die Politik des Sozialversicherungsstaates. ZeS-Arbeitspapier 12(99). https://www.econstor.eu/obitstream/10419/41537/1/561636702.pdf. Accessed 1 Mar 2017

Jun U, Heisterhagen T, Stratmann S (2017) Die Repräsentation von Armut durch politische Parteien. Voraussetzungen, ein theoretisches Analysemodell und empirische Untersuchungen im Lichte des Bundestagswahlkampfs 2013. In: Wiesendahl E (ed) Parteien und soziale Ungleichheit. Springer Fachmedien, Wiesbaden, pp 359–391

Kamke K (1998) The German health care system and health care reform. Health Policy 43 (2):171–194

Kauder B, Laring B, Potrafke N (2014) Was bringt uns die große Koalition? Perspekt Wirtsch 15 (1):88–101. https://doi.org/10.1515/pwp-2014-0005

Kemmerling A, Bruttel O (2006) New politics in German labour market policy? The implications of the recent Hartz reforms for the German welfare state. West Eur Polit 29(1):90–112

Konle-Seidl R, Eichhorst W, Grienberger-Zingerle M (2007) Activation policies in Germany: from status protection to basic income support. IAB, discussion paper, no 2007/6. https://www.econstor.eu/dspace/bitstream/10419/31868/1/525548033.PDF. Accessed 9 Jan 2014

Korpi W (1983) The democratic class struggle. Routledge & Kegan Paul, Boston

Leibfried S, Obinger H (2003) The state of the welfare state: German social policy between macroeconomic retrenchment and microeconomic recalibration. West Eur Polit 26(4):199–218. https://doi.org/10.1080/01402380312331280748

Lijphart A (1999) Patterns of democracy: government forms and performance in thirty-six countries. Yale University Press, New Haven

Mabbett D (2016) The minimum wage in Germany: what brought the state in? J Eur Publ Policy 23 (8):1240–1258. https://doi.org/10.1080/13501763.2016.1186210

Manow P (2001) Business coordination, wage bargaining and the welfare state: Germany and Japan in comparative historical perspective. In: Manow P, Ebbinghaus B (eds) Comparing welfare capitalism social policy and political economy in Europe, Japan and the USA. Routledge, London, pp 27–51

Marx P, Starke P (2017) Dualization as destiny? The political economy of the German minimum wage reform. Polit Soc 0(0):1–26. https://doi.org/10.1177/0032329217726793

McKenzie R, Lee D (1991) Quicksilver capital: how the rapid movement of wealth has changed the world. Free Press, New York

Münch U (1990) Familienpolitik in der Bundesrepublik Deutschland. Massnahmen, Defizite, Organisation familienpolitischer Staatstätigkeit. Lambertus, Freiburg im Breisgau

Neckermann P (1992) What went wrong in Germany after unification? East Eur Q 26(4):447–469

OECD (2013) Glossary of statistical terms. https://stats.oecd.org/glossary/detail.asp?ID=5183. Accessed 1 Jul 2017

OECD (2017a) Employment database, 2017. http://stats.oecd.org/Index.aspx?QueryId=64196#. Accessed 27 Mar 2017

OECD (2017b) Social expenditure: aggregated data. OECD Social Expenditure Statistics (database). https://stats.oecd.org/Index.aspx?DataSetCode=SOCX_AGG. Accessed 8 Sept 2017

Pabst S (1999) Sozialpolitische Entscheidungsprozesse in der Bundesrepublik Deutschland zwischen 1982 und 1989: Eine Literaturübersicht. ZeSArbeitspapier, No. 08/1999. https://www.econstor.eu/bitstream/10419/41489/1/566355078.pdf. Accessed 8 Jul 2017

Paterson W, Sloam J (2006) Is the left alright? The SPD and the renewal of European social democracy. German Polit 15(3):233–248

Peffekoven R (1997) Finanzpolitik im Konflikt zwischen Effizienz und Distribution. In: Lenel HO et al (eds). Ordo (Jahrbuch für die Ordnung von Wirtschaft und Gesellschaft, Bd. 48). Stuttgart 1997, pp 119–136

Renzsch W (1998) Financing Germany unity: fiscal conflict solution in a complex federation. J Federal 28(4):127–146

Rodrik D (1998) Why do more open economies have bigger government? J Polit Econ 106:997–1032

Rudolph H (1999) Geringfügige Beschäftigung: Das 630-DM-Gesetz: Was ändert sich für wen? Abschätzung der Betroffenheit von Arbeitgebern und Arbeitnehmern durch die rechtlichen Änderungen. *IAB-Kurzbericht, 11/1999.* http://www.iab.de/194/section.aspx/Publikation/i991102n02. Accessed 1 Mar 2017

Schludi M (2005) The reform of Bismarckian pension systems a comparison of pension politics in Austria, France, Germany, Italy and Sweden. Amsterdam University Press, Amsterdam

Schmidt M (2012) Der mittlere Weg der Liberalisierungspolitik? Deutschland im internationalen Vergleich. In: Eckard J, Sturm R (eds) Superwahljahr "2011" und die Folgen. Nomos, Baden-Baden, pp 285–305

Schröder G (1998) "Regierungserklärung des Bundeskanzlers am 10. November 1998 vor dem Deutschen Bundestag in Bonn: "Weil wir Deutschlands Kraft vertrauen." Datum: 11.11.1998, Doknr: 98074. https://www.google.ch/url?sa=t&rct=j&q=&esrc=s&source=web&cd=9&ved=0ahUKEwi7of-LmZ_WAhWEChoKHXzrDsYQFghTMAg&url=https%3A%2F%2Fwww.lmz-bw.de%2Ffileadmin%2Fuser_upload%2FMedienbildung_MCO%2Ffileadmin%2Fbibliothek%2Fschroeder_RE_1998%2Fschroeder_RE_1998.pdf&usg=AFQjCNEvBNYsD4TR-JwzWXkjANVZYTXewA. Accessed 1 Mar 2017

Schulze I, Jochem S (2009) Germany: beyond policy gridlock. In: Immergut EM, Anderson K, Schulze I (eds) The handbook of west European pension politics. Oxford University Press, Oxford, pp 660–711

Seeleib-Kaiser M (2002) A dual transformation of the German welfare state? West Eur Polit 25 (4):25–48. https://doi.org/10.1080/713601641

Seeleib-Kaiser M, Fleckenstein T (2007) Discourse, learning and welfare state change: the case of German labour market reforms. Soc Policy Adm 41(5):427–448

Starke P (2008) Radical welfare state retrenchment. A comparative analysis. Palgrave Macmillan UK, London

Streeck W (1995) German capitalism: does it exist? Can it survive? MPIFG discussion paper 95/5 ISSN 0944–2073. http://www.mpifg.de/pu/mpifg_dp/dp95-5.pdf. Accessed 1 Mar 2017

Streeck W (2009) Re-forming capitalism: institutional change in the German political economy. Oxford University Press, Oxford

Streeck W, Hassel A (2003) The crumbling pillars of social partnership. In Germany. Beyond the stable state. West Eur Polit 26(4):101–124

Streeck W, Thelen K (2005) Beyond continuity: institutional change in advanced political economies. Oxford University Press, New York

Taz (2009) Volker Kauder über die Modernisierung der CDU. 'Wir waren nie konservativ'. Die Taz, 5 Apr 2009. http://www.taz.de/!5165040/. Accessed 1 Dec 2016

Thelen K (2014) Varieties of liberalization: the new politics of social solidarity. Cambridge University Press, New York

Walwei U (2015) From deregulation to re-regulation: trend reversal in German labour market institutions and its possible implications. IAB discussion paper, no.10/2015. https://www.econstor.eu/handle/10419/108844. Accessed 1 Mar 2017

Weishaupt T (2010) Germany after a decade of social democrats in government: the end of the continental model? German Polit 19(2):105–122

Winter T (1989) Die CDU im Interessenkonflikt: Eine Fallstudie zur parteiinternen Auseinandersetzung über den Paragraphen 116 AFG. Leviathan 17(1):46–84

Winter T (1990) Die Sozialausschüsse der CDU: Sammelbecken für christdemokratische Arbeitnehmerinteressen oder linker Flügel der Partei? Leviathan 18(3):390–416

Zohlnhöfer R (1999) Der lange Schatten der schönen Illusion: Finanzpolitik nach der deutschen Einheit, 1990–1998. ZeS-Arbeitspapier, no 09. http://hdl.handle.net/10419/41497. Accessed 1 Mar 2017

Zohlnhöfer R (2001) Parteien, Vetospieler und der Wettbewerb um Wählerstimmen: Die Arbeitsmarkt-und Beschäftigungspolitik der Ära Kohl. Politische Vierteljahresschrift 42:655. https://doi.org/10.1007/s11615-001-0102-1

Zohlnhöfer R (2003) Partisan politics, party competition and veto players: German economic policy in the Kohl era. J Publ Policy 23(2):123–156

Zohlnhöfer R (2004) Destination anywhere? The German red–green government's inconclusive search for a third way in economic policy. German Polit 13(1):106–131

Chapter 6
Switzerland: Late Welfare State Catch-Up Processes and the Politics of Consensus

Switzerland has long been known as a small liberal state that refrains from de-liberalizing activities (Katzenstein 1985). Over time, however, Switzerland has displayed a shift from a liberal welfare state to one that closely resembles a conservative model (Obinger et al. 2010: 191). The welfare state modifications have been characterized by a variety of de-liberalizing reforms. The most recent period, in particular, saw another set of de-liberalizing reforms. How can we explain Switzerland's reform path, which involves a large number of de-liberalizing reforms in comparison to other OECD countries?

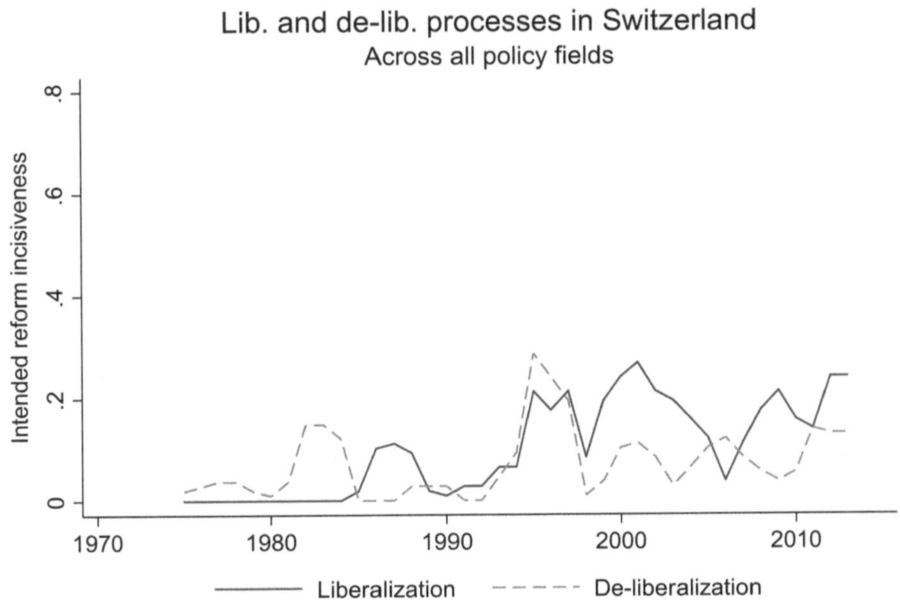

Fig. 6.1 Liberalization and de-liberalization processes in Switzerland across all policy field. Source: Liberalization Database (Armingeon et al. 2019)

© Springer Nature Switzerland AG 2019

A. Fill, *The Political Economy of De-liberalization*, Contributions to Political Science, https://doi.org/10.1007/978-3-030-01066-9_6

Switzerland has a unique political system with a very pronounced direct democracy and a well-marked federalism, all of which serves to raise doubts about whether classical political accounts are suited to explain de-liberalization processes in Switzerland. A *traditional partisan approach* would attribute Switzerland's de-liberalization process to the rise of the Social Democratic Party. However, Switzerland's policymaking process is embedded in a consociational democracy and incorporates all major political parties, interest groups, representatives of cantonal governments, experts, and the Swiss public, making it difficult for one party to override the others. Additionally, both the Swiss government and the parliament are typically dominated by center-right parties that keep the Social Democrats' ability to implement de-liberalizing reforms in check. The distribution of power presents a picture of a privileged group of employers that have much greater power than the trade unions. Hence, the Swiss policymaking process favors the interests of right-leaning parties and employers, which is at odds with *traditional partisan and power resources* approaches (Obinger et al. 2010: 191–194; Kriesi 1980: 111, 693; Korpi 1983; Häusermann et al. 2013). *Classical producer group* approaches such as the *Varieties of Capitalism School* attribute de-liberalizing policies on the labor market to employers' interest in certain skills on the part of laborers. Employers are said to foster cross-class coordination with unions in order to ensure long-term relationships between employers and workers, which in turn helps to promote diversified quality production that contributes to a comparative institutional advantage (Hall and Soskice 2001). However, major employer groups have continually chosen liberalization over de-liberalization. Throughout the 1990s, Swiss employers actively sought to decentralize collective bargaining and weaken the unions (Mach and Oesch 2003: 113–114). Thus, *conventional producer group* claims cannot explain why Switzerland has experienced phases of de-liberalization.

A *compensation hypothesis* explanation ascribes Switzerland's de-liberalization processes to the rise of liberalization. Even though Switzerland's liberalizing and de-liberalizing reforms often happened at the same time, de-liberalization also occurred in the mid-2000s without an accompanying liberalization, leaving this de-liberalization period unexplained (Rodrik 1998; Armingeon et al. 2019). *Corporatist-* and *consociational-democracy*-based accounts might be able to explain some de-liberalizing reforms, but others, such as the introduction of the *Swiss Immigration Initiative*, the introduction of the *Swissness Law,* and the partial rejection of the introduction of the *Cassis de Dijon* principle, occurred without significant liberal concessions, and sometimes even against the will of a large group of political actors (Armingeon and Fill 2016; Lijphart 1999; Lehmbruch 1967). Thus, we are still left with the question of how to explain Switzerland's distinct pattern of de-liberalizing reforms.

In order to answer this question, this case study will investigate Switzerland's distinct path of liberalization and de-liberalization. This section will also reveal the differences in Switzerland's de-liberalization process in comparison to Austria and Germany. The reform distribution displays 56.5% liberalizing reforms to 43.5% de-liberalizing reforms, measured based on the amount of all reforms enacted in Switzerland between 1973 and 2013. This puts Switzerland slightly ahead of Austria's policy distribution and behind Germany in terms of liberalizing reforms (Armingeon et al. 2019). In contrast to the other two case studies, however, part of

Switzerland's de-liberalization processes are comprised of policy reforms that constitute late welfare state expansion. Contrary to Austria and Germany, liberalization reforms in Switzerland empowered the left in some cases, and supported their attempts to receive de-liberalizing concessions because social democratic parties and unions threatened to introduce referenda if their interests were ignored. Even though this exchange broadly resembles the idea that de-liberalization is brought about in order to compensate for liberalization, the dynamic between the parties and unions is nevertheless different than the dynamics in Austria and Germany, where the unions were weakened throughout far-reaching liberalization periods. However, in Switzerland, the left was able to benefit from the liberalizing reforms thanks to the Swiss instruments of direct democracy. Hence, even though Switzerland pursued strategies of de-liberalization, the timing, gravity, and the political dynamics were different to those seen in Austria and Germany.

This chapter proceeds as followed: First, I will determine the starting point of Switzerland's liberalization and de-liberalization processes in order to set the reform path in context of the general development of the welfare state and the post-war economy. Afterwards, I will analyze the different reform periods against the claim of this book, which is grounded in public choice and modern partisanship approaches. In the conclusion, I will discuss further implications for this case study.

6.1 Switzerland's De-liberalization Processes: The Beginnings

Switzerland's de-liberalization process started in the early 1980s before liberalization processes had begun there. At this time, Switzerland was a frugal welfare state that offered a low level of benefits compared to other Continental European countries. In addition, the private market and individuals played a strong role in the health insurance market; only public pensions and disability insurance schemes were eligible for the entire population and therefore universal, while unemployment insurance and healthcare insurance were not yet mandatory[1] on the federal level. Compared to Austria and Germany, Switzerland's family policy was also very outdated (Obinger et al. 2010: 194–196).

Switzerland had effectively sheltered its economy during the post-war period and protected its national industries from international competition. Nevertheless, Switzerland successfully positioned itself on world markets as an export economy. As outlined by Katzenstein (1985), Switzerland pursued a strategy of liberal corporatism that they adjusted based on the global and national economies. The Swiss government never engaged in a Keynesian monetary approach, but rather relied on private adaptation strategies (Afonso and Mach 2011: 104).

[1] Some cantons already had mandatory unemployment insurance (Obinger et al. 2010: 194–195).

Post-war Switzerland has been displaying a consociational democracy with a stable corporatist system of interest facilitation (Lijphart 1999; Oesch 2011: 82–84). The most important interest groups in Switzerland have been either politically powerful, internationally oriented business groups or weak, somewhat decentralized labor unions. Thus, in terms of relative power the employers have had a slight upper hand over the unions, which are often referred to as junior bargaining partners. Swiss industrial relations have been characterized by fairly weak coordination modes, particularly with regards to the centralization of wage bargaining (Katzenstein 1985; Afonso and Mach 2011: 109). The most important employer association is the *Schweizerischer Arbeitgeberverband* (SAV), which is the peak level organization and mostly responsible for labor and wage matters. Another important employer organization is *Economiesuisse*, which mainly deals with tax, trade, and general economic policy issues (Afonso 2013: 98, 99; Oesch 2007). One of the largest trade union confederations is the *Schweizerischer Gewerkschaftsbund* (SGB), which unites about 50% of all trade union members; other members are spread across smaller trade union confederations, which are often organized along professional lines. However, the single unions hold more power than the peak level organization because the single unions collect member fees and therefore have greater financial resources (Oesch 2011: 83–88). Overall, the Swiss industrial relations landscape is a fragmented system of trade unions (Afonso and Mach 2011: 111–115).

In sum, de-liberalization processes in Switzerland started at a time when the country had a stingy welfare state system and when universal and mandatory social protections were scarce. The economy was highly protected, but business followed its own adjustment strategies while the state took a back seat. Industrial relations and corporatism were stable, but the unions were less powerful in comparison to Austria and Germany.

6.2 Liberalization and De-liberalization Between 1980 and 1990

The period between 1980 and 1990 was markedly different in Switzerland than in Austria and Germany. Switzerland did not engage in any liberalization reforms during this period. Even though the 1979 oil crisis temporarily impacted the Swiss labor market, the overall effect was limited. In the 1980s, Switzerland had one of the lowest unemployment rates in the OECD. In comparison to other European countries, the economy was doing well and Switzerland experienced a period of economic growth, budget surpluses, and decreasing levels of public debt. According to Obinger, Switzerland was in such good economic shape that no liberalizing reforms were necessary (Obinger et al. 2010: 202). Additionally, as laid out above, Switzerland was already a prime example of a liberal market economy with a lean welfare state, a decentralized bargaining system, and low tax rates, making further liberalization unnecessary.

6.2.1 *Liberalization and De-liberalization Policies Between 1980 and 1990*

Even though there were no far-reaching liberalization reforms in the welfare state, Switzerland implemented some liberal modifications in the banking and financial sectors. The Swiss capital market abolished the CHF 200 million ceiling on public sector loans to foreign borrowers. Also, the turnover tax on gold was abolished and the Swiss Parliament adopted a tax relief for families, which resulted in direct tax cuts of around 30% for middle-income families (this led to a loss in the Confederation's revenues of about CHF 365 million). Additionally, the rules against cartel abuse were strengthened (Armingeon et al. 2019).

Aside from liberalizing reforms, the Swiss government made a huge change in the welfare state, introducing several comprehensive de-liberalizing reforms. Most importantly, the government declared health insurance mandatory for all employees and separated it from accident insurance, introduced an obligatory unemployment insurance scheme, made the second pension pillar mandatory for all employees, and bolstered employment protection.

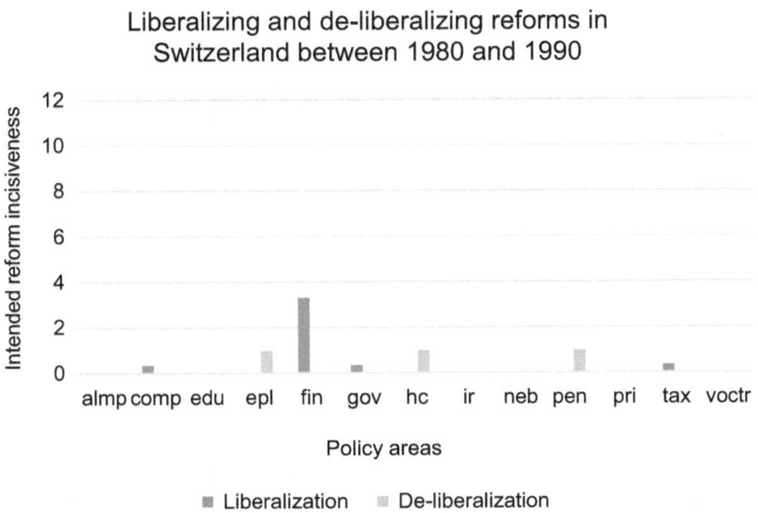

Fig. 6.2 Liberalizing and de-liberalizing reforms in Switzerland between 1980 and 1990 across all policy fields. Reforms are weighted according to the liberalization index (values: first-order changes: 0.33; second-order changes: 0.66; third-order and status quo changes: 1). Source: Liberalization Database (Armingeon et al. 2019)

6.2.2 Politics Between 1980 and 1990: The Calm Before the Storm

Two factors were decisive in Swiss politics in the 1980s. Firstly, as mentioned above, when compared to many European counterparts, Switzerland's welfare state in the late 1970s was underdeveloped, which clearly left room for growth. Secondly, the fact that the Switzerland's economy did comparatively well in the 1970s helped to bring about an impetus for social security expansion. In the course of this new expansion, the Social Democrats, trade unions, and employers became even more embedded in the social policymaking process (Obinger et al. 2005: 284–285). While employers and the right-leaning political parties were still convinced that a welfare state would only be viable as long as social expenditure was kept at a minimum, the Social Democrats (Sozialdemokratische Partei der Schweiz—SPS) and trade unions took up the topic of social protection and lobbied for policy expansion (Häusermann 2006a; Trampusch 2010). Trampusch (2010) indicates that the more the employers opposed the extension of social and labor market policies, the more active the unions became in the policy process. The left also benefited from the parliament, which very cautiously attempted to strengthen redistribution and social protections in the welfare state. Despite initially mixed opinions regarding welfare state expansions, all of the reforms were eventually agreed upon by all stakeholders and resulted in more de-liberalization than liberalization on the whole (Obinger et al. 2010: 206).

6.2.3 Comprehensive De-liberalization Policies Between 1980 and 1990

Early comprehensive de-liberalization processes in the 1980s can be described as a late welfare state expansion. In contrast to early de-liberalization processes in Austria and Germany, the reasons behind these processes were not only compensating measures for liberalizing reforms, but also expansion of the welfare state. The following section investigates how the most important de-liberalizing reforms came about.

6.2.3.1 Introduction of a Mandatory Unemployment Insurance Scheme and New Benefits

In 1976 the Swiss government issued a provisional decree making unemployment insurance compulsory (Obinger et al. 2005: 283–285). The reasons for these decisions were, firstly, the repercussions of the 1973 oil crisis, which had led to a rise in unemployment, and secondly, the low coverage rate of unemployed workers. The number of insured wage earners was 32% in 1975 (Moser 2005). After the Swiss government realized that full employment could not be taken for granted, it wanted to use mandatory insurance to tackle the problem of uninsured workers and the risk of unemployment (Armingeon 1999: 179). However, this legal change required an amendment of the constitution because it affected both employees and employers. A majority of political actors and interest groups backed the government's decision; the people voted to pass the amendment in 1976 (Moser 2005). The constitutional change resulted in an interim agreement which was only incorporated into the constitution in 1982. The main reason for this de-liberalizing change was the risk of persons becoming unemployed and not being adequately covered. The introduction of this insurance was a late welfare state expansion.

Throughout the 1980s, the unemployment insurance system was slightly modified through a number of de-liberalizing changes. In particular, a new compensation benefit in the event of employer insolvency was added in 1982. Moreover, the replacement rate was raised to 70% for singles and 80% for married couples and parents (Armingeon et al. 2019). Additionally, the government agreed to share employers' costs in the event of reduced hours and adverse weather conditions (meaning that these measures would prevent layoffs should an employer encounter financial difficulties as a result). However, these reform measures entailed not only de-liberalizing elements but also liberalizing aspects such as the introduction of activation policies (Obinger et al. 2010: 202). Hence, these reform measures led to a new unemployment system of "*tight controls with relatively generous benefits*" (Obinger et al. 2005: 283). As Obinger and others illustrated, the introduction of de-liberalizing aspects, which also served as welfare state expansion, was the result of a compromise that incorporated de-liberalizing policies in return for liberalizing policies (Obinger et al. 2005: 284, 285).

When the reforms were first envisaged, the social partners were not able to agree on a proposal for unemployment insurance. It was only when the parliamentary committee of the lower chamber amended the proposal and brought in activation measures in return for longer entitlement periods that the unions and the employers adopted the proposal. While the reform of mandatory unemployment insurance was clearly a late welfare state expansion, the introduction of a new benefit and the benefit extension happened in the context of unemployment insurance activation, and can therefore be considered part of a strategy of compensation (Häusermann et al. 2004). Hence, the second part of the unemployment insurance reform substantiates the argument that de-liberalization is often used to compensate liberalizing reforms—not only for voters but also to ease the political process between various actors.

6.2.3.2 Second Pension Pillar Becomes Compulsory for all Employees

The Swiss pension system underwent a major transformation in 1982. The second pension pillar was made compulsory for all workers in stable forms of employment earning more than CHF 25,000 annually (Häusermann 2010a: 167). How did this reform come about?

The reform of the occupational pension scheme dates back to the ongoing compromises between the left and right parties and between employers and unions that took place in the 1970s. At this time, the Social Democrats (SDS) and the SGB began to debate the issue of pension expansion, demanding a strengthening of the first pillar in particular. Employers and the center-right parties reacted to this demand by agreeing to an expansion of the second pillar as a counter-proposition rather than reinforcing the first pillar. The SDS and the SGB adjusted their demands accordingly (Häusermann 2010b). In 1972, a constitutional amendment led to the recognition of the three-pillar pension model coupled with a binding agreement that made occupational benefits mandatory and demanded that public and occupational pension benefits to be high enough to allow retired employees to maintain the standards of living they enjoyed while employed. Around 1975, many employers and pension funds repealed this pre-parliamentary compromise on grounds of that the rising costs were unsustainable. Employers argued that the ongoing worsening condition of the economy was irreconcilable with the initial pension claim. Against this background, a new bargaining round began in which the right-wing majorities in both chambers of parliament opted for a defined contribution Scheme (DC) that was more modest than the original defined benefit Scheme (DB) (Obinger et al. 2010: 203–204). Even though the Social Democrats and the trade unions could not get all of their demands met, they still agreed to the bill because they wanted the mandatory occupational pension benefits to pass (Häusermann 2010b; Obinger et al. 2010: 204). Häusermann (2010b) indicates that, even though some of the left's demands were ignored, they still considered the law to be an important victory. Overall, the law was the result of a compromise between traditional left- and right-wing groups in which greater de-liberalization of the first pension pillar was traded for more moderate de-liberalization of the second pension pillar. The introduction of this de-liberalization was an act of compensation because it prevented a potentially greater de-liberalization. As in Austria and Germany, early de-liberalizations in Switzerland occurred in the context of a policy reform deal which was agreed on by ideologically opposed political actors.

6.2.3.3 Dismissed Employees Have a Right to Be Informed Regarding the Reasons for Dismissal

In 1988, the Swiss government changed the employment protection laws against dismissal. While the employer could still end a professional relationship after an indefinite period without giving a special reason, the employee was now able to request the reasons for dismissal in writing (Schanze and Haunhorst 1995). How did this change come about?

The unions had long lobbied for de-liberalization in the Swiss employment protection legislation. In particular, after the 1973 oil crisis when unemployment was rising in Switzerland, the unions and the Social Democrats began promoting and demanding greater employment protection and a reduction in working hours. The employers responded very critically to both demands. While the government agreed to reduce the working hours from 46 to 45 hours a week in 1975, it did not increase employment dismissal protection. Even though the left did not revolt after their requests were not met, they continued to demand de-liberalizing employment protections for the dismissal of workers (Emmenegger 2010). Thus, in 1981, the Christian Democratic Trade Union Federation (CNG) submitted a popular initiative stressing the following: *"(1) dismissed employees can demand to be informed regarding the grounds for their dismissal; (2) regulation of collective dismissals; (3) the possibility of challenging a dismissal for being based on insufficient objective grounds; (4) postponement of dismissals in cases of hardship due to the personal situation of the employee; and (5) further restrictions on dismissals during sickness, accident, and pregnancy"* (Official Bulletin of the National Council 1985: 1087 cited in Emmenegger 2010: 199).

This popular initiative was not adopted by the federal government or the Preparatory Committees of both federal chambers; instead, the government proposed a slight revision to the Swiss Code of Obligations. While the Preparatory Committee of the National Council backed the government, the Swiss Council of States rejected the newly amended version. After lengthy negotiations, the two chambers were finally able to reach a solution and agree on a moderate version of the original proposal (Emmenegger 2010). The final proposition incorporated the claim that "*a dismissed employee can demand to be informed regarding the reasons for dismissal, compensation payments in cases of dismissal for insufficient objective grounds (misuse of rights), and an extension of the period during which an employee may not be dismissed due to sickness, accident, or pregnancy*" (APS 1988: 191,192 cited in Emmenegger 2010: 199). In the course of the negotiations, the CNG withdrew their popular initiative in return for the counter-proposal and, in 1988, the proposal was enacted.

The unions and the Social Democrats campaigned for more than 15 years for this de-liberalization policy to increase job security (Emmenegger 2010). The demand for this de-liberalization policy can be traced back to the unions' change of heart. As demonstrated by the results of Trampusch's in-depth study, the unions became more active in policymaking and changed their policy preferences once they were confronted with a labor market crisis (at least for Swiss standards) (Trampusch 2010).

However, the overall changes were adopted in exchange for the withdrawal of the initial proposal, which was farther-reaching. Thus, this de-liberalization also served as compromise, whereby one demand was met against the context of dropping larger demands (Emmenegger 2010). The Swiss left used the economic momentum of the day to propose late welfare state and labor market expansions. Against the threat of far-reaching de-liberalization, the right agreed to adopt modest reforms.

In sum, Swiss welfare state developments throughout the 1980s show important advances towards de-liberalization. Both the country's positive economic performance and the stronger engagement of Social Democrats and unions in pushing for the expansion of social policy helped to bring about de-liberalizing reforms, which were often agreed upon in a compromise-based policy process.

6.3 Liberalization and De-liberalization Between 1991 and 2000

The 1990s marked a turning point for the Swiss economy and the development process in terms of liberalization and de-liberalization. While Switzerland was able to manage the post-energy-crisis period in the 1980s well both economically and politically, and even expanded its welfare state and social policy, this course changed in the 1990s when the economic boom came to an end (Mach and Oesch 2003: 101–104). Due to high interest rates (between 1989 and 1992) and an abrupt increase in the exchange rate (between 1994 and 1996), growth rates stayed the same for six consecutive years (Ettlin and Gaillard 2001: 162 cited in Mach and Oesch 2003: 101–104). The economic crisis also impacted the labor market where unemployment rates were increasing beyond the levels of the 1930s (Mach and Oesch 2003: 101–104). The difficult economic situation coupled with rapid demographic changes resulted in large deficits in the state's budget for pensions and unemployment insurance. In 1995, the Swiss pension system experienced a deficit for the first time ever. Furthermore, the Swiss unemployment insurance system became strained when confronted with an acute increase in unemployment in the 1990s (from 0.5% in 1990 to nearly 5% in 1994, then hovering at this level until 1997 before declining again to 2% in 2000). Consequentially, the overall balance staggered into deficit in the mid-1990s, generating intense pressure for reform (Häusermann et al. 2004).

6.3.1 *Liberalization Policies Between 1991 and 2000*

From the 1990s on, Swiss policies became increasingly 'europeanized', which was equivalent to liberalization. After the Swiss public rejected membership in the European Economic Area (EEA), the government had to implement its liberalizing objectives without the dynamics of an EEA membership. The government's main objective was therefore to liberalize the internal market because the lack of competition on the domestic market was seen as one of the main drivers of Switzerland's economic problems (Lipp 2012: 111–117; Mach and Trampusch 2011: 20–22). The government launched an economic revitalization program focused around 'competitiveness abroad through increasing competition on domestic markets'. The Federal Council emphasized the need to introduce the same structural economic reforms that an EEA membership would have imposed. The economic revitalization program contained measures designed to adapt Swiss legislation to European standards, such as liberalization of public utilities, reinforcement of competition policy, the abolition of certain protectionist measures, and the introduction of a value added tax (VAT). At the same time, the government negotiated and concluded bilateral agreements with the EU in 1999 (on the free movement of persons, technical trade barriers, research, public procurement, transport, and agriculture) and in 2004 (Dublin and Schengen agreements related to security and asylum, banking secrecy, police collaboration, as well as agreements concerning agricultural products, the environment, media, education, and other fields) (Mach and Trampusch 2011: 20–22; Armingeon and Emmenegger 2007: 196, 197).

One of the most important reform changes was the liberalization of the *Cartel Act*. Before 1995, cartels had been widely tolerated on Swiss domestic markets as they were considered to be valuable for the collective rather than merely special interests. The new legislation did not abolish cartels altogether, but it established a Competition Commission (ComCom) with a mandate to act against anti-competitive practices. Since 1995, according to the *Cartel Act,* horizontal agreements between firms effectively hinder competition (Baudenbacher 2011; Armingeon and Emmenegger 2007: 196, 197). In addition to the *Cartel Act*, several new laws such as the *Law on Domestic Markets* and the *Law on Public Procurement* further supported the government's attempt to promote a market-economic renewal of the Swiss economy. The 1995 *Law on Trade Restrictions* objected to lower technical barriers to trade (Lipp 2012: 122–124; Armingeon and Emmenegger 2007: 196–198).

As a consequence of these new laws, national network companies were reformed and began to pursue liberalization. Telecommunications were liberalized in 1991; postal and telecom services provided by the Swiss public telecom company (*Postal Telegraph and Telephone—PTT*) were separated into two distinct companies (*Swisscom* and *Die Post/La poste*). The Swiss national railways were converted into a private enterprise in 1999 (with the state remaining the sole proprietor) (Obinger et al. 2010: 208; Armingeon and Emmenegger 2007: 196–198). Tax harmonization laws in 1993 and 1995 set out new principles for tax legislation which the cantons were required to integrate. In a national referendum in 1993, the Swiss people (and the cantons) accepted the introduction of value-added tax (VAT) from 1995 onwards. The standard rate was set at 6.5%, and the government was given authority to raise it by an additional percentage point to help finance the public pension scheme (AHV/AVS). In 1998, a flat-rate tax (8.5%) on business profits replaced a progressive taxation scheme (Obinger et al. 2010: 208).

The liberalizing changes in competition policy and privatization also influenced liberalizing developments on the labor market and in the welfare state. The welfare state policy reforms were mostly a compromise between the right and left factions that linked cutbacks to higher contributions (Obinger et al. 2010: 208). Over the course of the liberalizing reforms, the unemployment replacement rate dropped from 80 to 70% and a new 5-day waiting period before receipt of benefits was added. The new two-year limit on entitlements that were previously unlimited was combined with an extension of active labor market policies. Several cantons established reintegration measures either at the level of unemployment assistance, or at the level of social assistance, or as a completely new measure (Bertozzi and Bonvin 2001: 39 cited in Obinger et al. 2010: 212).

In 1995, the 10th AHV/AVS revision brought about major changes with the objectives of introducing greater gender equality and a more flexible retirement age. The retirement age for women was raised from 62 to 63 in 2001 (Obinger et al. 2010: 208).

6.3.2 De-liberalization Policies Between 1991 and 2000

Even though the 1990s sparked a lot of liberalization processes in Switzerland, they also saw some de-liberalization. In this period, federal unemployment insurance was subject to several reforms, all of which resulted in greater contributions (Obinger et al. 2010: 209, 210). In 1993, the contribution rate was raised from 0.4 to 2% of wages, and in 1995 it was raised again to 3%. In addition, a special 'solidarity surcharge' was introduced on higher incomes in 1995 to combat Switzerland's budgetary woes. While these contributions did help to balance the budget initially, that effect lasted only until 1996. In a new attempt to curb spending, the Swiss parliament adopted more reductions on the expenditure side and introduced higher contributions (Obinger et al. 2010: 209, 210). The parliament also implemented the first comprehensive healthcare reform in 80 years. In 1994, the government introduced mandatory health insurance for the entire population (Obinger et al. 2010: 216).

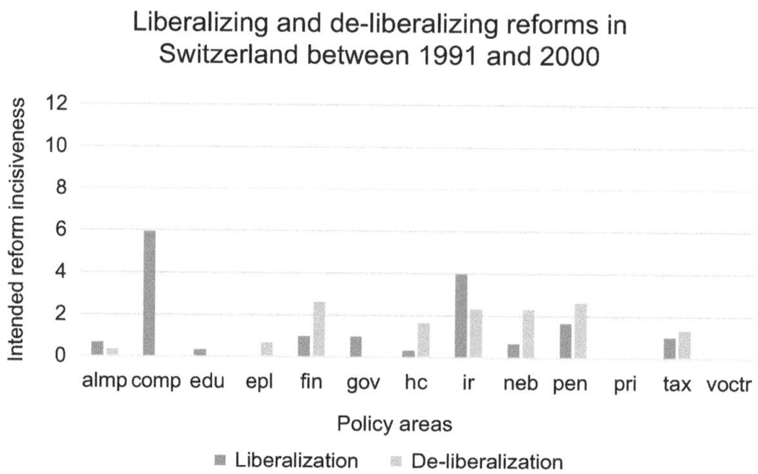

Fig. 6.3 Liberalizing and de-liberalizing reforms in Switzerland between 1991 and 2000 across all policy fields. Reforms are weighted according to the liberalization index (values: first-order changes: 0.33; second-order changes: 0.66; third-order and status quo changes: 1). Source: Liberalization Database (Armingeon et al. 2019)

6.3.3 Politics Between 1991 and 2000: Dichotomous Reform Adjustments

At the beginning of the 1990s, the Swiss people voted against becoming a member of the European Economic Area (EEA) (Afonso and Mach 2011: 103). Switzerland's difficult economic situation and the rejection of the EEA membership became an impetus for reform. At the onset of the 1990s, activists who had built an influential coalition seized the moment and advertised liberalizing reforms (Armingeon and Emmenegger 2007: 196). This group mainly consisted of representatives from the administration, business owners, business associations, and famous economists. The objectives for liberalization were the result of international and European influences, as well as the work of well-known Swiss economists such as Aymo Brunetti, who became the Chief Economist of the State Secretariat for Economic Affairs. As part of this liberalization consensus, the government filled new posts with independent experts and economists who helped design liberalizing propositions. Many policy proposals were drafted in direct reference to European laws and took other countries' liberalization processes into account. These drafts and proposals were mainly drawn up by a small group of experts, while the unions and other opposing groups were excluded from the process. Yet, the government offered some strategic concessions to the 'losers and opposing groups' in their proposals (Häusermann et al. 2004; Obinger et al. 2010: 207; Armingeon and Fill 2016). Over the course of these reforms, the federal government launched an 'economic revitalization reform program' to foster international competition and tighten Switzerland's fiscal policy programs in order to boost Swiss competitiveness; particularly since Switzerland was not able to use an EEA membership as a catalyst for liberalization (Mach and Trampusch 2011: 20–22; Häusermann et al. 2004; Obinger et al. 2010: 207; Armingeon and Fill 2016).

During the 1990s, employers began to pressure the trade unions for decentralization on the labor market. Although Switzerland already had a fairly flexible labor market and a decentralized system of industrial relations and collective bargaining, the unions were still put on the spot. The difficult economic situation and the neoliberal shift in business and politics pressured the unions, particularly when employers demanded less binding collective bargaining and decreased labor market regulations (Oesch 2011: 89–90). In addition, Switzerland concluded the first bilateral agreement with the European Union in 2000. This agreement allowed for the free circulation of European workers in Switzerland, thus further increasing the pressure on the unions. However, this additional pressure created some leeway for the unions to negotiate concessions, which resulted in so-called 'flanking measures' (Afonso et al. 2010). According to Armingeon and Emmenegger (2007: 195,196), this strategy of fostering international mobility while simultaneously setting national regulations is an example of the hybrid character of Swiss economic and social policy. Before this agreement, Swiss immigration policy had already been partially deregulated in 1992 (Flückinger 1998: 388 cited in Obinger et al. 2010: 208).

The willingness to reform the economic policy sector lasted until the late 1990s when Switzerland signed its first bilateral agreement with the EU in 1999 (Baltensperger 2005; Linder 2011: 57, 58). The majority of liberalization reforms took place in the fields of network industries, competition and cartel laws, budget consolidation, and tax reforms (Baltensperger 2005; Häusermann et al. 2004). Reforms in the welfare state and on the labor market took a different reform path than the competition-finance-policy nexus because welfare state reforms were both liberalizing and de-liberalizing in nature. A typical example of this double reform path includes pension policies that were restricted with regards to age but also modernized and expanded in their generosity. The unemployment insurance system was also reformed according to both dynamics, while family policy was primarily expanded. However, both the benefit levels and family policies had been decidedly stingy before the 1990s, and therefore did not leave much room for liberalization (Bonoli and Häusermann 2011: 188–193).

The period between 1991 and 2000 was shaped by a difficult economic situation and far-reaching liberalization processes aimed at curbing budget expenditures and boosting Switzerland's competitiveness. Liberalization processes in the welfare state were compensated through de-liberalizing policies in order to appease the reform opposition. The 1990s also defined the relationship between Switzerland and the European Union, which did not end in membership, but rather in Switzerland keeping the EU at arm's length (Afonso and Mach 2011: 103–104, 107–108).

6.3.4 *Comprehensive De-liberalization Between 1991 and 2000*

Between 1991 and 2000, Switzerland introduced several comprehensive de-liberalizing measures. In some cases the demand for the specific de-liberalization had already been in place for a longer period of time, but was only implemented against the context of new liberalization. Liberalizing measures therefore served indirectly as impetus for reform.

6.3.4.1 Health Insurance Is Made Compulsory for All Citizens

In 1994, basic health insurance became mandatory for all Swiss citizens. The starting point for this reform dates back to 1991, when the Swiss healthcare funds decided to raise their premiums to 20%, whereupon the Swiss government decided it was time to intervene. As a result, the government issued a temporary, limited, emergency measure before starting the lengthy process of reform. While aspirations for greater redistribution and risk pooling were widely shared among various political interest groups, the goal of curbing expenditures was controversial and became the crux of the debates (Obinger et al. 2010: 215). The proposed changes even provoked an optional referendum that was introduced by the Communist Party of Labor and attempted, in particular, to eliminate patient co-payments of CHF 10/day in the case of hospitalization. The referendum was approved by nearly 80% of voters (Obinger et al. 2010: 215).

The government, under increasing pressure, worked closely with a group of experts to improve the chances of passing healthcare reform. The government's main goal was to create an interest overlap between the different political actors in order to bolster support for this reform (Obinger et al. 2010: 216). Hence, the initial goals for healthcare reform were two-sided: on the one hand, the government wanted to introduce greater solidarity across society (meaning between ages and genders) but also higher subsidies for lower-income groups; on the other hand, the government wanted to cut costs through greater competition between the healthcare funds; the government also sought to make it easier for insured persons to choose and switch their health insurance providers (Obinger et al. 2010: 287, 288). The proposed changes included the establishment of mandatory health insurance, the switch from cash benefits to benefits in kind, and the introduction of more competition in order to curb expenses and negotiate lower prices for treatment. Additionally, the government proposed, as mentioned above, equal premium prices for a basic insurance package for every citizen across different genders and ages, matched with higher subsidies for lower-income groups. The discussion and amendments process in parliament took 3 years. The final agreement resulted in the introduction of mandatory insurance, the expansion of the benefit catalogue,[2] the enhancement of redistribution within the Swiss healthcare system, and increased competition. Even though the reform was challenged by an optional referendum, which criticized it for introducing too much regulation, the population adopted the reform by a small majority in 1994 (Obinger et al. 2010: 216).

This healthcare reform brought about both de-liberalizing and liberalizing changes. While the advantages and disadvantages of the Swiss healthcare system had been debated for a long time, the topic became particularly salient in the 1990s when expenditures for healthcare and inequality for consumers rose exponentially. Thus, even though the majority of political parties agreed that reform was necessary, the parties still had different stances on how much de-liberalization was needed. The Free Democratic Party (*Freisinnig-Demokratische Partei der Schweiz—FDP*), the Christian Democratic Party (*Christlichdemokratische Volkspartei der Schweiz—CVP*) and the SPS were ready to accept greater de-liberalization, meaning more state involvement and solidarity, while the Swiss People's Party (*Schweizerische Volkspartei—SVP*) only considered minor changes of equity as necessary. Hence, in order to accomplish a reform that the majority would agree on, the proposal had to cover a broad spectrum of interests (Uhlmann and Braun 2009). By adopting liberalizing elements in order to spur competition and bring costs down, which were at the forefront of the government's policy goals, and by introducing de-liberalizing elements to increase solidarity, the government was able to appeal to the majority of the interested parties. This reform is therefore a clear case of compensating reform strategy where de-liberalization and liberalization are combined in a single reform in order to overcome political disharmony.

6.3.4.2 Pension Credits for Women Who Stop Working in Order to Care for Children (or Elderly Relatives)

In the 1990s, the Swiss pension system was a subject to major reforms: the 10th AHV review. The earlier pension scheme was partially based on a Bismarckian male breadwinner model. Hence, one of the main drivers of reform was the controversial topic of equal treatment of men and women in old-age pensions, flexible pensions, and

[2]Preventing the withholding of benefits to chronically ill (Obinger et al. 2010: 216).

financial relief for lower-income groups (Obinger et al. 2010: 213, 214). The actual negotiations on reform also emphasized the topic of cost containment. The first cautious reform proposal barely touched on the topic of gender equality and did not make it through the parliament. It was opposed by Swiss women's organizations, (female) MPs, the Social Democrats, and the Swiss Liberal Party (LPS) (Obinger et al. 2010: 213). The topic of pension reforms produced two major political camps: the first group, which included the trade unions (SGB), the Social Democratic Party, women's associations, the FDP, the Liberal party, and the main employers' associations from the export-oriented sectors of the Swiss economy, supported the introduction of individualized splitting of contributions and educational benefits in the 10th reform. The second group, consisting of conservative members such as the CVP, the Protestant People's Party (EVP), the SVP, and the Employers Association of Small Businesses (SGV), opposed this proposition (Häusermann 2006a: 171–182). The final bill was heavily modified by incorporating various new aspects, attempting to split up the different views on new policy alteration, and, most importantly, by introducing both liberalizing and de-liberalizing elements (Obinger et al. 2010: 213; Häusermann 2006a: 171–176). Hence, in 1994, the government finally reached a compromise on the adjusted pension proposal. The central law, which was enacted in 1995, introduced liberalizing features such as the increase of the retirement age for women from 62 to 64 over a period of 8 years, and flexible retirement with strong linear cuts, as well as de-liberalizing elements such as educational pension credits for those raising children up to 16 years of age[3] (Häusermann 2010a: 170).

The pension reform was made possible by introducing cost-cutting liberalizing elements together with modernizing de-liberalizing elements, thus adhering to various political interests.

6.3.4.3 Creation of Cantonal Tripartite Commissions to Monitor the Labor Market

Similar to the Austrian case, the opening of the labor market to foreign workers was extremely politically controversial in Switzerland. Swiss labor parties and trade unions in particular were critical of providing labor market access to European Union member states. The topic began to become especially salient in the lead-up to vote on Switzerland's possible membership in the European Economic Area in 1992 (Afonso 2013: 134). The opposition group, mainly represented by the SVP, predicted an 'invasion of foreigners' on the Swiss labor market. The potential negative effects on the labor market were clearly a key motive for the rejection of the membership (Kriesi et al. 1993). The wage differentials between Switzerland and its neighboring countries were claimed to be a major reason for the no vote (Afonso 2013: 134).

[3]Eldercare can also be transferred towards pension credits but does not automatically count as an education pension period (Häusermann 2010a: 170).

Even though the Swiss public refused to join the EEA, the Swiss government still started negotiations on a bilateral agreement with the EEA; part of the agreement foresaw the opening of the labor market to EU foreigners. As part of the agreement, the Swiss government also entered into talks with domestic parties and social partners on how to organize a possible labor market opening. The free movement of workers was certainly among the most tenuous issues in both negotiations. The SVP in particular wanted to restrict labor market access to EU foreigners; however, the European Union had a firm position on the labor market, which meant that if Switzerland wanted to participate in the single market, it had to agree to the free movement of workers. The employers were in favor of opening up the labor market because they were in need of skilled workers (Afonso 2013: 135).

Both the unions and many voters feared that their working and wage conditions would deteriorate under the confrontation of direct competition from European workers. Thus, the unions threatened to launch an optional referendum against the bilateral agreements[4] if their labor market protection demands were not met. The unions were especially under pressure because the Swiss labor market had few institutionalized protections for workers, making the threat of working conditions and wage deterioration even more significant. The unions started a campaign around their demands and were able to strengthen their position within the political spectrum (Afonso 2013: 135, 136).

The Swiss government was under pressure trying to successfully conclude the bilateral agreements with the European Union. Thus, it was too risky for the government to ignore the demands of the unions and to accept an optional referendum supported not only by the trade unions but also by the Swiss People's Party. The government opted instead for a compromise that yielded to the conditions of the trade unions in order to reach an agreement with the European Union.

The compromise with the unions resulted in the establishment of the so-called 'flanking measures' (*Flankierende Massnahmen*) (Fischer 2002). These measures mainly focused on the extension of collective labor agreements and included the following points:

(1) A law on posted workers requires foreign companies to hold their workers to the same conditions as workers residing in Switzerland. (2) The extension of collective labor agreements is eased in special circumstances, such as in the case of demonstrated and repeated abuse of wage standards (order imposing extensions of collective agreements). (3) Minimum wages can be arranged through standard contracts of employment. (4) Tripartite commissions consisting of representatives of labor, capital, and the government, are to be set up in each canton to monitor labor market developments and to decide when special regulations should be applied (Fischer et al. 2002). Additionally, the government was able to negotiate a gradual opening of the Swiss labor market with a transitional period and safeguard clauses. The gradual opening included limitation measures on the inflow of workers during the first 2 years (Afonso 2010).

[4]The European Union was not willing to make concessions on the labor market and wanted to enact all demands in one agreement including several policy fields (Afonso 2013: 135–136).

Thus, this de-liberalization is a clear case in which liberalization policy was compensated for by de-liberalization policies in order to pass legislation. The unique Swiss political system and the pronounced direct democracy allowed the left to mobilize power resources in light of threatening liberalization.

In conclusion, the 1990s saw many important welfare changes in Switzerland, including liberalizing as well as de-liberalizing measures. The de-liberalizing measures shaped the Swiss welfare state based on socially conservative ideology, but provided also for some modernization. The most significant changes included the implementation of mandatory health insurance, pension reform, and the bilateral agreements with the European Union (Obinger et al. 2010: 218; Afonso 2013: 234, 235). Thus, the 1990s clearly demonstrate Switzerland's aspirations to reform the welfare state, which happened against the context of de-liberalizing reforms.

6.4 Liberalization and De-liberalization Between 2001 and 2007

At the turn of the new millennium, the Swiss economy was doing well. The unemployment rate fell from 5.2% in 1997 to 1.7% in 2001. However, unemployment rose again in 2004 to 3.9% before falling back down to 2.8% in 2007. After the enactment of tight fiscal policies and several privatizations, the federal government was able to balance its finances.

6.4.1 Liberalization Policies Between 2001 and 2007

The Swiss government continued its emphasis on tightening fiscal policy and pursuing supply-side reforms. The government also undertook significant liberalizing reforms in the area of agriculture. Switzerland's strong economic protectionism was no longer reconcilable with the market rules of the World Trade Organization (WTO) and the European Union. Thus, the government reduced its subsidies for agriculture and abolished the milk quota (Armingeon and Fill 2016; Obinger et al. 2010: 220). In the field of competition policy, the Swiss government enacted financial penalties for illegitimate, uncompetitive behavior along the lines of European Union policy rules. The Swiss parliament pushed for further liberalization in the telecommunications and electricity sectors (Obinger et al. 2010: 220–220). As a part of these reforms, the insurance market, the postal service, and the healthcare sector were slightly liberalized. In the early 2000s, the Swiss government adopted a constitutional 'debt brake' via majority vote that was aiming at keeping the federal budget in check (Obinger et al. 2010: 220, 221).

In terms of the welfare state, the government reversed some de-liberalizing measures that had been enacted during the economic crisis of the 1990s. The state cut down insurance contributions to 2% and reduced the duration of unemployment benefits from a maximum of 520 days to 400 days.[5] The minimum duration to be eligible for unemployment benefits was increased from 6 to 12 months of employment. Also, the solidarity contribution on high wages was abolished.[6] Moreover, the government lowered the interest rate for occupational pension funds while raising the retirement age for early retirement occupation benefits from 55 to 58 (Armingeon et al. 2019). Access to the labor market was broadened after Switzerland was integrated into the Schengen and Dublin treaties, which were agreed upon in the second bilateral agreement. Overall, the reforms clearly followed the leading liberalizing example of the European Union (Obinger et al. 2010: 220–222).

6.4.2 *De-liberalization Policies Between 2001 and 2007*

Many of the de-liberalizing changes in the 2000s were first-order de-liberalization reforms, however, one comprehensive de-liberalizing reform occurred in the field of employment protection legislation when state-funded maternity leave was introduced. Moreover, the minimum interest rate for occupational pension funds was raised from 2.25 to 2.5%.

In the field of health insurance, cantons started to reduce premiums for people earning steady incomes and for families (Armingeon et al. 2019).

[5]Excluding persons older than 55 years and employees working in cantons where the unemployment rate is above 5% (Armingeon et al. 2019).

[6]With an exception clause that allows the government to levy it if the unemployment insurance fund is facing a debt of more than CHF 5 billion (Armingeon et al. 2019).

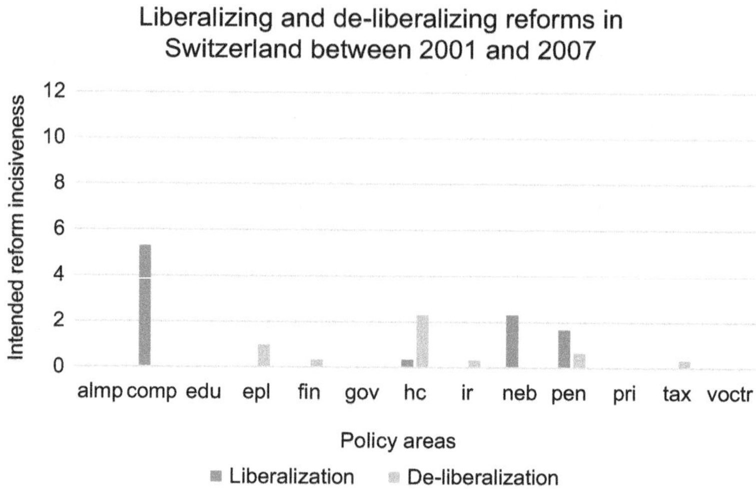

Fig. 6.4 Liberalizing and de-liberalizing reforms in Switzerland between 2001 and 2007 across all policy fields. Reforms are weighted according to the liberalization index (values: first-order changes: 0.33; second-order changes: 0.66; third-order and status quo changes: 1). Source: Liberalization Database (Armingeon et al. 2019)

6.4.3 Politics Between 2001 and 2007: Moving Towards more Social Policy?

The policy course of the 2000s maintained an emphasis on liberalization focusing on both fiscal consolidation and policy convergence with European Union laws. Swiss politics, however, changed significantly in 2003 when, for the first time in over 40 years, the partisan composition of the Swiss federal government was altered; the SVP gained a seat from the Christian Democrats, indicating a shift to the right in Swiss politics (Obinger et al. 2010: 220, 221). Despite this change, the government continued its retrenchment and expansion policies, displaying both liberalizing and de-liberalizing reforms. However, when compared to the previous period, Switzerland's overall liberalization remained limited while the introduction of state-funded maternity leave was a major step towards de-liberalization. Based on optional referenda, it seems as though the zeal for liberalization in the welfare state slowly came to an end after the 2000s, in particular the areas of pensions and unemployment benefits enjoyed public support against retrenchment (Obinger et al. 2010: 230).

6.4.4 Comprehensive De-liberalization Policies Between 2000 and 2007

The most important comprehensive de-liberalization reform between 2000 and 2007 was the introduction of paid maternity leave, which will be discussed in detail below.

6.4.4.1 Introduction of Paid Maternity Leave

The topic of state-funded maternity leave had long occupied Switzerland: Switzerland had introduced a constitutional obligation to implement maternity insurance in 1945. Various attempts were made to introduce state-funded maternity leave up to the early 2000s, but all of them were rejected (Criblez and Manz 2011: 119). In 1964, the government opposed the introduction of motherhood insurance. In 1984, the Swiss people voted against a similar initiative for motherhood insurance in a popular vote. In 1999, both the right-wing and the liberal parties rejected the creation of a parliamentary bill promoting maternity leave schemes in a referendum. Consequentially, paid maternity leave was sparsely available and only on the basis of private-sector agreements. Finally, in 2004, a popular vote led to the introduction of a nationwide maternity leave scheme (Kuebler 2007: 219). The maternity leave included a replacement rate of 80% of previous earnings for a leave period of 14 weeks. How did this come about?

After the parliamentary defeat in 1999, the Social Democratic Party, the Green Party, and various female members of parliament continued to demand an appropriate regulation for maternity leave. The group of maternity leave proponents pressured the government to create a new proposal that would receive support from the majority of the parties. This intent led to a parliamentary bill that was prepared by members of all four governmental parties (FDP, CVP, SPS, and SVP) and was intended to establish maternity leave; in contrast to the earlier proposal from 1999, this proposition was strictly limited to women who were employed. The bill was even supported by employers and adopted in a majority vote (Häusermann 2006b; Criblez and Manz 2011: 120; Kuebler 2007: 228). While the Social Democrats and the Greens have long pursued the goal of maternity leave, the right-wing and conservative parties (excluding the SVP) and the employers only welcomed the idea after it was linked to economic efficiency.

The CVP and FDP adopted a new approach on family policy that coupled gender equality with economic arguments. The parties promoted the benefits of female employment for the labor market (Criblez and Manz 2011: 120, 121). The CVP's manifesto made reference to female employment, stating that they wanted to achieve full employment with the help of working women. The CVP argued further that it aimed to raise the economic power of women in Switzerland, and therefore aspired to promote childcare facilities, flexible working schemes, paid maternity leave, and all-day schools. The FDP based its reasoning mainly on economic grounds, stating that female employment would have a positive economic effect due to larger fiscal revenues, more economic growth, and greater financial independence of women; however, contrary to the CVP, the FDP still considered childcare to be a private responsibility (Criblez and Manz 2011: 125). The Swiss employer's organization, which had previously sought the support of ProFamilia in order to produce a new white paper on family policies, joined the pro-parental-leave supporters. ProFamilia concluded that the creation of day care facilities, allowing high-skilled mothers to stay in or re-enter the labor market, could be a possible solution to overcome the shortage of highly qualified labor that employers had been facing since the 1990s.

Debates for maternity leave had been on the table for a long time. However, de-liberalization only came about when it was linked to competitive economic goals which were pushed to the forefront by both liberal and conservative parties as well as employers. The proposal for maternity leave had to be adapted several times so that it would be accepted by a majority of political parties and voters.

In sum, the 2000s mainly saw a continuation of strict fiscal policies and a focus on supply-side reforms. In addition, the government pursued several reforms in the public sector. Switzerland dismissed its post-war compromise, which was built around a sheltered economy, by reducing its protectionism for domestic industries. Yet, the country also enacted some de-liberalizations in the welfare state.

6.5 Liberalization and De-liberalization Between 2008 and 2014

After 2007, Switzerland's reform path entered into another period of both liberalizing and de-liberalizing reforms. While some liberalization continued in the field of agriculture, Swiss politics partly rejected the implementation of a law that tried to introduce the *Cassis de Dijon* principle in 2015. Moreover, Switzerland strengthened the *Swissness Law*, which was introduced in 2013 and set out rules under which a product can be labeled 'Swiss'. Additionally, a revision of the *Cartel Act* which was aimed at restricting certain types of cartels, failed in 2014. Most importantly, in 2014 the Swiss people accepted a constitutional amendment—the Initiative Against Mass Immigration—which regulated the influx of foreign workers to the Swiss labor market in favor of national workers. The turn away from comprehensive liberalization could be explained by the rise of political actors supporting limited liberalization (Armingeon and Fill 2016).

6.5.1 Liberalization Policies Between 2008 and 2014

In 2008, the liberalization reforms continued in the field of agriculture: the state reduced its budgetary expenditures for market price support by around 30%. In 2012, subsidies were further reduced and payments to the dairy sector were abolished. From 2008 onwards, Switzerland engaged in various tax reforms such as an increase in tax allowances for second earners. In addition, another new tax policy, adopted in 2008, aimed to reduce or eliminate double taxation for investors who owned at least 10% of the capital of a company. In 2013, the Swiss Post turned into a publicly-traded company with the state as its main proprietor (Armingeon et al. 2019).

In terms of the welfare state, the duration of unemployment benefits was aligned to the time of contribution, meaning benefits cannot be received longer than a person has made insurance contributions. In 2013, the labor law was revised with regards to nightly opening hours for shops: gas stations were now allowed to sell goods at night (Armingeon et al. 2019).

In the healthcare sector, the state raised the co-payment for medicines from 10 to 20%. In, 2012, a new organization—Swiss DRG SA—was established to develop and maintain a national schedule of Swiss diagnostic-related groups, initially based on the German DRG model. This new program governs payments for compulsory social insurance schemes (Armingeon et al. 2019).

6.5.2 De-liberalization Policies Between 2008 and 2014

After 2007, Switzerland introduced several new de-liberalizing laws. In 2008, a new law was enacted to more strictly combat under-the-table work. The law obliges cantons to set up control organs and implement tougher penalties (Armingeon et al. 2019).

In the banking sector, several de-liberalizing laws were introduced to more thoroughly regulate and monitor the banking sector. As part of this process, the federal banking commission was transformed into an independent bank regulator: the FINMA (Swiss Financial Market Supervisory Authority) (Armingeon et al. 2019). The government also tightened the reporting requirements for insurance companies. In 2013, the Swiss people passed a people's initiative that introduced a cap on managers' salaries.

In 2009, a new tax law granted tax allowances to parents who pay for external childcare. Furthermore, in 2010, unemployment insurance contribution rates were increased from 2 to 2.2%. In, 2014, the population accepted a federal popular initiative against mass immigration (German: *Eidgenössische Volksinitiative Gegen Masseneinwanderung)* which was intended to limit immigration through the use of quotas (Armingeon et al. 2019).

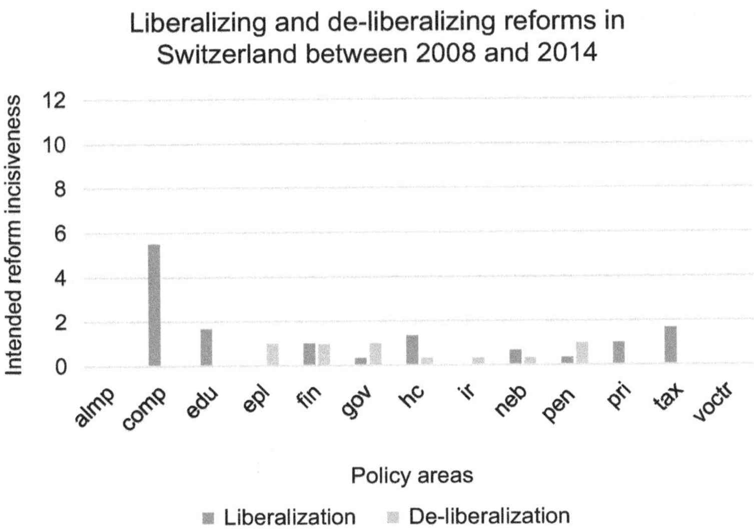

Fig. 6.5 Liberalizing and de-liberalizing reforms in Switzerland between 2008 and 2014 across all policy fields. Reforms are weighted according to the liberalization index (values: first-order changes: 0.33; second-order changes: 0.66; third-order and status quo changes: 1). Source: Liberalization Database (Armingeon et al. 2019)

6.5.3 Politics Between 2008 and 2014: Business as Usual

After 2007, the momentum of far-reaching liberalization came to an end. There were several reasons for this: in the areas of politics and economics, actors who had been in support of de-liberalization, such as interest organizations, became stronger. Furthermore, the Swiss population had a change in heart towards de-liberalization and began rejecting various liberalizing reforms and adopting de-liberalizing measures (Armingeon and Fill 2016). Another factor, presented by both Jan Atteslander, a chief economist at *Economiesuisse,* and Ernst Baltensperger, an academic expert on the Swiss economy, was the outstanding performance of the Swiss economy. Baltensperger is convinced that liberalization processes mainly come about in times of strong economic pressure, while Atteslander states that it is very difficult to advocate for liberalizing reforms when a country is leading in various economic rankings (Interview Economiesuisse 2016; Interview Baltensperger 2016). Thus, politics after 2007 departed from comprehensive liberalization processes in the welfare state and shifted towards a mix of de-liberalization and status quo preservation.

6.5.4 Comprehensive De-liberalization Policies Between 2008 and 2014

In the period after 2008, the only comprehensive de-liberalization policy that was enacted has been the Federal initiative against mass immigration. However, the final implementation of this policy has been far less comprehensive than the original initiative.

6.5.4.1 The Swiss Federal Popular Initiative Against Mass Immigration

On February 9, 2014, the Swiss population voted to pass the popular initiative to stop mass immigration (MEI). The MEI aimed to reintroduce limits on labor immigration from the European Union through quotas. In principle, the initiative was incompatible with the bilateral agreements between Switzerland and the European Union, which includes the free movement of workers.

Almost 3 years after the popular vote, the Swiss government opted for a light implementation of the MEI. The final implementation of the MEI contains primary measures to empower national workers instead of introducing quotas for European nationals. In particular, the implementation of the MEI ordered employers to only publish open vacancies exclusively with regional Swiss job centers (RAV) for a specific period, giving unemployed Swiss citizens and EU nationals residing in Switzerland holding specific work permits a privileged position; however, this new obligation only applies to industries with high unemployment rates. The final implementation differs vastly from the original text of the referendum. The preliminary initiative implied far-reaching de-liberalization measures that clearly threatened access to an open labor market and endangered the bilateral agreements that were in place (Federal council 2016; Abberger et al. 2014; Sciarini et al. 2015; Kläser 2014; Deloitte 2016; NZZ 2016).

How did this de-liberalization come about? All of the governing parties (with the exception of the Swiss People's Party), employers, and the unions[7] vehemently opposed this initiative. The Federal Council and the Swiss Parliament advised the population to reject this initiative; however, the population accepted the MEI with a slight majority of just 50.3%. The main promoter of the MEI was the right-wing SVP. The SVP promoted the MEI based on potential problems such as an overcrowded country consisting of many non-Swiss citizens, the increasing number of Muslims in the Swiss population, an increase in poverty due to immigration, and an expansion of urbanization and construction sites throughout Switzerland (Bernhard et al. 2014). Even though one could argue that this policy was introduced to cater towards the population's demands and thereby increased the electoral viability of the Swiss People's Party, the fact that this policy has not been implemented successfully is much more interesting and shows that a successful introduction of de-liberalization has to be supported by the majority of political actors. The actual outcome of the initiative contains only modest changes. While the government was obligated to implement the MEI as closely in accordance with the initial written initiative as possible, the outcome does not comply with any great de-liberalization promises or closed labor markets (NZZ 2016; Deloitte 2016). Thus, one might argue that far-reaching de-liberalization, which would potentially bear great changes, requires the political representation of a coalition between parties and interest organizations in order to be implemented successfully.

In sum, in the period after 2007, Switzerland continued on a path of liberalizing policies from earlier while also attempting to maintain the status quo. Moreover, Switzerland introduced some de-liberalizations, particularly in the field of financial policies and regulation. Nevertheless, the MEI cannot be considered a major de-liberalizing reform because the government was not able to fully implement all of the changes laid out by the MEI, instead opting for a milder version that was welcomed by nearly all of the political parties and interest groups apart from the SVP. Thus, this period demonstrated that the introduction of significant de-liberalization needs the political support of a majority of governing actors and as well as the people's endorsement.

---

[7]Almost all unions and parties opposed the MEI; however there were some regional exceptions, particularly in the Italian canton of Ticino (Abberger et al. 2014; Sciarini et al. 2015).

6.6 Conclusion: The Swiss Case Study

While Switzerland's de-liberalization dynamics differ from those of Austria and Germany, they still support the main argument of this book. In contrast to Austria and Germany, Switzerland's early de-liberalization processes denoted a late welfare state expansion, and yet most of these early de-liberalization processes came about in the form of compensating measures. These de-liberalizations either occurred in response to the threat of more comprehensive de-liberalization, or otherwise de-liberalizing reforms were accompanied by liberalizing reforms as part of a traditional de-liberalizing strategy. Unlike *producer group theory*, many votes in Switzerland have indicated that neither the early or later de-liberalizations were dependent on employers, who often showed a dismissive attitude towards de-liberalizing policies in the early stages of their formulation.

Throughout the 1990s, after the late welfare state expansion came to a halt, employers pressured unions to conclude fewer binding collective agreements and deregulate the labor market, which clearly deviates from the core claim of the *Varieties of Capitalism* approach. In contrast to Austria and Germany, however, the trade unions and the Social Democrats were able to seize the momentum of liberalization and demand de-liberalizing concessions through the instruments of direct democracy. The most prominent example of using direct democracy to enable de-liberalization occurred during the bilateral agreements with the EU when the left started to threaten a counter-referendum if their demands for protective measures were not met. Yet, it was not only the left who brought about de-liberalizations. Protective measures for the economy and society have been proposed by a variety of political actors and interest organizations; in some cases, the leftist parties and the unions had varying opinions on the introduction of de-liberalizing policies, and at times disagreed with one another or faced internal splits, casting doubt on a traditional partisan or power-resource approach (Häusermann et al. 2013; Korpi 1983).

Similar to Austria and Germany, the zeal for liberalization abated temporarily in the mid-2000s after far-reaching liberalization reforms had been introduced earlier both in terms of the economy and in the area of social protection. Political actors and voters returned to a state of modest de-liberalization combined with preservation of the status quo. These new trends took place without far-reaching liberalization, which forces us to question the validity of *compensation hypothesis* as a means of explaining de-liberalization in Switzerland (Rodrik 1998). In the most recent period, however, Switzerland has once again begun pursuing a dual path of liberalizing and de-liberalizing reforms.

Switzerland's unique political system makes it remarkably different to Germany and Austria. This also becomes evident when we looking at de-liberalization procedures. In contrast to Austria and Germany, political strategies of de-liberalization are in Switzerland mainly used to compensate for and ease reform processes rather than alleviating blame for earlier reforms. Due to Switzerland's consociational democracy consensus, decisions are of prime importance. Thus, strategies of compensation, denoting the application of liberalizing and de-liberalization policies, can help to overcome conflict. Additionally, phases of liberalization and de-liberalization are less linked to governmental periods than in Austria and Germany.

The Swiss case also underlined the fact that de-liberalization policies require a majority appeal from a political coalition, otherwise it becomes difficult to enact de-liberalization. The introduction of the MEI particularly demonstrated that de-liberalization necessitates broad political agreement between parties and interest groups to be successfully implemented.

Overall, the Swiss case largely supports my argument, but mainly consists of compensating strategies of de-liberalization. In contrast to Austria and Germany, some de-liberalizing reforms were initiated by the unions and not by the governing parties, yet they often served as compensation for liberalization. Another aspect that sets Switzerland apart from Austria and Germany is the fact that Switzerland had an extremely frugal welfare state in the early 1980s; nevertheless, the dynamics of welfare state expansion still often occurred within the context of liberalization, which accordingly supports my argument.

Table 6.1 Overview of the different policy reform periods in Switzerland

Policy period	Government and period	Share of lib.	Share of de-lib.	Social expend. (as a percentage of GDP)
Compensation period: De-liberalizing policies are introduced in order to avoid blame during periods of liberalization	1980–1990	50.0%	50.0%	1985: 12.8% 1990: 13.2%
Liberalization period: Economic pressure and new political strategies lead to full-fledged liberalization; however, some liberalization also allows for de-liberalization in Switzerland	1991–2003	60.0%	40.0%	1995: 15.1% 2000: 16.3%
Post-liberalization period: After the public views liberalization proceedings negatively, governments introduce more de-liberalization policies	2004–2007	43.5%	56.5%	2005: 15.6%

Source: Liberalization Database (Armingeon et al. 2019; OECD 2017)

References

Abberger K, Dibiasi A, Siegenthaler M, Sturm J (2014) The Swiss mass immigration initiative: the impact of increased policy uncertainty on expected firm behaviour. KOF Stud 53. https://doi.org/10.2139/ssrn.2516227. Accessed 8 Mar 2017

Afonso A (2010) Europeanisation, policy concertation and new political cleavages: the case of Switzerland. Eur J Ind Relat 16(1):57–72

Afonso A (2013) Social concertation in times of austerity. Amsterdam University Press, Amsterdam

Afonso A, Mach A (2011) Coming together but staying apart: continuity and change in the Swiss and Austrian varieties of capitalism. In: Becker U (ed) The changing political economies of small west European countries. Amsterdam University Press, Amsterdam, pp 99–124

Afonso A, Fontana M, Papadopoulos Y (2010) Does Europeanisation weaken the left? Changing coalitions and veto power in Swiss decision-making processes. Policy Polit 38(4):565–582
APS, Année Politique Suisse (1988) Année Politique Suisse. Schweizerische Politik 1988 (24. Jahrgang). Forschungszentrum für schweizerische Politik, Bern
Armingeon K (1999) Swiss labour market policy in comparative perspective. In: Klöti U, Yorimot K (eds) Institutional change and public policy in Japan and Switzerland. Universität Zürich, Zürich, pp 179–193
Armingeon K, Emmenegger P (2007) Wirtschaftspolitik in der Schweiz: Erosion eines Modells. In: Scholtz H, Nollert M (eds) Schweizer Wirtschaft—ein Sonderfall? Seismo, Zürich, pp 189–227
Armingeon K, Fill A (2016) Trajectories of liberalization and de-liberalization: actors matter. The cases of Austria, Germany, and Switzerland. Working paper presented at the annual conference of the Swiss Political Science Association at the 22 Jan 2016
Armingeon K, Baccaro L, Fill A, Galindo J, Heeb S, Labanino R (2019) Liberalization database 1973–2013 (20170619). Available online July 2019
Baltensperger E (2005) Mut Zum Aufbruch—10 Jahre Danach. Orell Füssli, Zürich
Baudenbacher C (2011) Steigt die Schweiz in die kartellrechtliche Champions League auf?: Die Verankerung eines Kartellverbots allein gibt dem Kartellgesetz nicht mehr Biss. Neue Zürcher Zeitung, 23 Sept 2011, sect. Wirtschaft. http://www.nzz.ch/aktuell/wirtschaft/uebersicht/steigt-die-schweiz-in-die-kartellrechtliche-champions-league-auf-1.12619551. Accessed 8 Mar 2017
Bernhard L, Bühlmann M, Gerber M, Schubiger M (2014) APS-Inserateanalyse der eidgenössischen Abstimmungen vom 9. Februar 2014 Bern. Année Politique Suisse, Institut für Politikwissenschaft
Bertozzi F, Bonvin J (2001) Wiedereingliederungsmassnahmen zu Gunsten der Arbeitslosen in der Schweiz: Unterschiedliche lokale Erfahrungen. Soziale Sicherheit (CHSS) 1:39–40
Bonoli G, Häusermann S (2011) Swiss welfare reforms in a comparative European perspective: between retrenchment and activation. In: Trampusch C, Mach A (eds) Switzerland in Europe—continuity and change in the Swiss political economy. Routledge, Oxon, pp 186–205
Criblez L, Manz K (2011) Neue Familienpolitik in der Schweiz—für die Familie, für die Frauen—oder für die Wirtschaft? In: Rita C, Forster E (eds) Ungleiche Geschlechtergleichheit. Geschlechterpolitik und Theorien des Humankapitals. Budrich, Opladen, pp 113–130
Deloitte (2016) Swiss Parliament decides on a very light implementation of the mass immigration initiative. http://blogs.deloitte.ch/tax/2016/12/swiss-parliament-decides-on-a-very-light-implementation-of-the-mass-immigration-initiative-.html. Accessed 1 Apr 2017
Emmenegger P (2010) Low Statism in coordinated market economies: the development of job security regulations in Switzerland. Int Polit Sci Rev 31(2):187–205
Ettlin F, Gaillard S (2001) Die lange Krise der 90 Jahre: Eine wett-bewerbsfähige Wirtschaft braucht eine stabilisierende Geldpolitik. In: Furrer J, Gehring B (eds) Aspekte der schweizerischen Wirtschaftspoli-tik. Ruegger, Chur/Zürich
Federal Council (2016) Implementation of the popular initiative 'Stop Mass Immigration'. https://www.admin.ch/gov/en/start/documentation/dossiers/implementation-initiative-stop-mass-immigration.html. Accessed 1 Jun 2017
Fischer A (2002) Wirtschaftsbranche, Gewerkschaftsstarke und Interessengesätze der Arbeitgeber: Der Fall Der Flankierenden Massnahmen Zur Personenfreizügigkeit. Revue Suisse de Science Politique 8(3/4):85–100
Fischer A, Nicolet S, Sciarini P (2002) Europeanisation of non-EU countries: the case of Swiss immigration policy towards the EU. West Eur Polit 25(4):143–170
Flückinger Y (1998) The labor market in Switzerland: the end of a special case? Int J Manpow 19 (6):369–395
Hall P, Soskice D (eds) (2001) Varieties of capitalism: the institutional foundations of comparative advantage. Oxford University Press, Oxford
Häusermann S (2006a) Reform opportunities in a Bismarckian latecomer: restructuring the Swiss welfare state. Draft chapter presented at the 2nd project meeting, 16–18 Jun 2006, CES, Harvard, Cambridge. http://citeseerx.ist.psu.edu/viewdoc/summary?doi=10.1.1.466.3632. Accessed 1 Feb 2017

Häusermann S (2006b) Changing coalitions in social policy reforms: the politics of new social needs and demands. J Eur Soc Policy 16(1):5–21
Häusermann S (2010a) The politics of welfare state reform in continental Europe. Modernization in hard times. Cambridge University Press, Cambridge
Häusermann S (2010b) Solidarity with whom? Why organized labor is losing ground in continental pension politics. Eur J Polit Res 49:223–256
Häusermann S, Mach A, Papadopoulos Y (2004) From corporatism to partisan politics: social policy making under strain in Switzerland. Swiss Polit Sci Rev 10(2):33–59
Häusermann S, Picot G, Geering D (2013) Partisan politics and the welfare state. Recent advances in the literature. Br J Polit Sci 43(1):221–240
Interview, Baltensperger (2016) Ernst Baltensperger. University of Bern, Bern, 14 Mar 2016
Interview, Economiesuisse (2016) Jan Atteslander: EconomieSuisse, Zürich, 3 Mar 2016
Katzenstein P (1985) Small states in world markets industrial policy in Europe. Cornell University Press, Ithaca
Kläser J (2014) The Swiss public initiative against mass immigration (Masseneinwanderungsinitiative), caught between constitutional sovereignty and Pacta Sunt Servanda. Eur J Migr Law 16(4):559–564
Korpi W (1983) The democratic class struggle. Routledge & Kegan Paul, Boston
Kriesi H (1980) Entscheidungsstrukturen und Entscheidungsprozesse in der Schweizer Politik. Campus Verlag, New York
Kriesi H, Sciarini P, Passy F (1993) Analyse de La Votation Federale Du Decembre 1992. Analyse vox. gfs/Universite de Geneve, Geneve/Berne. https://www.google.ch/url?sa=t&rct=j&q=&esrc=s&source=web&cd=1&ved=0ahUKEwis_pHKhNzWAhUHXRoKHdOvCdYQFggrMAA&url=http%3A%2F%2Fwww.gfsbern.ch%2FDesktopModules%2FEasyDNNNews%2FDocumentDownload.ashx%3Fportalid%3D0%26moduleid%3D677%26articleid%3D1138%26documentid%3D776&usg=AOvVaw0AqEp0FlqqFeOhq6Ad0rTB. Accessed 9 Jan 2014
Kuebler D (2007) Understanding the recent expansion of Swiss family policy: an idea-Centered approach. J Soc Policy 36(2):217–237. https://doi.org/10.1017/S0047279406000572
Lehmbruch G (1967) Proporzdemokratie. Politisches System und politische Kultur in der Schweiz und in Österreich. Recht und Staat Heft 335/336
Lijphart A (1999) Patterns of democracy: government forms and performance in thirty-six countries. Yale University Press, New Haven
Linder W (2011) Europe and Switzerland: Europeanization without EU membership. In: Trampusch C, Mach A (eds) Switzerland in Europe—continuity and change in the Swiss political economy. Routledge, Oxon, pp 43–61
Lipp S (2012) Standort Schweiz im Umbruch. Etappen der Wirtschaftspolitik im Zeichen der Wettbewerbsfähigkeit. NZZ Verlag, Zürich
Mach A, Oesch D (2003) Collective bargaining between decentralization and stability: a sectoral model explaining the Swiss experience during the 1990s. Indust Bezieh 10(1):160–182
Mach A, Trampusch C (2011) The Swiss political economy in comparative perspective. In: Trampusch C, Mach A (eds) Switzerland in Europe—continuity and change in the Swiss political economy. Routledge, Oxon, pp 11–27
Moser J (2005) Expanding the welfare state after the golden age: the case of Switzerland. TranState working papers no 28. http://hdl.handle.net/10419/28278. Accessed 1 Mar 2017
NZZ, Neue Zürcher Zeitung (2016) Nationalrat stimmt MEI-Umsetzung deutlich zu. Neue Züricher Zeitung, 1 Sept 2016. https://www.nzz.ch/schweiz/umsetzung-der-masseneinwanderungsinitiative-rueckweisungsantrag-von-amstutz-wird-klar-abgelehnt-ld.117950. Accessed 15 Jun 2017
Obinger H, Armingeon K, Bonoli G, Bertozzi F (2005) Switzerland. The marriage of direct democracy and federalism. In: Obinger H, Leibfried S, Castles FG (eds) Federalism and the welfare state. New World and European experiences. Cambridge University Press, Cambridge, pp 263–304
Obinger H, Starke P, Moser J, Bogedan C, Gindulis E, Leibfried S (2010) Transformations of the welfare State. Small states, big lessons. Oxford University Press, Oxford

OECD (2017) Social expenditure: aggregated data. OECD social expenditure statistics (database). http://www.oecd.org/social/expenditure.htm. Accessed 8 Sept 2017
Oesch D (2007) Weniger Koordination, mehr Markt? Kollektive Arbeitsbeziehungen und Neokorporatismus in der Schweiz seit 1990. Swiss Polit Sci Rev 13(3):337–368
Oesch D (2011) Swiss trade unions and industrial relations after 1990. A history of decline and renewal. In: Trampusch C, Mach A (eds) Switzerland in Europe: continuity and change in the Swiss political economy. Routledge, London, pp 82–102
Official Bulletin of the National Council (1985) Bern: Eidgenössische Drucksachen—und Materialzentrale
Rodrik D (1998) Why do more open economies have bigger government? J Polit Econ 106:997–1032
Schanze E, Haunhorst K (1995) Security of tenure in conventional and flexible employment regimes: a neoinstitutional perspective. Eur J Law Econ 2:179–197
Sciarini P, Lanz S, Nai A (2015) Till immigration do us part? Public opinion and the dilemma between immigration control and bilateral agreements. Swiss Polit Sci Rev 21:271–286. https://doi.org/10.1111/spsr.12167
Trampusch C (2010) The welfare state and trade unions in Switzerland: an historical reconstruction of the shift from a liberal to a post-liberal welfare regime. J Eur Soc Policy 20(1):58–73. https://doi.org/10.1177/0958928709352539
Uhlmann B, Braun D (2009) Explaining policy stability and change in Swiss health care reforms. Swiss Polit Sci Rev 15(2):205–240

Chapter 7
Conclusion

Over the past 40 years, Austria, Germany, and Switzerland have undergone major reform transformations towards both liberalization and *de-liberalization*. In all three countries, de-liberalizing reforms have been enacted in the form of compensation measures or in response to unhappy voters and interest groups. What makes these reforms paradigmatic is the fact that de-liberalizing reforms came about due to endogenous political reasons. Furthermore, strategies of de-liberalization are more often applied in the areas of welfare state and labor market policies than is assumed by the extant literature (Streeck and Thelen 2005). I do not argue that de-liberalization occurs as frequently and with the same intensity as liberalization, or that all three countries follow the same path of de-liberalizing reform strategies. What this study does show, however, is that de-liberalizing reforms make up a significant percentage of the reform politics in Austria, Germany, and Switzerland, and that all three countries engaged in de-liberalization to various extents, at different times, and across diverse policy fields.

7.1 Summary of Findings

Intrigued by the question of *what drives de-liberalization*, I analyzed de-liberalizing policy reforms in Austria, Germany, and Switzerland between 1973 and 2015. Contrary to the common wisdom of many political economy accounts (Streeck and Thelen 2005; Baccaro and Howell 2017; Bretschger and Hettich 2002), this book has established that industrialized countries engage not only in liberalizing reforms but also in a significant amount of de-liberalizing reforms. Thereby, this study also shows that ideas like the *race to the bottom hypothesis* or the *efficiency hypothesis,* which focus on functionalist factors such as globalization or European integration, are not applicable when it comes to the reform trajectories of the case study countries.

© Springer Nature Switzerland AG 2019

A. Fill, *The Political Economy of De-liberalization*, Contributions to Political Science, https://doi.org/10.1007/978-3-030-01066-9_7

Moreover, in my evaluation of reform policies in Austria, Germany, and Switzerland, I demonstrate that the occurrence of de-liberalization hinges on endogenous factors. Political parties, which are primarily motivated by gaining office and holding on to power, use de-liberalizing policies in politically salient policy fields in two ways: Firstly, they engage in de-liberalizing reforms in order to compensate their political opposition and voters, which allows them to pass liberalizing reforms. Secondly, political parties use de-liberalizing policies to mitigate blame after liberalizing reforms have been implemented, to distance themselves from earlier liberal reforms that are now seen in a negative light, and to take credit among voters and interest organizations for new de-liberalization reforms in order to gain or retain office. They do so by reversing existing liberalizing policies or introducing new de-liberalizing policies that allow them to take credit for these new adjustments and help political parties to be voted into office and stay there. Therefore, this analysis illustrates that liberalization, despite common beliefs, is *not a stable political outcome*. If public support for liberalization withers and both voters and trade unions express negative feedback, as they did in Austria and Germany, political actors will react to this feedback accordingly. Consequentially, they will try to reconcile the public and trade unions with de-liberalizing policies—even against the will of employer groups.

The extent of de-liberalizing reforms depends on the involved actors' ability to form coalitions, as well as on the public's demand for de-liberalization. This means that the public not only has to be in favor of de-liberalization, but also that a portion of the governing parties and interest groups have to support de-liberalizing reforms in order for these reforms to be successful. In the majority of the cases analyzed in this study, comprehensive de-liberalizing reforms were supported by trade unions.

When we compare Austria, Germany, and Switzerland, all three countries lend support to the argument that de-liberalizing reforms are enacted for the purposes of compensation and blame mitigation; however, there was naturally some variation within the cases. The Austrian case confirmed the theoretical argument: Austria was the least liberalized country and experienced extensive de-liberalization throughout the compensation period and the post-liberalization era. The complex entanglement between parties and interest groups helped to create powerful coalitions that endorsed de-liberalization. The German case also broadly supports the main notion of this argument. The extent of de-liberalization in Germany was smaller, which can be attributed to the difficulty in forming a coalition in support of de-liberalization policies. Switzerland deviates from the main argument somewhat: in comparison to Austria and Germany, Switzerland showed mostly compensating strategies of de-liberalization and not necessarily blame mitigating strategies, which can be ascribed to Switzerland's strong direct democracy.

Categorically in line with Culpepper's argument of 'quiet politics' (Culpepper 2011), this book demonstrates that reform dynamics differ strongly between politically salient policy fields and non-salient policy fields. Politically salient policy fields are of high interest to voters and interest groups, and therefore, political parties tend to de-liberalize policies in these fields. Quiet policy fields have rarely been de-liberalized. Contrary to politically salient policy fields, quiet policies have only been subject to de-liberalizing reforms after the financial crisis revealed institutional dysfunctions. Hence, de-liberalizing reforms to the welfare state, the labor market, and industrial relations are generally dependent on endogenous political strategies; they are shaped by politics rather than by functional pressures or new social risks. Furthermore, the European Union did not play an important role in determining de-liberalization outcomes. The endogenous influence is particularly emphasized by the fact that, in many cases, the de-liberalizing reforms I analyzed had been debated for a long time, and yet were only enacted as compensating reforms or after liberalizing reforms had become very unpopular. The political element of de-liberalizing reforms is also underscored by the point that social democratic parties were not the only parties using de-liberalizing strategies, but also parties with other ideological backgrounds. Hence, despite functional pressures to liberalize, political actors will employ de-liberalizing strategies in policymaking if voters demand it and if powerful coalitions support de-liberalization. Yet, as the case studies have shown, while de-liberalization makes up a significant percentage of the reforms enacted, it is not always on par with the overall extent of liberalizing reforms.

7.2 What About Alternative Explanations?

At the beginning of this volume, I asked the question, "*How can we explain the various reform paths of de-liberalization policies in Austria, Germany, and Switzerland?*"

A *compensation hypothesis* approach would argue that de-liberalization is introduced together with rising liberalization in order to mitigate the negative effects of liberalization and to secure the approval of the public for liberalization (Rodrik 1998). However, while global integration was continuously rising throughout the 1990s and 2000s in all three countries, as the reform developments in the politically non-salient policy fields show, de-liberalization did not increase simultaneously, as it should have according to this approach.

Furthermore, traditional political theories such as *traditional partisanship theory* and *power resource accounts* have problems explaining the divergent de-liberalizing reform paths of Austria, Germany, and Switzerland (Korpi 1983; Häusermann et al. 2013). These theories would attribute the occurrence and the extent of de-liberalizing reforms to the power of social democratic parties and unions. However, the most far-reaching liberalizations without de-liberalizing compensations were introduced under a social democratic government in Germany, while many comprehensive de-liberalizing reforms were often introduced under grand coalitions or multiple party governments in all three countries. A minimum wage was introduced in Germany under a grand coalition, as were the *Pension 63* and the *Mother Pension* reforms (Mabbett 2016; Butterwegge 2016). The enactment of an *Anti-Wage-Dumping Law*, a means-tested basic income scheme, and an anchoring of the social partners into the constitution in Austria all occurred under a grand coalition government (Obinger et al. 2010: 62, 63; Eurofund 2014). In Switzerland, obligatory healthcare and the expansion of the pension system were introduced under a broad government coalition that was made up of left- and right-leaning parties (Obinger et al. 2010: 216, 217). Furthermore, a *power resource approach* cannot fully account for de-liberalizing reforms since certain unions were not always proponents of de-liberalization as the German case showed (Korpi 1983; Mabbett 2016). Even though comprehensive de-liberalizing reforms were very often supported by various union organizations, some unions also opposed de-liberalizing measures as demonstrated by the complicated case of the introduction of the German minimum wage. In this case, IG Metall was against the introduction of the statutory minimum wage in the beginning (Mabbett 2016). Thus, neither *traditional partisan approaches* nor *power resource approaches* can explain the different de-liberalizing reform paths seen in these three countries.

The *Varieties of Capitalism* approach would attribute de-liberalizing reforms in Austria, Germany, and Switzerland to the employer's interest in stabilizing welfare and labor market arrangements. Protective welfare and labor market institutions are said to foster skill development, which in turn leads to a comparative institutional advantage of coordinated market economies, including the three case study countries (Hall and Soskice 2001). Yet, the findings in this study deviate greatly from VOC-based explanations. In all three countries, de-liberalization has often been met with harsh criticism from the employers' side. Swiss and German employers even actively sought to decentralize the local systems of industrial relations (Baccaro and Howell 2017; Mach and Oesch 2003). Additionally, employers rarely supported de-liberalization initiatives; the only instances where de-liberalizations were supported by business associations occurred when labor markets were opened to EU foreigners and the Austrian Chamber of Economics, as well as small and medium employers from the service sector in Germany, demanded protective wage measures (Eurofund 2014; Mabbett 2016; Bosch 2015). Hence, overall, *Varieties of Capitalism* cannot explain de-liberalizing reform paths in these three countries. Thelen's *producer group approach* (2012, 2014) is also unable to shed light on the different de-liberalization paths we see in Austria, Germany, and Switzerland. Thelen would attribute de-liberalizing reforms to the power of trade unions and their ability to build political coalitions, as well as on the specific competitive interest of employer organizations; yet de-liberalizing reforms were initiated by governing parties rather than by interest groups. Thus, *producer group theories* also fail to produce a viable answer to my question.

Other institutional accounts such as *corporatism- and consociational-democracy-*based explanations would attribute the outcome of de-liberalizing reforms to compromise-based solutions, or to the intentions of political actors and interest organizations to cushion market-driven change (Armingeon 2002: 162,163; Schmidt 2006: 334; Katzenstein 1985). Switzerland, which is a consociational democracy, experienced the highest relative share of de-liberalizing reforms measured against the overall amount of reforms per country. This finding is in line with these approaches. Yet, while compromise-based solutions are part of the explanation for de-liberalizing change, consociational-democracy- and corporatist-based explanations cannot account for the de-liberalizing reform changes in Austria and Germany that occurred after 2006 and after 2011, respectively. In both countries, de-liberalization was introduced after public support for liberalization abated. The German government changed its liberalizing course after the Social Democrats were severely punished for their liberalization efforts and German inequality became a salient topic, leading to new demands for more social protections for the public (Mabbett 2016; Marx and Starke 2017). The Austrian government returned to traditional social democratic policies in conjunction with the unions after the Austrian right-conservative government lost backing for their liberalizing endeavors (Obinger et al. 2010: 62, 63). Thus, de-liberalization was introduced without liberalization and against the will of employers (Obinger et al. 2010: 216, 217; Mabbett 2016).

Having demonstrated why these alternative explanations cannot provide adequate answers to the research question, one may still ask whether the exogenous shock of the 2008 financial crisis and the ensuing Great Recession affected patterns of de-liberalization? The chronology of the events in Austria, Germany, and Switzerland that led to de-liberalizing reforms after 2008 speaks against crisis-based explanations. In Austria, the endorsement for de-liberalizing policies had already begun towards the end of the black-blue coalition, when the government and the opposition campaigned for the upcoming election. In their 2006 election campaign, the Austrian Social Democrats promised to repeal university fees and to find a solution for caregivers, while the discussion surrounding the anti-wage dumping law had already begun during the Eastern European Enlargement in 2004 (Krings 2013; Leidenfrost 2010; Obinger et al. 2010: 216, 217). In Germany, discussions surrounding the introduction of a statutory minimum wage commenced when the *Hartz* reforms were introduced. In 2006, the DGB advocated for the introduction of a statutory minimum wage of EUR 7.50 per hour at its annual congress. Additionally, political discussions on the introduction of the minimum wage were not linked to the crisis (Marx and Starke 2017; Eurofund 2009). The initiative against mass immigration in Switzerland was framed in an anti-immigration context and not as a result of to the 2008 economic crisis (Abberger et al. 2014). It is therefore unlikely that recent comprehensive de-liberalizations arose as response to the Great Recession.

Hence, as we have seen, while these accounts provide interesting insights, they are not able to fully explain the different de-liberalizing paths of the countries in the case studies. Against this backdrop, this book presents an argument that allows for dynamic change. Based on rational choice approaches, modern partisanship theory, and path dependency accounts, I have argued that political parties, who primarily seek to gain and retain office, engage in de-liberalizing reforms in order to compensate their political opposition and voters for liberalizing reforms. After far-reaching liberalizing reforms have been enacted and the public support for liberalization has withered significantly, political parties engage in de-liberalization in order to mitigate blame for earlier liberalizing reforms and to take credit among voters and interest organizations for new de-liberalization reforms in order to gain or retain office. The extent of de-liberalizing reforms depends, in particular, on the possibility of forming coalitions in support of de-liberalization, and on the public support for de-liberalization. As the case studies in this book have indicated, this argument is largely able to explain the different de-liberalizing reform paths of Austria, Germany, and Switzerland, but also requires further research before it can be applied on a wider basis.

7.3 Outlook

This study shows that countries engage not only in liberalization but also de-liberalization. Contrary to liberalization reforms, the introduction of de-liberalizing policy reforms occurs mainly as a result of endogenous political reasons, meaning that governing parties use de-liberalization as a political strategy. In recent years, governing parties have begun to actively campaign around potential de-liberalizing reforms in the welfare state and on the labor market in order to gain an advantage of their political competition. At this point, we cannot know if de-liberalization will be advanced by political competition and voters, if de-liberalization will be strengthened in the context of welfare state chauvinism, or if liberalizing welfare state policies will soon return. However, recent political reform announcements, such as a generous increase in pension benefits in Austria (DiePresse 2017), the strengthening of the Posted Workers Directive against further social dumping in Switzerland (NZZ 2017) and Angela Merkel's decision against a raise in retirement age in Germany (DieZeit 2017) demonstrate once more that the topic of de-liberalization is certainly deserving of further scientific research and scrutiny.

References

Abberger K, Dibiasi A, Siegenthaler M, Sturm J (2014) The Swiss mass immigration initiative: the impact of increased policy uncertainty on expected firm behaviour. KOF Stud 53. https://doi.org/10.2139/ssrn.2516227. Accessed 8 Mar 2017

Armingeon K (2002) Interest intermediation: the cases of Consociational democracy and corporatism. In: Keman H (ed) Comparative democratic politics: a guide to contemporary theory and research. SAGE, London, pp 143–166

Baccaro L, Howell C (2017) Trajectories of neoliberal transformation. Cambridge University Press, Cambridge

Bosch G (2015) Der holprige Weg zum gesetzlichen Mindestlohn in Deutschland. Sozialer Fortschritt Unabhängige Zeitschrift für Sozialpolitik, vol 64. Duncker & Humblot, Berlin, pp 173–181. ISSN 0038-609X, ZDB-ID 20886

Bretschger L, Hettich F (2002) Globalisation, capital mobility and tax competition: theory and evidence for OECD countries. Eur J Polit Econ 18(4):695–716

Butterwegge C (2016) Das großkoalitionäre Rentenpaket – ein Mittel gegen die Armut im Alter? In: Butterwegge C (ed) Reichtumsförderung statt Armutsbekämpfung. Eine sozial- und steuerpolitische Halbzeitbilanz der Großen Koalition. Springer Fachmedien Wiesbaden, Wiesbaden, pp 11–18

Culpepper P (2011) Quiet politics and business power—corporate control in Europe and Japan. Cambridge University Press, Cambridge

DiePresse (2017) SPÖ und ÖVP beschließen gestaffelte Pensionserhöhung. DiePresse, 22 Aug 2017. http://diepresse.com/home/innenpolitik/5272497/SPOe-und-OeVP-beschliessen-gestaffelte-Pensionserhoehung. Accessed 1 Sept 2017

DieZeit (2017) Ökonomen kritisieren Merkels Nein zur Rente mit 70. DieZeit, 5 Sept. http://www.zeit.de/politik/deutschland/2017-09/verdi-chef-frank-bsirske-angela-merkel-rentenalter-oekonomen. Accessed 10 Sept 2017

Eurofund (2009) Germany: 'Wage formation'. https://www.eurofound.europa.eu/observatories/eurwork/comparative-information/national-contributions/germany/germany-wage-formation. Accessed 1 Feb 2017

Eurofund (2014) Austria: anti-wage dumping and social dumping law updated. https://www.eurofound.europa.eu/news/news-articles/working-conditions-labour-market-industrial-relations-law-and-regulation/austria-anti-wage-dumping-and-social-dumping-law-updated. Accessed 1 Feb 2017

Häusermann S, Picot G, Geering D (2013) Partisan politics and the welfare state. Recent advances in the literature. Br J Polit Sci 43(1):221–240

Hall P, Soskice D (eds) (2001) Varieties of capitalism: the institutional foundations of comparative advantage. Oxford University Press, Oxford

Katzenstein P (1985) Small states in world markets industrial policy in Europe. Cornell University Press, Ithaca

Korpi W (1983) The democratic class struggle. Routledge & Kegan Paul, Boston

Krings T (2013) Von der "Ausländerbeschäftigung" zur Rot-Weiß-Rot-Karte: Sozialpartnerschaft und Migrationspolitik in Österreich. Österr Z Polit 42(3):263–278

Leidenfrost J (2010) The demise of "Minoritenplatz-Schleicherei" eighty-four months of Wende higher education policy in Austria. In: Bischof G, Plasser F (eds) The Schüssel Era in Austria. Innsbruck University Press, Innsbruck, pp 283–320

Mabbett D (2016) The minimum wage in Germany: what brought the state in? J Eur Publ Policy 23 (8):1240–1258. https://doi.org/10.1080/13501763.2016.1186210

Mach A, Oesch D (2003) Collective bargaining between decentralization and stability: a sectoral model explaining the Swiss experience during the 1990s. Indust Bezieh 10(1):160–182

Marx P, Starke P (2017) Dualization as destiny? The political economy of the German minimum wage reform. Polit Soc 45(4):1–26. https://doi.org/10.1177/0032329217726793

NZZ, Neue Zürcher Zeitung (2017) "Macron möchte Lohndumping in der EU eindämmen." Neue Züricher Zeitung, 23 Aug 2017. https://www.nzz.ch/international/treffen-in-salzburg-macron-moechte-mit-kern-gegen-sozialdumping-in-der-eu-vorgehen-ld.1312299. Accessed 15 Sept 2017

Obinger H, Starke P, Moser J, Bogedan C, Gindulis E, Leibfried S (2010) Transformations of the welfare state. In: Small states, big lessons. Oxford University Press, Oxford

Rodrik D (1998) Why do more open economies have bigger government? J Polit Econ 106:997–1032

Schmidt M (2006) Demokratietheorien—Eine Einführung. Verlag für Sozialwissenschaften, Wiesbaden

Streeck W, Thelen K (2005) Beyond continuity: institutional change in advanced political economies. Oxford University Press, New York

Thelen K (2012) Varieties of capitalism: trajectories of liberalization and the new politics of social solidarity. Annu Rev Polit Sci 15:137–159

Thelen K (2014) Varieties of liberalization: the new politics of social solidarity. Cambridge University Press, New York

FSC
www.fsc.org
MIX
Papier | Fördert
gute Waldnutzung
FSC® C083411

Kolibri 360 GmbH
Ferdinand-Jühlke-Straße 7
99095 Erfurt, Deutschland
produktsicherheit@kolibri360.de